Hiking through History
Pennsylvania

Hiking through History Pennsylvania

Exploring the State's Past by Trail

Bob Frye

FALCONGUIDES

GUILFORD, CONNECTICUT

FALCONGUIDES®

An imprint of The Rowman & Littlefield Publishing Group, Inc.
4501 Forbes Blvd., Ste. 200
Lanham, MD 20706
www.rowman.com
Falcon and FalconGuides are registered trademarks and Make Adventure Your Story is a trademark of The Rowman & Littlefield Publishing Group, Inc.

Distributed by NATIONAL BOOK NETWORK

British Library Cataloguing-in-Publication Information available

Library of Congress Cataloging-in-Publication Data

Names: Frye, Bob, 1967- author.
Title: Hiking through history Pennsylvania : exploring the state's past by
    trail / Bob Frye.
Description: Guilford, Connecticut : FalconGuides, 2018. | Includes index. |
    Identifiers: LCCN 2017054757 (print) | LCCN 2017056685 (ebook) | ISBN
    9781493036837 (e-book) | ISBN 9781493030101 (pbk.)
Subjects: LCSH: Hiking—Pennsylvania—Guidebooks. |
    Trails—Pennsylvania—Guidebooks. | Historic
    sites—Pennsylvania—Guidebooks. | Pennsylvania—Guidebooks.
Classification: LCC GV199.42.P4 (ebook) | LCC GV199.42.P4 F784 2018 (print) |
    DDC 796.5109748—dc23
LC record available at https://lccn.loc.gov/2017054757

♾™ The paper used in this publication meets the minimum requirements of American National Standard for Information Sciences—Permanence of Paper for Printed Library Materials, ANSI/NISO Z39.48-1992.

Printed in the United States of America

Contents

The Hikes

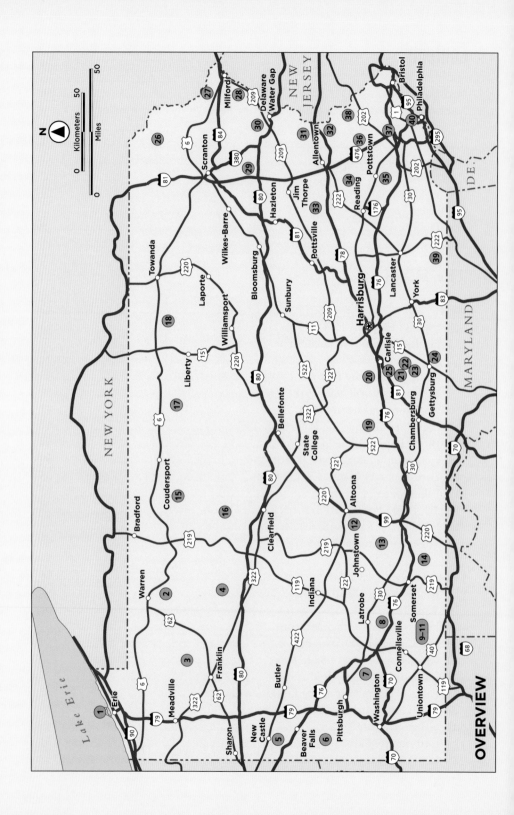

OVERVIEW

Acknowledgments

Even the person least interested in history probably knows that Gettysburg was the site of a famous battle. Or that Valley Forge was where George Washington's soldiers spent a miserable winter. Or that any place with the name "Fort" in front of it has a military background.

But where at such places does it make the most sense to explore on foot? Philadelphia is pretty big, after all, with a lot of old structures.

A thanks is in order to all the guides, interpreters, public affairs folks, and others who helped break those sites down and offered suggestions on where to walk and what to see.

Appreciation is due, too, to those who offered advice on lesser known but certainly important and definitely interesting historic sites. If the Battle of Bushy Run had turned out differently, for example, the fate of Fort Pitt and ultimately Pittsburgh could have been different. Yet the battlefield itself is somewhat hidden these days. Without some advice, I might have overlooked it.

Thank you to all those who work to preserve our historic sites. Some are paid; many are volunteers. All are critical. You can't appreciate where you are if you don't know where you came from, and by keeping our history safe and accessible, these people serve us all.

And lastly, thanks to my wife, Mandy, my constant hiking companion, who made walking these miles and exploring these places so memorable.

Foreword

Pennsylvania is steeped in a rich history and abundant natural resources. Add to that one of the largest trail systems in the country, and you have the makings of a great book. *Hiking through History Pennsylvania* is just that—a rich compilation of all the good things that stepping out into our state's great outdoors has to offer. It's all here: a blessing of natural resources melded with so many historical tales, all linked together by two masters of connections—the trail and, of course, Bob Frye.

An award-winning outdoors writer and skilled newspaperman, Bob truly is an author who walks the walk and can paint an evocative picture with his words, connecting readers to the sights and sounds of the great outdoors. He does both with knowledge and facts accrued through many years of hiking and biking, camping, fishing, and hunting. Bob experiences nature in a deep, profound way and brings others along on his journeys.

It's no secret to those of us in the outdoor recreation field that combining history and heritage with walking is a favorite activity for many outdoors enthusiasts. And now, using his words to entice and excite, Bob makes that connection for us, exploring forty places around the state where you can get up close with some of Pennsylvania's and America's preeminent historic sites, from Valley Forge to Gettysburg, from Flight 93 to Bushy Run.

Through Bob's eyes and prose, *Hiking through History Pennsylvania* takes readers to many places that are special to me, from my Audubon days at the John James Audubon Center at Mill Grove; to the iron furnace history of my local state park, Pine Grove Furnace; to stories of our canal systems at Hugh Moore Park and Delaware Canal State Park. For you lovers of Pennsylvania state parks, which I clearly am, Bob picks twenty of the best with historical roots.

Trails are our mini-highways, enriching municipalities across the state and taking travelers to adventure, peace of mind, and good health. Encircling lakes and paralleling streams, they are an open invitation to the hiker and biker, jogger, and birder in our state and local parks. They bring the state forest to the visitor, where anglers and hunters can reach those secluded spots to search for their elusive prey.

To all, they provide needed escape from the daily grind.

Trails of Pennsylvania vary as much as the terrain they traverse. A trail's value is in the eye of its user, and we have so many trails and so many users. That's why Pennsylvania has emerged as a national trails leader.

Bob's latest undertaking is a must-read for the history-loving hiker. Walk with him as you connect to our wonderful past through the beauty of our trails!

—Cindy Adams Dunn, Secretary,
Pennsylvania Department of Conservation and Natural Resources

Introduction

Pennsylvania is known as the "Keystone State" and, apropos of a history book, has been since the earliest days of the nation. A keystone, in architectural terms, is the central, wedge-shaped stone in an arch that holds the other stones in place. So it is with Pennsylvania.

It's located right about in the middle of the original thirteen colonies, looking north to south. It was smack dab in the middle of things in terms of early American political, economic, and cultural activities, too. Philadelphia, for example, was at that time the country's largest, most opulent city. It's no wonder two of the most famous documents in American history—the Declaration of Independence and the US Constitution—were penned here.

Even before then, when the British and French were battling for control of the North American continent, Pennsylvania and its western frontier were crucial to both sides.

The state lost none of its importance with the passage of time, either. Another of America's most legendary documents—the Gettysburg Address—was finalized and delivered in Pennsylvania, at the site of what was the Confederacy's deepest push into Union soil. Before and after that, some of the innovations that would power America and turn it into an economic force were made here.

An abundance of unusual and fascinating history is also found within the state's borders. The founder of America's forestry system, who set the direction for conservation of our woodlands? His magnificent home is here. The world's first center for raptor conservation? You'll find it here. The memorial to a crash resulting from a terroristic attack—the twenty-first-century version of Pearl Harbor—which, far from marking the country's defeat, instead reveals America's fighting spirit? It's here, too.

What's amazing is how often so much of that history is connected. The Battle of Bushy Run and the fate of Fort Pitt are separate incidents, to be sure. But one wouldn't have turned out like it did without the other.

There are other historic sites across the state, of course, all special in their varied ways. The ones contained in this book, though, offer something extra—opportunities to explore by hiking. And make no mistake, there's something real and powerful to be said for exploring such sites on foot.

The pace of the world today is faster than it's ever been. Things are unlikely to slow down either; technology will see to that. But to be able to slow down and explore the past? There's value there, and fun, too.

I hope you'll use this book to explore, learn, and reconnect, all while stretching your legs and covering some ground at the speed of history.

How to Use This Guide

The hikes in this book are listed by region, going west to east, so you can find one in particular or perhaps determine how best to link a few together for a weekend-long or cross-state adventure.

Each of the forty chapters contains some important information. For starters, there's historical information. Stories tell you what it is that makes each site worth visiting, be it a military achievement or failure, industrial remnants, one-of-a-kind architecture, or something else.

There's also a description of the hike connected with the sites. They go into some detail on why the trail is located where it is, what its connection to the site is, or why it exists. It's accompanied by turn-by-turn directions from the trailhead to the end of the hike.

Along with that, each chapter tells you just how long the hike is, how difficult, when best to hike it, and who else you might share the path with. There's contact information, too, for the organization or agency that manages the historic site—in case you want more information—and details on costs to explore.

We tell you how to get to the trailhead, too.

Finally, each hike is accompanied by a map. They're not meant to replace topographical or even road maps, but they do provide some sense of what the hike looks like and where it leads.

Hiking Tips

Few things are as fun as hiking, especially when a trip afield can be combined with exploring history.

Assuming everyone enjoys themselves along the way, that is, and returns home happy and healthy. There's no guaranteeing that, unfortunately. Accidents happen. People twist ankles. They get sunburned. Bugs bite. Children grow tired.

But you can minimize the chances of things going wrong with a little planning.

- Carry water and snacks. Water is, or should be, a no-brainer. And we're not talking just one of those tiny water bottles either. Get yourself a backpack with a hydration bladder or carry larger water bottles in a pack. You may not drink it all, but it's better to have more than you need than not enough. As for snacks, they can give you a boost mid-hike. They're especially helpful when hiking with children.
- Pack some essentials. A thin, light rain jacket and pants can save the day—and keep a hike fun rather than turn it into an endurance event—if the weather turns sour. Rain gear is especially critical if you're wearing cotton clothing. Cotton is

not the best choice for hiking; it loses its ability to insulate when wet. So if you have a choice, opt for synthetics. But in any case, dry is better than wet.

- If you'll be hiking on the edges of warm weather, in spring and fall or even winter, dress in layers and be sure to have gloves and a hat. Your head is one of the places your body loses heat fastest. Cover your dome to stay warm.

- When the sun is shining, and especially when you'll be on a hike that is exposed to the sun, pack sunscreen. Apply some before leaving your vehicle, then take it along. That way, if you sweat it off, you can reapply mid-hike. Lip balm is good to have for the same reasons. Carry sunglasses and wear a hat, too.

- Carry insect repellent. Hopefully you've treated your clothes with permethrin before leaving, to keep ticks at bay. Apply bug spray to your skin to keep mosquitoes away. Carrying a little bottle with you, be it spray or cream, allows you to reapply it as needed.

- Protect your feet. Nothing will kill the joy of a hike faster than developing blisters halfway in. Wear liner socks next to your feet, with wool socks over those. Then wear good hiking boots. The cushion provided by all those layers is incredibly valuable.

- Take along a first-aid and emergency kit. It would be almost impossible to get lost or even have to spend any time alone on some of these hikes. Others, though, are more remote, where a fall or twisted ankle could leave you having to fend for yourself or even spend a night outdoors. Then there's always the chance of just getting a cut or scratch, too. Be prepared for such situations. You don't need a full-scale bug-out bag, but something with some Band-Aids, pain killers, and a way to start a fire is helpful. A knife or multi-tool is good to have as well.

- Pack this book—it's easier to reference it on-site than try to remember what you read about earlier—and perhaps a journal. If you see something that makes you want to explore further later, you can jot a note to yourself. A little bit of money and, of course, your phone can come in handy, too.

- Stay on trails. They're blazed where they are for a reason—they represent the safe way through, or keep sensitive areas from being trammeled, or protect historic sites. Respect what it is that brought you there in the first place.

- Lastly, before heading out, be sure to tell someone back home where you're going, who you're going with, and when you expect to be home. Then, when you return home, notify the person that you're back safe. All that information will be critical should some emergency arise that causes people to have to look for you. The more they know about your outing, the faster they can find you and the sooner you'll get help.

One will range in size from a poppy seed on the small end to a sesame seed on the big end. Another is capable of growing to 60 inches long. The third can top 700 pounds.

They are blacklegged ticks, venomous snakes—namely, timber rattlesnakes and copperheads—and black bears, the three kinds of wildlife that hikers in Pennsylvania should pay some attention to, for safety's sake.

Ticks

The seed-size critter is the blacklegged tick, commonly called the deer tick. Ticks are dangerous because they can carry *Borrelia burgdorferi*, which is infamously the bacterium that causes Lyme disease.

It's a serious threat in Pennsylvania. The state has led the nation in reported cases of Lyme every year since 2011. Some parts of the state are worse for ticks than others—the west-central portion of the state was worst in 2016, the latest year for which records are available—but the threat of ticks is real everywhere.

Now, should these bugs be enough to keep you out of the woods? No. Treated promptly, tick bites are little more than an annoyance.

Left untreated, though, they can lead to serious ailments, from fever, chills, headaches, and fatigue to dizziness, short-term memory loss, arthritis, and facial palsy. An irregular heartbeat is even possible.

So it pays to know how to protect yourself against them, what to do if you find a tick on your body, and what symptoms to be on the lookout for.

To prevent tick bites, the US Centers for Disease Control recommends:

- Use repellent that contains 20 percent or more DEET, picaridin, or IR3535 on exposed skin for protection that lasts several hours.
- Use products that contain permethrin on clothing. Treat clothing and gear, such as boots, pants, socks, and tents with products containing 0.5 percent permethrin. It remains protective through several washings. Pre-treated clothing is available and may be protective longer.
- Bathe or shower soon after arriving home, preferably within 2 hours, being sure to do a full-body tick check. The groin, armpits, belly button, ears, backs of knees, waistline, and hairline are all likely spots for ticks to hide. Parents should check children.
- Check gear and pets, too. Ticks like to hitch rides, then attach to people later.
- Tumble dry clothes in a dryer on high heat for 10 minutes to kill ticks on dry clothing after you come indoors.
- If your clothes need to be washed first, use hot water. If hot water isn't an option, wash them, but then tumble dry on low heat for 90 minutes or high heat for 60 minutes.

- If you discover a tick on your body, use fine-tipped tweezers to grasp it as close to the skin's surface as possible. Pull upward with steady, even pressure. Don't twist or jerk the tick; this can cause the mouthparts to break off and remain in the skin. If this happens, remove the mouthparts with tweezers. If you are unable to remove the mouth easily with clean tweezers, leave it alone and let the skin heal. After removing the tick, thoroughly clean the bite area and your hands with rubbing alcohol, an iodine scrub, or soap and water. Dispose of a live tick by submersing it in alcohol, placing it in a sealed bag/container, wrapping it tightly in tape, or flushing it down the toilet. Never crush a tick with your fingers.
- Finally, while it usually takes a tick being attached to a host 24 to 36 hours to transmit disease, if any symptoms show up, consult a doctor.

Snakes

Pennsylvania is home to three venomous snakes: the timber rattlesnake, copperhead, and massasauga.

The last of the three, the massasauga, is the rarest. In fact, it's endangered and only known to exist in two of the state's sixty-seven counties, and even then in just parts of them, so you won't have to worry about it. They typically stretch 18 to 40 inches.

Copperheads are the mid-size snake of the three, reaching lengths of 24 to 36 inches. They've been verified in about three-quarters of the state, though they were more widespread historically, so there's a chance they could be almost anywhere.

Timber rattlesnakes, meanwhile, are the granddaddy of Pennsylvania's venomous snakes. Capable of reaching 60 inches in length, they're found in all but the most extreme western and southeastern counties.

The timber rattlesnake—which comes in yellow and black color phases—is the species that most recently claimed a human life. In 2015 a 39-year-old man putting wood on a campfire startled a timber rattler, which bit him. He developed respiratory problems on the way to the hospital and died.

That's the rare exception, though.

The Pennsylvania Fish and Boat Commission—with responsibility for snakes in the state—said it hardly ever hears of more than two or three snake bites per year. In many years there are none. The state's Department of Conservation and Natural Resources, meanwhile, said the fatal 2015 bite was the first of its kind in more than twenty-five years.

Still, some common sense is in order. To avoid getting bitten, by a timber rattlesnake or any other snake, the Fish and Boat Commission offers some recommendations:

- Most rattlesnakes rattle when approached or feel threatened. If you hear rattling nearby, retreat and proceed by another route, or proceed only after identifying its location.
- Do not attempt to displace or capture the snake. Timber rattlesnakes are not an aggressive species and will avoid human contact if given the opportunity to flee or retreat under cover.

- Never walk barefoot or with open shoes (sandals) when hiking through Pennsylvania's wild lands.

- Keep your dogs leashed when hiking whenever practical. Be watchful of what they investigate, especially when unleashed. While most dogs will avoid a rattlesnake, don't make any assumptions. A rattlesnake will strike if it feels threatened and is approached too closely.

- Timber rattlesnakes may seek temporary shelter as well as food, like rodents, in outdoor man-made structures, including wood piles, construction debris, and the like. If one is found, realize that its occupancy is only temporary, and that in a few days it will move to another location, probably the natural environment from where it came.

- Be especially mindful of snakes from July through September, when mating season has males on the move.

Black Bears

Pennsylvania's black bear population is large and growing. A dozen years ago, the Pennsylvania Game Commission estimated the number of bears within the state at 15,000. Six years ago it was up to 18,000. Today the population is thought to number 20,000 animals, spread across virtually every county in the state.

So, yeah, they're all over the place.

They get big, too. Records kept by hunting organizations like the Boone & Crockett Club show that Pennsylvania black bears are routinely among the largest in the world. In parts of Canada, for example, where the living is hard, a big bear might weigh 200 pounds. In Pennsylvania—where there is not only a great variety of wild foods, but also all kinds of domestic ones—omnivorous male bears routinely top 400 pounds. Each year, hunters kill several weighing more than 600 pounds. The largest taken in recent years exceeded 800.

For all that, they are—generally speaking—not aggressive toward people. Most avoid encounters when possible, and will often sneak away before you even know they're around.

The Game Commission, though, offers advice on what to do if you encounter a bear while outdoors:

- If you see a bear, alert it to your presence. Make noise and give it ample time and space to turn and leave. Avoid being caught up in the excitement of seeing a bear and inadvertently letting the bear get too close before surprising it.

- If you have a close encounter, back away slowly while facing the bear, so you always know where the bear is and how it's reacting. Slowly backing away diffuses the situation and gives the bear room to flee.

- While unexpectedly encountering a bear can be startling, remain calm. Avoid sudden movements and talk calmly to the bear while retreating. Don't turn and run or attempt to climb a tree. Running may prompt the bear to give chase, and climbing a tree could be interpreted as a threat to any cubs that are present, as cubs often climb trees when startled. Move toward your camper, house, or vehicle if nearby.

- Pay attention to what the bear is doing. Bears use all of their senses to figure out what you are. That might involve standing upright or moving closer in an attempt to detect odors in the air currents. Don't consider this a sign of aggression. Once a bear identifies you, it will usually leave. If it begins to slowly approach you, face the bear, wave your arms wildly and shout while continuing to back away. The idea is to intimidate the bear into retreating. Swing a stick, your backpack, or whatever is handy if the bear gets close.

- If suddenly surprised, some bears may feel threatened and give warning signs that they are uncomfortable. They may clack their jaws together or sway their head; those are signs for you to leave. Some bears have been known to charge to within a few feet when threatened. If this occurs, wave your arms wildly and shout at the bear.

- Finally, if you have no other choice, fight back. Bears have been driven away when people have fought back with rocks, sticks, binoculars, and even their bare hands.

Leave No Trace

Pennsylvania is blessed to have a lot of public land, at least by Northeastern standards. It's home to many, many historic sites, too. All are popular to one degree or another. And that's almost a problem. Increasing numbers of people spending more and more time in fewer and fewer places can lead to sites being almost literally loved to death. It's why state park officials are looking into whether to limit visitation to some sensitive areas.

Hikers can do their part to maintain access to areas while still protecting them by remembering the seven main principles of "leave no trace." They are as follows:

- Plan ahead and prepare. That means visit during off-peak times when possible and in small groups, and be prepared for weather and emergencies.

- Travel (and camp) on durable surfaces. That means using established trails, walking single file on trails to avoid widening them, and otherwise keeping your impact small.

- Dispose of waste properly. OK, as a day hiker you won't be leaving human waste behind, at least in most cases. And many hikes have bathrooms along the way. But there are exceptions. Know how to handle things in places where you're on your own.

- Leave what you find. Have you ever heard the phrase, "Take only pictures, leave only footprints?" It applies to historical hikes as much as anywhere. Leave natural objects and historical artifacts as you find them.

- Respect wildlife. A white-tailed deer is a lovely creature, for example. But it's a wild one, too, and should be treated as such. Don't pick up or collect baby wildlife, or try to approach too closely to any animal. Observe them from a distance, take photos, but leave them alone.

- Be considerate of others. You'll encounter other history buffs when visiting the sites in this book. Some will want the same experience as you; others will be looking for something different, perhaps with less walking, or with pedaling replacing walking. Be courteous and share the trail.

- Finally, minimize campfire impacts. There are a few sites in this book where camping is permitted. Use only established fire rings in such places to make sure those who follow after you have the same opportunity for adventure.

Trail Finder

Best Hikes for Military History

7. Fort Pitt Museum and Point State Park
8. Bushy Run Battlefield
10. Fort Necessity National Battlefield
24. Gettysburg National Military Park
25. U.S. Army Heritage and Education Center
38. Washington Crossing State Park and Delaware Canal State Park
39. Valley Forge National Historical Park

Best Hikes for Industrial History

3. Oil Creek State Park
5. McConnells Mill State Park
9. Friendship Hill National Historic Site
12. Allegheny Portage Railroad National Historic Site
15. Kinzua Bridge State Park
17. Pennsylvania Lumber Museum
19. Greenwood Furnace State Park
20. Little Buffalo State Park
21. Kings Gap Environmental Education Center
22. Pine Grove Furnace State Park
31. Hugh Moore Park
32. Boulton Historic Site and Jacobsburg Environmental Education Center
35. Hopewell Furnace National Historic Site and French Creek State Park

Best Hikes for Conservation History

16. Woodring Farm
27. Promised Land State Park
28. Grey Towers National Historic Site
33. Hawk Mountain Sanctuary

Best Hikes for Man-Made Tragedies

13. Johnstown Flood National Memorial
14. Flight 93 National Memorial

Best Hikes for Natural History

2. Hearts Content National Scenic Area
4. Cook Forest State Park
18. Leonard Harrison State Park
26. Lacawac Sanctuary
29. Ricketts Glen State Park

Best Hikes for Artistic and Recreational History

6. Raccoon Creek State Park
11. Fallingwater
30. Delaware Water Gap National Recreation Area
36. John James Audubon Center at Mill Grove

Best Hikes for Lighthouses

1. Presque Isle State Park

Best Hikes for Agricultural and Pioneer History

34. Daniel Boone Homestead
37. Norristown Farm Park

Best Hikes for Political History

23. Caledonia State Park
40. Independence National Historical Park

MAP LEGEND

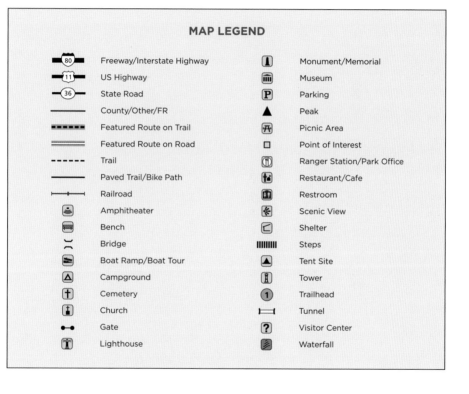

🛣 80	Freeway/Interstate Highway	📍	Monument/Memorial
11	US Highway	🏛	Museum
36	State Road	Ⓟ	Parking
	County/Other/FR	▲	Peak
▪▪▪▪▪▪	Featured Route on Trail	🪑	Picnic Area
	Featured Route on Road	□	Point of Interest
- - - - -	Trail	🏢	Ranger Station/Park Office
	Paved Trail/Bike Path	🍴	Restaurant/Cafe
⊢——⊣	Railroad	🚻	Restroom
🎭	Amphitheater	🔭	Scenic View
🛋	Bench	◰	Shelter
⌣	Bridge	⦀⦀⦀⦀⦀	Steps
🚤	Boat Ramp/Boat Tour	🔺	Tent Site
⛺	Campground	🗼	Tower
✝	Cemetery	①	Trailhead
⛪	Church	⊢—⊣	Tunnel
•—•	Gate	❓	Visitor Center
🗼	Lighthouse	〰	Waterfall

West

1 Presque Isle State Park

Start: At the parking lot for the Perry Monument and exhibit and scenic boat tours
Distance: 4 miles
Type: Out and back
Hiking time: 3 hours
Difficulty: Easy
Best season: May to October
Traffic: Hikers only, at least by rule, on the Sidewalk Trail; vehicles and bicycles for a short way on the park road

Fees and permits: None to hike the trail or see the Perry Monument; fee to climb the lighthouse on those occasions when it's open (check with the state park)
Maps: Available at www.dcnr.state.pa.us/stateparks/findapark/presqueisle
Trail contact: Presque Isle State Park, 301 Peninsula Dr., Ste. 1, Erie 16505-2042; (814) 833-7424; www.dcnr.state.pa.us/stateparks/findapark/presqueisle

Finding the trailhead: From I-79 North in Erie, take exit 182 to merge onto West 26th St./US Route 20 West. Turn right onto Route 832 and follow it roughly 1.5 miles—here it becomes Peninsula Drive—into the park. GPS: N42 09.292' / W80 05.508'

The Hike

Likely few of the 4 million people who visit Presque Isle State Park annually—nearly as many as travel to Yellowstone in a calendar year—know it. But the park is never the same place twice.

It's a long, narrow peninsula that on a map looks like a crooked left index finger with the flesh before the first knuckle swollen from an errant hammer blow. Buffeted by the winds and tides of Lake Erie, it's constantly shifting shape, its sands coming and going with the years.

In a couple of other ways, though, it's timeless.

It was here, from Misery Bay, that Commodore Oliver Hazard Perry and his Lake Erie Squadron recorded a first in naval history and helped save a young nation. It's also here that a towering remnant of the region's industrial past—a lighthouse once notoriously inaccessible by road—still operates.

Connecting the two historic sites is a path known as the Sidewalk Trail, a flat, narrow, mostly paved walkway. A mud and wooden plank thoroughfare until being paved in 1925, it once served a utilitarian purpose. Lighthouse keepers who needed to reach the city of Erie for supplies would walk it to Misery Bay, where they kept a boat docked to finish the trip. Up until 1927 children followed the same route to school. The only difference was that rather than pilot their own craft across the bay, the Lifesaving Service, later called the US Coast Guard, provided a ride.

Today the trail is a pleasant walk connecting the lighthouse—open periodically for tours, for a fee—and the monument to Perry's achievements.

Hikers and bikers on the pathway leading to the Perry Monument, visible in the background. Kiosks tell the story of Perry and the battle.

In getting from one to the other, hikers have to watch out for poison ivy and ticks. The terrain to the sides of the trail can be low and wet, too, so insect repellent is necessary. But hikers are also often treated to sightings of white-tailed deer, squirrels, wild turkeys, rare wildflowers like purple lupine, and all sorts of birdlife, from great blue herons to bald eagles. If you really want to explore that nature, other trails wind through the area, 1,000 acres of which are managed as an "ecological reservation."

And while you're in the area, consider a visit to Erie's Maritime Museum (www.flagshipniagara.org), which is home to a replica of Perry's ship, the *Niagara*.

The History

Presque Isle is a place of beauty today. In past years it was the site of both heroism and tragedy, and loneliness and hard work.

The heroism and tragedy resulted from the War of 1812. Great Britain—still stinging over the loss of the American colonies—was a thorn in the side of the new nation. It was basically kidnapping American sailors at sea and pressing them into service on its own ships, while also causing all manner of grief and mischief inland from Canada. War resulted.

Control of the Great Lakes—in an age before railways and highways—was critical to controlling travel and commerce, so the US government commissioned the building of a fleet of warships in Erie in September 1812. Two 110-foot vessels were built, along with five smaller ones. Four other commercial craft were also pressed into service.

Sent to command the new flotilla the following March was Commodore Oliver Hazard Perry. Son of a sailor, he'd gone to sea himself at 14 years old and been captain of his own ship by age 24. Despite his accomplishments, probably few in the world thought he could win. His boats were crewed by about 500 men. Some were sailors. The rest were Marines, US Army soldiers, local militia, and free black men. Few had been in a naval battle; most had never even been on a ship.

The British Navy, meanwhile, was seasoned and powerful. It reigned supreme worldwide. Never, historians say, had one of its squadrons suffered an unqualified defeat.

Against Perry, though, it did.

Perry took nine ships into battle against six from the British Navy on September 10, 1813, near Put-in-Bay, Ohio. Things didn't go well initially. The American cannons were limited in range, so Perry's crew took a beating just getting into the fight. His flagship, the *Lawrence*, was so severely damaged that Perry had to climb into a rowboat with a handful of crew, row under fire to the battleship *Niagara*, and take command from there. He raised his personal battle flag—which proclaimed "Never give up the ship"—and led the Americans to victory. His message relaying the news became famous: "We have met the enemy and they are ours."

It came at a cost, though.

Perry's crew returned to Presque Isle. The wounded were treated at the county courthouse, which was turned into a makeshift hospital. The remainder spent the winter of 1813-14 aboard ship in Little Bay. Conditions were crowded and squalid. One surgeon aboard ship wrote that he was "reduced to a skeleton and will never cross this or any other lake again." Many men got sick; some died and were buried in Graveyard Pond. Things got so bad that the bay was renamed Misery Bay, the moniker it still carries today.

The victory opened the way for America to take control of the continent once and for all. Perry didn't see much of that. He died of yellow fever in Venezuela on his birthday in 1819. But his achievement is remembered at a monument erected at Misery Bay on September 10, 1926. It stands 101 feet tall and measures 8.5 feet wide at the bottom and 6.5 feet at the top. Its bronze top, once lit by a natural gas flame—which often was extinguished by wind—now features a solar-powered, multicolored LED light.

Meanwhile, at the other end of the Sidewalk Trail—and testament to loneliness and hard work—is an icon of the industrial city that Erie became. The city once held

The Presque Isle Lighthouse. Originally 40 feet tall, it was later raised to 57 feet. Tours are sometimes possible.

Hikers follow the Sidewalk Trail toward the Presque Isle Lighthouse.

500 manufacturing plants, including the world's largest horseshoe and pipe organ factories. Raw materials and finished goods alike were moved by ship then, at a time when there was no such thing as electronic navigation. The Presque Isle Lighthouse was one of hundreds on the Great Lakes that provided that service, alerting sailors to where they were in relation to potential hazards.

The lighthouse was 40 feet tall when originally built in 1873. It was raised to 57 feet in 1896 to increase visibility. Its light was a Fresnel (pronounced fresh-nel) encased in brass and lit by a single oil lantern. It projected light for 13 nautical miles.

Keeping it lit was labor intensive. The lighthouse keeper had to maintain it every four hours, sunset to sunrise, from April through November. He did it alone, too. Until the road to Presque Isle was built in 1927, the keeper and his family lived alone except for the few occasions when a supply ship would arrive. Charles Waldo, who spent seven years there, and whose wife Mary bore the first child on the peninsula, called it "the loneliest place on earth."

Today the lighthouse lamp still operates for the sake of small boats. It's lit by an electric bulb operating on a timer. The lighthouse, meanwhile—which was built five bricks thick to withstand the cold and has rounded corners inside—serves as a residence for park staff.

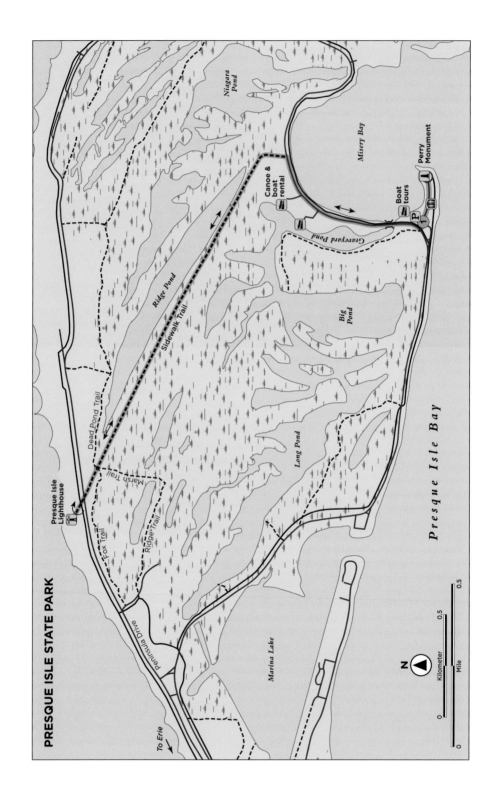

PRESQUE ISLE STATE PARK

Niagara Pond

Misery Bay

Perry Monument

Canoe & boat rental

Boat tours

Graveyard Pond

Ridge Pond

Sidewalk Trail

Dead Pond Trail

Big Pond

Marsh Trail

Long Pond

Presque Isle Lighthouse

Fox Trail

Ridge Trail

Peninsula Drive

To Erie

Marina Lake

Presque Isle Bay

N

Kilometer

Mile

0   0.5

0   0.5

Miles and Directions

0.0 From the parking lot entrance, walk past the educational kiosks to the Perry Monument. There are a few grills and picnic tables here, as well as restrooms.

0.1 Arrive at the monument.

0.3 After backtracking from the monument to the parking lot, turn right to walk the park road.

0.4 Cross over a bridge. Graveyard Pond is on the left.

0.6 On the left is a kayak and bicycle rental. Paddlers can enter the park's lagoons here, a neat place to see wildlife.

0.8 Sidewalk Trail enters the woods on the left. Use caution when crossing the road. The trail here is narrow but paved. Watch for lots of wildlife.

1.8 Notice the bat house on a pole on the left, built as a home for bats that eat pesky mosquitoes.

1.9 Sidewalk Trail intersects Marsh Trail and Fox Trail on the left and Dead Pond Trail on the right. Continue straight.

2.0 The trail hits the park road. Watch for traffic and cross over to reach the lighthouse. There are educational displays here. You can also walk onto the beach to see Lake Erie and get a beach view of the lighthouse. Turn around at the lighthouse and retrace your steps to the monument parking lot.

4.0 Arrive back at the parking lot.

2 Hearts Content National Scenic Area

Start: At the Hearts Content day-use area parking lot
Distance: 1.2 miles
Type: Loop
Hiking time: 1 hour
Difficulty: Easy
Best season: April to October

Traffic: Hikers only
Fees and permits: None
Maps: Available at www.alleghenysite.com/wp-content/uploads/2011/11/map3.pdf
Trail contact: Allegheny National Forest, 4 Farm Colony Dr., Warren 16365; (814) 723-5150; www.fs.usda.gov/allegheny

Finding the trailhead: From Warren, take Route 6 to the Mohawk Avenue exit (look for a sign for Hearts Content). Go south, then bear right onto Pleasant Drive for 11.5 miles. Turn left onto Route 2002 and go 3.7 miles. The entrance to Hearts Content is on the left. GPS: N41 41.525' / W79 15.133'

The Hike

One benefit of old-growth forests? Easy walking.

You'll notice that while cruising through Hearts Content National Scenic Area. Trees reaching 140 feet or higher into the sky do a great job of keeping much sunlight from reaching the forest floor. That limits the amount of underbrush. When you add in lots of white-tailed deer—forestry officials believe there have been too many here for too long—they can keep what does grow from getting rolling. The result is a national forest section that seems manicured, almost vacuumed even, and certainly park-like.

That's welcome here, though.

The larger Allegheny National Forest is big, by Eastern standards, at more than 500,000 acres. But it's fragmented, broken into several pieces, with each of those pieces home to varying amounts of oil and gas development. That makes undisturbed tracts like this all the more special.

When you walk here, though, pay attention not only to the trees still standing, but those on the forest floor, too. One defining characteristic of old-growth forest is the logs that have fallen and are rotting into the earth. At first, they seem dead, just pieces of trees that didn't make it. But they support a whole ecosystem of their own. Look at the thick moss growing on them, like lime-colored shag carpet. It supports bugs and other life; they in turn feed birds that can only survive in such locations. Fungi of all kinds grow on the logs, too.

You'll cross the West Branch Tionesta Creek along the way, but always on bridges, so there are no tricky areas. Do bring bug spray, though, as some of these low spots can get swampy enough to breed mosquitoes.

Hearts Content National Scenic Area has been a National Natural Landmark since 1977.

Finally, before leaving, check out the small pavilion with a squared-off log and informational panels on old-growth forest and the men who worked it. There's also a pavilion here with tables, if you packed lunch. It is a lovely spot for a picnic.

The History

You won't find any old buildings in Hearts Content National Scenic Area. No, the history here is too old for that.

More than 150 years before the British built Fort Pitt in Pittsburgh, and 160 or so before the Americans declared their independence, and almost 250 before the first shots were fired in the Civil War, some of the trees growing in Hearts Content had already taken root. Shoot, some of the trees got their start around the same time the Pilgrims landed on Plymouth Rock in 1620.

That's old.

The history here, then, is of the natural sort. That it survived is a miracle or, at least, the result of some good-natured, if self-centered, luck.

Pennsylvania was once covered in giant virgin forests. An estimated 8 million acres of forest covered this region of Pennsylvania alone when the first European settlers arrived. But then, in the late nineteenth and early twentieth centuries, those vast forests were subjected to devastation. Hemlocks were cut down to provide bark for tanneries and wood for construction. White pines 140 feet and taller were chopped down to become masts for clipper ships. Hardwoods were turned into furniture.

Timber operators set out to take all of it. The thinking of the time was that the forests were inexhaustible. Cut one patch of trees down and just move on to the next—that was the mindset. Conservation? There was no time for that. The area around Hearts Content felt the bite of the axe, as surely as did any other. As early as the 1830s, Warren County had more than one hundred sawmills in operation.

It took a hardy breed of man to cut those trees down, square them off, and get them out of the woods and downriver to markets. If you doubt that, check out the squared log on display under the pavilion at the trailhead, and imagine the effort it took to shape it like that. Then think about what it took to move those logs. Typically, crews bound a bunch of the giant logs together to form massive "creek rafts" 100 feet long by 15 feet wide. They'd literally ride those downstream until they hit a larger river, where as many as nine "creek rafts" were joined to form one "river raft" 300 feet long. They'd build a shanty atop that for cooking and sleeping and pilot the rafts to the state's biggest cities. There the logs were dismantled and sold.

Amazingly, one tiny patch of woods survived.

The William H. Wheeler family, partners in one of the area's many logging operations, had a home here. Not wanting to be surrounded by nothing but stumps, they left 20 acres of the big timber closest to their home standing. That area is now Hearts Content. It passed into public ownership in 1922, when descendants of Wheeler and Henry Dusenbury, a partner, donated the 20-acre site to the US Forest Service "for public use and enjoyment." Another 100 acres were added over time.

Today the Hearts Content Scenic Area is a National Natural Landmark, having been given that distinction in 1977. It's home to 300- and 400-year-old white pines and hemlocks, trees that tower into the sky. The forest around them doesn't look exactly like it might have when the Pilgrims arrived on the East Coast. The chestnut trees that also would have been a big presence here are gone, killed by blight. And—as the tremendous logs on the forest floor show—nature is always changing.

But this area is ancient, and for that reason historic in its own way.

Miles and Directions

0.0 Start at the gravel parking area for the day-use area.

0.2 The Short Loop Trail goes to the right. Stay left on the main loop.

0.4 Come to a memorial for the Wheeler and Dusenbury families, who donated 20 acres of virgin timber here to the federal government.

0.5 Cross a bridge over West Branch Tionesta Creek. Soon you will cross the creek again, this time on a plank bridge.

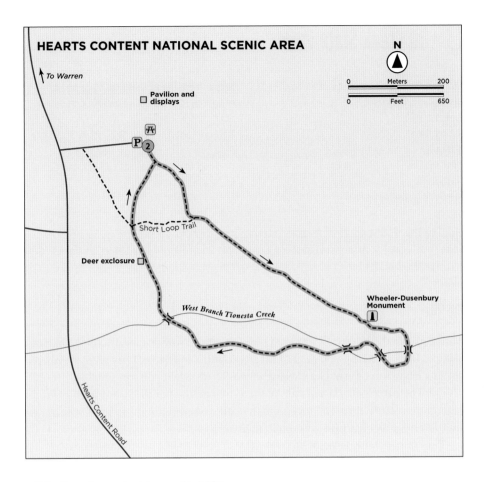

HEARTS CONTENT NATIONAL SCENIC AREA

N

To Warren

Pavilion and displays

P 2

Short Loop Trail

Deer exclosure

West Branch Tionesta Creek

Wheeler-Dusenbury Monument

Hearts Content Road

| 0 | Meters | 200 |
| 0 | Feet | 650 |

0.6 Cross the creek again on a tiny bridge.

1.0 Look on the left for a deer exclosure, a spot where fencing has been erected to keep white-tailed deer out, so that the species they otherwise prefer to browse on can grow.

1.1 The trail Ys at a spot where it's easy to miss the turn to the right. That's the one you want, though. To go left would take you to the picnic area. Instead, turn right to close the loop, then turn left and retrace your steps to the parking lot.

1.2 Arrive back at the parking area.

3 Oil Creek State Park

Start: At the Petroleum Centre Train Station
Distance: 5.6 miles
Type: Loop
Hiking time: 3.5 hours
Difficulty: Moderate to difficult
Best season: April to October
Traffic: Hikers and bicyclists
Fees and permits: None

Maps: Available at www.dcnr.state.pa.us/
cs/groups/public/documents/document/
dcnr_003502.pdf
Trail contact: Oil Creek State Park, 305 State
Park Road, Oil City 16301-9733; (814)
676-5915; www.dcnr.state.pa.us/stateparks/
findapark/oilcreek

Finding the trailhead: From Franklin, follow Route 8 North for about 12 miles. Turn right onto State Park Road. Follow it to the Petroleum Centre Train Station and Visitor Center, on the left. GPS: N41 31.098' / W79 41.000'

The Hike

At first glance the oil barrels scattered throughout the woods appear to be giant rustic planters, like something you might find at a country craft store. They seem weathered, but in a chic kind of way. Get closer, though. That's when you can smell it.

Oil. The barrels, blackened still by the crude petroleum that was pulled from the ground here more than 150 years ago, remain soaked through, as your nostrils will attest. You can feel it, too, if you touch their sides.

They aren't alone, though.

The Oil Creek valley—which was for a time as wild and wicked a place as any on earth—was built in a hurry. Men eager to find fortune didn't have time even to build brick buildings in the boom towns that sprang up. They certainly didn't have time or the inclination to clean up after themselves when the boom ended either. The barrels and other detritus of their passing—rotting tin buildings, stone foundations, odds and ends of rusting machinery—remain throughout the park.

They're visible and sometimes jarring reminders. You'll be walking through the woods of Oil Creek State Park, enjoying what seems to be an idyllic, if not exactly remote, forest when you suddenly stub your toe on an ancient pipeline.

That's what makes this hike so unique, though. It's interesting to see what's left behind, to know what the area was like when oil was king, and to see how it's come back after what was nothing short of environmental devastation.

The hike begins and ends in Petroleum Centre, at the train station visitor center. On the way back, near the end of the hike, you'll walk past a dozen or more informational panels telling about the area. They make up what's known as the Petroleum Centre Walking Tour. You'll notice we're walking it backwards; the arrows on those

A hiker on Oil Creek State Park's Gerard Hiking Trail stops for a look back after passing by an old barrel and other debris left over from the area's oil boom.

signs point the opposite direction. Don't worry about that. There's no real order to them, and this gives us the chance to see them before we're done.

Otherwise, the hike largely follows Gerard Hiking Trail—a wonderful backpacking trail in the park, if you're ever inclined to do an overnighter—and the park's paved bike trail. It winds past a "historical tableau," almost a period movie set, along the way.

One thing worth noticing is what existed before the oil drillers and what's still here now that they're gone: Oil Creek itself. When the oil boom was going full tilt, it ran black, courtesy of oil that escaped and other pollution purposely freed in an era when environmental protections weren't even a thought. The oil left it dead for decades, its fish and other aquatic life gone. Today, though, it's a wonderful place to fish, paddle, and just enjoy.

Nature, and life, can conquer all, given the chance.

The History

Mud, murder, and madness. Riches, railroads, and riots. Pollution, poverty, and—at the very root of it all—petroleum. Pennsylvania's Oil Creek valley spawned them all.

When Col. Edwin Drake drilled the world's first commercial oil well here, hitting black gold at 69.5 feet in August 1859, he literally changed the course of history. As one writer later put it, "The oil rush changed the pace of the world and greased the wheels of the machine age. It lit up the future, fueled wars, speeded peace and is still flowing strong."

Ah, but the cost. The Oil Creek valley, which spawned fortunes, also birthed chaos. Men were making money at a dizzying pace.

Consider the case of John Benninghoff. He was a subsistence farmer in the valley in 1865, living primarily on what he could grow. But when wells were successfully drilled on his 240-acre property—a bit of a surprise, as previously no one knew it was possible to work on slopes like his—he leased his ground in small lots. He not only charged exorbitant lot rents, but also collected one-quarter of the oil from each well. In no time at all, he was earning $6,000 a day—the equivalent of about $85,000 today.

James McCray did even better. A farmer who owned the bluff behind where the state park office now sits, was making $9,000 a day—the equivalent of almost $128,000 every 24 hours—in 1871.

Drillers were making money, too, and would-be oil barons poured in from all over. They secured themselves a piece of unproven ground and went to work, giving birth to the name "wildcatters" for their rogue ways.

To serve them, towns sprang up all around the valley, populated by blacksmith and cooper shops, grocery stores, bakeries, saloons, brothels, and other businesses. Each village—Petroleum Centre, Pioneer, and Funkville, among others—was more hastily constructed than the last. With rules in place saying that any building found to be sitting above oil had to be moved within thirty days, structures were quickly built from green wood and, when necessary, just as quickly moved. Only one building in the entire valley was ever made of stone or brick in the oil rush days.

Life, sadly, was considered no more valuable or worthy of preservation than the buildings. The valley not only drew drillers and those looking to serve them, but others willing to prey on them. Petroleum Centre became known as the wildest town east of the Mississippi. It's said that California gold rush veterans who visited called the Oil Creek valley the roughest, most perverse place they'd ever seen.

Crime was rampant. Benninghoff had $200,000 stolen from his home in what was the area's greatest robbery. A waitress was shot and killed in 1866 in the Temple of Fashion saloon, and the newspapers of the day barely noted it. Sandbagging—hitting someone in the head from behind with a wet bag of sand—was regularly practiced. A story in the *Oil City Derrick*, a newspaper of the day, said that Petroleum Centre "could have given Sodom and Gomorrah points in wrecking weak mortals and sending them to the devil by the shortest cut."

All coexisted in a world that was grimy, smoky, and dirty. Oil fouled Oil Creek. Fires were devastating, and routine. And the mud? It was a hallmark of everyday life. A traveler passing through the region in 1865 described it as the "great leveler of distinction." He wrote, "The wealthy capitalist of New York, still more wealthy oil prince of the creek and the laborer working for the modest sum of $5 to $10 a day can scarcely be distinguished from each other under the mask of mud worn by each."

The Petroleum Centre Train Station allows visitors to explore Oil Creek State Park by train.

Another called the streets of bottomless, clinging, sticky mud "wholly unclassable, almost impassable, scarcely jackassable."

The boom towns didn't last. By the 1870s, the valley was dotted with ghost towns, as those who had struck it rich and those who hadn't all moved on, to enjoy their windfall or seek it out.

Visitors today can see much of what they left behind in the state park. Be sure to stop by the Drake Well Museum and Park (www.drakewell.org). It tells the story of the region in numerous ways, including indoor and outdoor exhibits and historic structures spread over three sites.

Miles and Directions

0.0 Start at the Petroleum Centre Train Station and Visitor Center. There are some exhibits inside the building (open noon to 5 p.m. on Saturday and Sunday) and train rides for those who buy a ticket. Leave the station and walk about 80 feet to the gravel Stevenson Hill Road. Turn right and follow the road.

0.2 Turn right into the woods onto Gerard Hiking Trail. Follow the yellow blazes. Note right away the old pipelines underfoot (sometimes painted to make them noticeable), old oil barrels, the remains of tin buildings, and more.

0.3 Cross a small footbridge.

0.4 The trail Ts. Go right to follow the yellow blazes.

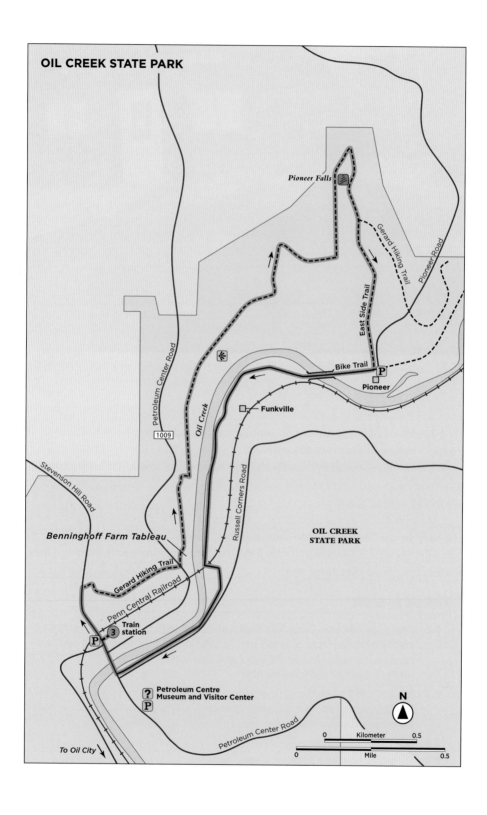

OIL CREEK STATE PARK

Pioneer Falls

Gerard Hiking Trail

Pioneer Road

East Side Trail

Petroleum Center Road

1009

Oil Creek

Bike Trail

P

Pioneer

Funkville

Russell Corners Road

OIL CREEK
STATE PARK

Stevenson Hill Road

Benninghoff Farm Tableau

Gerard Hiking Trail

Penn Central Railroad

Train
station

3

P

Petroleum Centre
Museum and Visitor Center

?

P

To Oil City

Petroleum Center Road

N

0   Kilometer   0.5

0   Mile   0.5

0.5 See an old foundation on the right. Just after crossing another bridge, cross Petroleum Center Road (Route 1009), then cross another bridge over Benninghoff Run.

0.6 The trail Ts. Go straight to follow the yellow blazes. Arrive at the Benninghoff Farm Tableau, which has oil derricks and an engine house. When the famous "Ocean Well" was sunk here in 1865, proving that it was possible to drill even on steep hillsides, the farmer who owned the land began earning $6,000 a day in leases.

0.8 Come to a Y junction. Go right on Gerard, following the yellow blazes. Soon the trail Ys again. Go right on Gerard. The trail gets narrower and steeper here.

1.1 Notice the old foundations to the left and right.

1.4 A bench on the right offers an overlook of Oil Creek.

1.6 Look for an ancient collapsing building on the right.

2.0 Pass another old building on the right.

2.1 Cross a small footbridge.

2.3 Come to Pioneer Falls. This is a scenic spot to stop for a drink or snack.

2.8 The trail Ys. Gerard Trail, with its yellow blazes, goes left, up a set of stairs. Instead, go right and follow the white blazes of East Side Trail.

3.2 The trail Ys. Go left toward Pioneer Road parking lot.

3.3 By an old concrete structure, hit Pioneer Road. Go right on this gravel lane.

3.4 Cross through the Pioneer Road parking lot and turn right onto the park's paved bicycle trail. Soon you will pass an informational panel identifying the location of the village of Pioneer. It's the first known spot where vacuum recovery was used to draw forth oil.

3.5 Cross over Oil Creek on the bridge.

3.7 East Side Trail goes to the left, marked by white blazes. Stay straight on the paved bike trail.

3.8 Pass a marker identifying the location of Funkville.

4.6 Look for a replica of a barge on the left. Look right to see a view of the Benninghoff Farm Tableau, then follow the trail beneath a railroad bridge.

4.7 The trail meets Russell Corners Road. Go right.

5.2 Russell Corners Road comes to a T at Petroleum Center Road (Route 1009). Go right on Petroleum Center, walk across the bridge, then cross the road to the left to get to the wooden boardwalk. Follow it (this is the Petroleum Centre Walking Tour, which we're doing sort of backwards, though that doesn't matter. This way allows you to hit it from this direction).

5.3 At the end of the boardwalk, turn right and backtrack slightly to hit the boardwalk closest to the bridge. Follow the boardwalk to the end, turn left to cross the road, and follow the boardwalk back again.

5.5 Note the cement steps here. They're remnants of the only brick building that existed in Petroleum Centre. Then turn right.

5.6 Arrive back at the train station visitor center to close the loop.

4 Cook Forest State Park

Start: At the Cook Forest State Park office
Distance: 5.2 miles
Type: Loop
Hiking time: 3.5 hours
Difficulty: Moderate to difficult
Best season: April to October
Traffic: Hikers only
Fees and permits: None

Maps: Available at www.dcnr.pa.gov/State Parks/FindAPark/CookForestStatePark/Pages/Maps.aspx
Trail contact: Cook Forest State Park, 113 River Rd., PO Box 120, Cooksburg 16217-0120; (814) 744-8407; www.dcnr.pa.gov/StateParks/FindAPark/CookForestStatePark/Pages/Maps.aspx

Finding the trailhead: Follow Route 36 north from Sigel for about eight miles. Turn right onto River Road and go just a few hundred feet. The park office and parking are on the left. GPS: N41 19.947' / W79 12.468'

The Hike

This hike is designed to take you to two of Cook Forest State Park's most majestic features, the Forest Cathedral and the nearly 90-year-old fire tower.

That requires some climbing, though.

Starting at the park office, the hike enters the woods just beyond the children's fishing pond—and the rustic cabins built by the Civilian Conservation Corps in the 1930s—and goes immediately uphill on Indian Trail. There are log steps for a portion of the way. Still, this will test your aerobic fitness.

The trails, though, are wide, flat, and often carpeted in pine needles. One benefit of old-growth timber is lack of competing understory. Be sure to look up and down along the way. The absolute tallest trees aren't identified—park officials fear too much traffic would cause harm—but it's cool to see the giant, knotty roots underfoot and the trees sprouting from those roots stretching into the sky. Be sure to check out some of the house-size boulders in here, too. Some are fun to climb on if you want to go off-trail just a bit.

Near the intersection of Indian Trail and Longfellow Trail, meanwhile, look for the marker—appropriately enough, attached to a giant tree—identifying the Forest Cathedral as a National Natural Landmark. Then get ready to do some more climbing.

You'll backtrack a bit, then drop down to Toms Run, ultimately crossing Forest Road. After that the hike goes largely uphill on its way to the fire tower. It's not uphill the entire way; there are some level stretches, too. But it's uphill more often than not, which only makes sense, right? No one builds a lookout tower in a valley.

Boulders are piled atop one another in the Forest Cathedral in Cook Forest State Park.

On the way to the top of the ridge, the hike—now on paths that double as the Deer Park Trail/North Country National Scenic Trail—passes through some old and some newer forests. White-tailed deer are more common here.

Just beyond Seneca Trail, you'll encounter some more interesting rock formations. Next you trade walking through the open woods to winding among close-growing mountain laurel. Emerge from there and, before getting to the fire tower, you'll pass a parking lot with restrooms and then Seneca Point Overlook. You have to detour just a couple of hundred yards to check out the overlook, but it's worth it. The view is not entirely panoramic; vegetation can block it a bit. But it's worth seeing while you're here.

After visiting the fire tower, backtrack to Seneca Trail and follow it steeply downhill. Use caution here; there are a few drop-offs on the right that bear watching. But the descent offers a peek at the Clarion River, portions of which are in the National Wild and Scenic Rivers System. You'll cross Route 36 again to wind back up at the park office and close the loop.

Cook Forest State Park is, like a few other spots in Pennsylvania, home to some magnificent old-growth forest. This forest is special even among those in one way, though.

John Cook was the first permanent white settler to arrive in this area. He showed up with his family of ten children in 1828, looking to build an east-west canal on the Clarion River. That never came to be. He did log some of his 765 acres, though, cutting the timber with a water-powered mill and floating the logs to Pittsburgh for sale. One of his sons took over later, building additional sawmills, adding flour and planing mills, a store, and more. Around 1870 he built the Cook homestead, now known—and still standing—as the Inn at Cook Forest. His descendants ran the lumbering operation as A. Cook Sons Co.

Nowhere along the way were all the trees cut in this area, though. Some stands were left untouched. So in 1927, at the urging of Gov. Gifford Pinchot and conservation groups, the state bought 6,055 acres from A. Cook Sons for $647,000 and turned it into Cook Forest State Park. It was the first Pennsylvania state park created specifically to preserve a natural area.

Today some of that virgin forest remains. The area known as the "Forest Cathedral" is especially impressive, encompassing what is thought of as the finest stand of old-growth white pine in the eastern United States. It's here you'll find—potentially, as it's not marked—the tallest known tree east of the Great Smoky Mountains, a white pine that reaches 185 feet.

That's not the only history to be found here, though. Cook Forest State Park is also home to an 87.5-foot fire tower near the Seneca Point Overlook. Built in 1929, it offers a 15- to 20-mile view of the surrounding countryside. It's a tall window into the past.

According to the Forest Fire Lookout Association, there were once 8,000 or so towers across the country, all built to help spot blazes. A national rush to build them started in 1910, the year of the "Big Blowup," when hurricane-force winds fanned fires already burning in Idaho, Montana, and Washington. Some 3 million acres burned in more than 1,700 individual fires. Eighty-five people died.

Pennsylvania's tower boom occurred soon after, starting in the 1920s. Roughly 460 were built across the state in the 1920s and 1930s, at the urging of Pinchot and later the Civilian Conservation Corps.

Most of those towers—across Pennsylvania and the country—are gone. The Lookout Association estimates only 2,000 or so remain, with less than half actually staffed. Many of those are monitored by volunteers. Pennsylvania has fewer than 100 of its towers left. This one stands, but is no longer in use. It was officially retired in 1966.

It's possible to walk up to it any time, though, and occasionally even get in it. Park educators lead fairly regular tours to the tower. Often, the observation cabin perched at its very top is open then.

The fire tower at Cook Forest State Park is not officially in service any more, but visitors can sometimes climb to the top to take in the view.

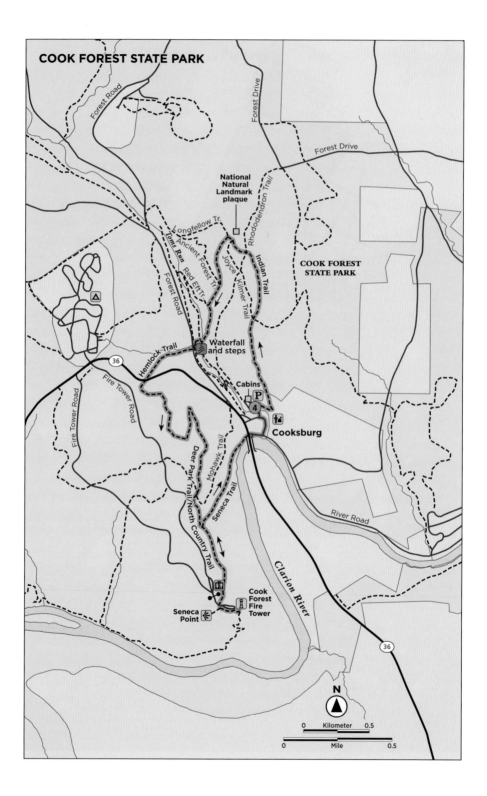

Paying a visit may offer a window to the future, too. Pennsylvania's Department of Conservation and Natural Resources—which manages state parks and forests—is looking to build as many as twenty-five new towers across the state. The thinking is that while aerial monitoring of potential fires is effective, it's also costly. Towers might allow for more routine, and cheaper, surveillance. So, perhaps, towers like this one will again someday be common.

This tower in Cook Forest will always be historic, though, and all the more iconic for standing guard over a forest that's been around since the days of the American Revolution.

Miles and Directions

0.0 Start at the park office. Walk toward the children's fishing pond and cross the bridge.

0.1 Enter the woods on the right via Indian Trail. Follow the yellow blazes.

0.6 Look on the right for giant boulders stacked atop one another.

0.9 Indian Trail meets Joyce Kilmer Trail. Stay straight on Indian Trail.

1.1 Look for rock formations on both sides of the trail.

1.2 Indian Trail meets Rhododendron Trail. Stay straight on Indian.

1.3 Indian Trail meets Longfellow Trail at the plaque marking the Forest Cathedral as a National Natural Landmark. Go left on Longfellow, following the blue and yellow blazes.

1.6 Ancient Forest Trail goes right. Stay left on Longfellow and go down the stairs.

1.8 Red Eft Trail goes right. Turn left on Longfellow.

2.0 Cross Toms Run via a bridge, then turn left and go up the steps.

2.1 Cross Forest Road and enter the woods on Baker Trail/Hemlock Trail.

2.2 Follow the trail left at what looks like a hitching post.

2.4 Cross Route 36 and enter the woods on Baker Trail/Deer Park Trail.

2.7 The trail bends left. Follow the blazes.

3.6 Deer Park Trail meets Mohawk Trail. Stay straight on Deer Park.

3.7 Seneca Trail goes off to the left. Stay straight on Deer Park, passing through a boulder field.

4.1 Parking area with restrooms on the right. Continue straight up the hill, then bear left toward the fire tower (to the right is Seneca Point Overlook).

4.2 Come to the fire tower. Check it out, then return the way you came to the Seneca Trail junction.

4.7 Turn right to go downhill on Seneca Trail.

5.1 Cross Route 36 and walk River Road back to the start.

5.2 Arrive back at the park office.

5 McConnells Mill State Park

Start: At the Point parking lot
Distance: 2.3 miles
Type: Loop
Hiking time: 2 hours
Difficulty: Moderate to difficult
Best season: May to October
Traffic: Hikers only, though there is some vehicle traffic around the mill and bridge
Fees and permits: None

Maps: Available at www.dcnr.pa.gov/ StateParks/FindAPark/McConnellsMill StatePark/Pages/Maps.aspx
Trail contact: McConnells Mill State Park, c/o Moraine State Park, 225 Pleasant Valley Rd., Portersville 16051-9650; (724) 368-8811; www.dcnr.pa.gov/StateParks/FindAPark/ McConnellsMillStatePark/Pages/default.aspx

Finding the trailhead: From New Castle, follow Route 422 east for about 9 miles. Turn right onto McConnells Mill Road and go approximately 1 mile to the Point parking lot on the right. GPS: N40 57.473' / W80 10.163'

The Hike

Slippery Rock Creek can be wild where it cuts through the gorge here at McConnells Mill State Park. In spring, when snowmelt causes the stream to run high and fast, and at other times of high water, it's a favorite of kayakers trained to run whitewater. That explains the life preserver rings you'll encounter at various points along this hike. Don't think the boaters are the only ones who get to experience adventure, though. The hiking here can be thrilling, but also rather challenging, too.

You'll notice it right away. Leave the parking lot and descend some fairly steep, often wet and slippery stairs to Alpha Pass Trail. From there the trail is rocky, rooty, and winding. And that's the easy part.

The trail takes you to the old gristmill. Be sure to explore it before going on. There's a little respite starting there. The hike leads downstream along the eastern bank of Slippery Rock Creek, and the path for the first quarter mile or so is relatively wide and groomed.

Then things change. The gorge here is fairly deep. The hillsides slant down to the water, if not precipitously, at least at enough of an angle to make things interesting. They're covered in rock, too, with those stones ranging from giant boulders to bowling ball–size ankle turners. Mix in the roots that snake along the top of the rocks and hard-packed earth and you'll take a lot of steps before you ever set your foot down completely flat.

Ah, but the scenery. Periodically along the hike you'll come to spots where it's possible to get right to the streambank. The views are gorgeous, especially if the sunlight is filtering down through the leaves, bright green in summer, orange and red and yellow in fall. The fishing can be good, too, if you want to bring a rod.

The 1874 covered bridge at McConnells Mill State Park accommodates hikers, bikers, and even automobiles today.

At the halfway point you'll hit a road that dead-ends here. You'll cross a bridge—an entirely sufficient affair structurally but also a comparatively plain Jane one compared to the Howe covered bridge—to reenter the woods and follow the creek back upstream. If anything, the trail on this side is even more rugged. If you have ever thought of using a walking stick, this would be the place to do it.

The hike eventually brings you back to the Howe bridge. You'll cross it to get back to the mill, then retrace your steps to the start.

As for when to make this hike? The rough nature of the trail and the surrounding countryside is what makes it so beautiful. But it's also what makes it moderately tricky under even the best conditions. Pick a dry, sunny day—when the rocky terrain isn't so slick—to make this hike.

If you can do it in late September, all the better. McConnells Mill State Park hosts a heritage festival the last full weekend of the month. It features local artisans, crafters, bluegrass and Celtic music, children's activities, mill tours, food, and more. It's a busy weekend here, to be sure. But then, most weekends are. The "Point" parking lot where this hike begins is sometimes full, so be prepared to park elsewhere if necessary.

But do stop by. This hike will challenge you, but the rewards are worth it.

The History

The covered bridge at McConnells Mill State Park is every bit as old as you might imagine. It was originally built in 1874. And yet, it's a product of the industrial age. How's that for a twist?

The bridge is what's known as a "Howe" truss. It's one of just four like it—and the longest—remaining in Pennsylvania. It's called the Howe truss after William Howe, who patented the design in 1840. It was the first to marry iron with wood. It proved sturdy, and by the late 1800s most railroad bridges were of the Howe design.

What really made it stand out, though, was how it could be built. Howe bridges could be made with green wood. A year later, as the wood aged and shrank, builders could return and tighten the iron rods with turnbuckles to snug it up. Most importantly, Howe's design allowed for factory production. Workers in a New England foundry could make the iron rods, nuts, and angler blocks. They could be shipped around the country, where bridge builders could—using almost any wood—finish their bridge.

The Slippery Rock Creek gorge, meanwhile, is exhibit A for why such bridges existed. They were critical for pioneers. Otherwise, crossing any stream—let alone one as wild as Slippery Rock Creek—was hard and often outright dangerous. Of course, they served other purposes, too. Because they offered shelter, covered bridges held town meetings, rallies, and even church services. Robbers used them to hide before springing upon unwary travelers. And couples used them, for, well, romance. They were known as "kissing bridges."

As for why to cover a bridge? Simple efficiency. The roof protects the bridge's supporting structure—the sides and trusses—from rot.

Originally built in 1852, McConnells Mill was expanded and refurbished over the years.

As for why a bridge here, that's tied to the mill. Bridges were money makers. In a time before government took over construction of infrastructure, people who lived at stream crossings built their own bridges, then charged others to use them. Mill owners—located along streams because of the power they provided—built bridges to make it convenient for farmers to bring in grain.

The first mill built here predated the bridge, having been built in 1852 by Daniel Kennedy. It burned in 1867, and was rebuilt a year later. The mill got a real boost into the future in 1875, though, when the McConnell family bought it. They "modernized" it in the 1880s, replacing the waterwheel with water turbines and the grinding stones with rolling mills. They operated the mill until 1928, when a slowdown in business put it under. It eventually passed to the state and was refurbished in 1960 to its current condition.

The mill is open to self-guided tours on a regular basis. A walk through shows just what a process milling really was. The machines here could turn wheat into flour in about 30 minutes, without a whole lot of manual manipulation. It all took place on four floors, with farmers pulling in with raw grains in one spot and leaving with

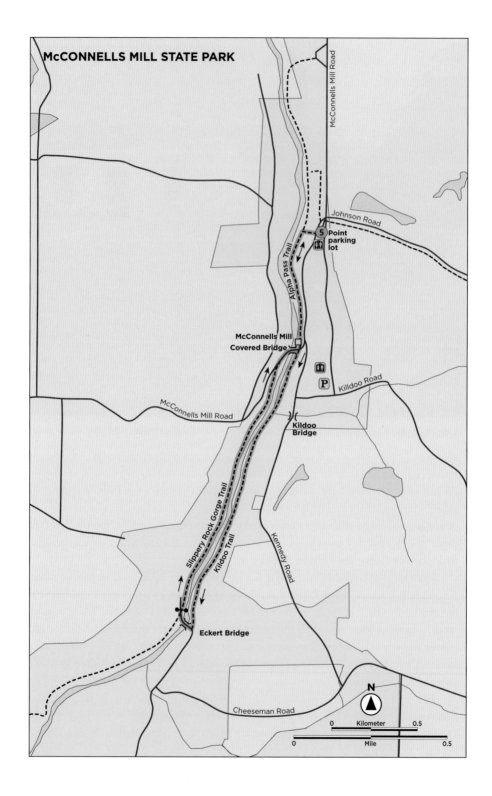

McCONNELLS MILL STATE PARK

McConnells Mill Road

Johnson Road

5 Point parking lot

Alpha Pass Trail

McConnells Mill Covered Bridge

Killdoo Road

P

McConnells Mill Road

Kildoo Bridge

Slippery Rock Gorge Trail

Kildoo Trail

Kennedy Road

Eckert Bridge

Cheeseman Road

N

0   Kilometer   0.5

0   Mile   0.5

ground flour in another. Visitors can walk through the mill and see how the whole process worked. A series of dozens of informational signs explain the process along the way.

One of the more interesting signs explains how mills like this one gave rise to the sayings "rule of thumb," "to show one's mettle" and "to go through the mill." Where did they come from? You'll have to stop by to find out.

Miles and Directions

0.0 Start at the Point parking lot. Go down the steps on the far side of McConnells Mill Road and turn left onto Alpha Pass Trail. Soon you will see a bench on the right overlooking Slippery Rock Creek.

0.1 Come out at the tiny parking lot by McConnells Mill. Explore the mill, then continue straight.

0.2 To the right is the covered bridge. Go left, following the creek downstream on Kildoo Trail.

0.4 Cross a small bridge.

1.0 Look for a small waterfall on the left.

1.1 Go down a few steps and come to Eckert Bridge. Turn right, cross the bridge, then reenter the woods on the right on Slippery Rock Gorge Trail.

1.2 Look for a waterfall on the left. Soon after, you will see a small beach on the right.

1.3 Pass rock formations on the left.

1.5 Climb some rocky stairs.

1.9 Come to a bench on the left. The trail then meets McConnells Mill Road. Turn right, cross the covered bridge, then retrace your steps back to the start.

2.3 Arrive back at the starting point.

6 Raccoon Creek State Park

Start: At the parking lot across the street from the Raccoon Creek State Park office
Distance: 1.1 miles
Type: Loop
Hiking time: 1 hour
Difficulty: Easy
Best season: April to October
Traffic: Hikers only
Fees and permits: None

Maps: Available at www.dcnr.pa.gov/StateParks/FindAPark/RaccoonCreek StatePark/Pages/Maps.aspx
Trail contact: Raccoon Creek State Park, 3000 State Rte. 18, Hookstown 15050-1605; (724) 899-2200; www.dcnr.pa.gov/StateParks/FindAPark/RaccoonCreek StatePark/Pages/default.aspx

Finding the trailhead: From Burgettstown, follow Route 18 north for about 8.5 miles. Turn left on Cabin Road to the state park office. The parking lot is on the left. GPS: N40 30.179' / W80 25.468'

The Hike

The trail that takes you to the remains of the Frankfort Mineral Springs Resort is neither a long nor a difficult one.

It begins across the road from the park office, in a small parking lot on Cabin Road. There's room for maybe a dozen cars here. That's usually plenty, except on nice weekends. Then—or when the park, its Friends group, or other organized hiking groups schedule an outing—the springs can draw a crowd. In that case, park at the office and just walk to the trailhead.

The trail goes uphill just a bit at the start, on a grassy track, then parallels a small trickle of a stream and Route 18. That means you'll hear traffic noise along the way. Still, wildlife is common. White-tailed deer, including fawns, aren't unheard of in spring and early summer. Squirrels, chipmunks, and assorted songbirds frequent the area, too. You'll cross the creek and a few small wet spots, sometimes on bridges, sometimes by stepping from rock to log to rock in the span of just a few feet.

The approach to the spring is neat in that, when looking up, the way suddenly seems dark. Not foreboding, but definitely dark. That's the impact of the cave. Stop and check out the waterfall and the seeping water of the spring.

It's here that you first notice the remains of the old spa. There are rock walls, a bridge, and a walkway. They lead to a set of stairs. Climb the stairs and you'll arrive at an old foundation, where many of the stones used in the buildings once here are scattered about like dice tossed by giants.

Crossing Heritage Trail, the hike then proceeds back into the woods, through some ferns and then evergreens. It curls back downhill to the right and rejoins the trail you walked earlier. In no time at all, you're back to the start.

The "healing waters" that made Frankfort Mineral Springs Resort so famous as a spa trickle out of the walls at this cave.

Before leaving the park, though, if you want to get in some additional walking, drive to the park's wildflower reserve, located off Route 30 to the east. It's not large, accounting for just 314 of the park's 7,572 acres. Yet it's said to contain one of the most diverse and unique stands of wildflowers in Pennsylvania. A call to the reserve in advance can get you a breakdown, by month, of what's flowering and when. Late April to early May and August through September are the peak times, though.

The reserve has a visitor center and 5 miles of trails. One of the trails will take you past Hungerford Cabin, the getaway for famous *Pittsburgh Post-Gazette* political cartoonist Cy Hungerford.

The History

Raccoon Creek State Park lies just 25 miles or so from Pittsburgh. Distance-wise anyway. But in other ways?

It's much more pastoral and long has been, even as far back as the early 1800s. It's no surprise that city dwellers—starting before Pittsburgh became an industrial center and then long after it was a place of dark, smoky skies and thick air—often saw a trip there as an escape of sorts. It didn't hurt that the area had healing powers. That was the reputation anyway, at least at Frankfort Mineral Springs.

The actual spring sits in a U-shaped ravine off what is now Route 18 in the park. There's a cave, or grotto, that's been carved out of the hillside over eons by water.

Ruins of the old Frankfort Mineral Springs Resort at Raccoon Creek State Park

You don't always notice that water in equal measure. The stream—pulling water from aboveground sources—can all but dry up in some years. That's why the waterfall here is an iffy thing, impressive one time, a trickle the next.

What never goes dry is the Frankfort Mineral Springs itself. Its water, which comes from an underground reservoir, flows year-round, leaking out of the rock wall in several spots. It's not a torrent by any means. But it's consistent and a testament to the power of water over time. Look at the stones set below these natural faucets. They're bowl-shaped, the depressions in them the result of water pounding away, like a relentless little hammer, minute after minute, day after day, year after year.

Notice, too, the orange color of the rock wall behind the water. It's that way because of the natural iron content in the spring water. And that's what made this area so appealing to Pittsburghers and travelers from elsewhere.

The first recorded documentation of the spring dates to 1772. It's thought that Native Americans knew of it long before then, though. It was first treated as a source of healing, officially, a little later, in 1823. A Dr. William Church tested the water and found it contained a variety of minerals. Carbonate of magnesia, a laxative, was one. Those minerals indeed made it curative, he said in an article in a Philadelphia medical journal. "Drinking the water, with the use of the cold shower bath, has been of great service to persons laboring under chronic rheumatism, dyspepsia, asthma caused by gastric irritation, general debility of the system, and to convalescents from bilious fever, and liver complaints," he wrote.

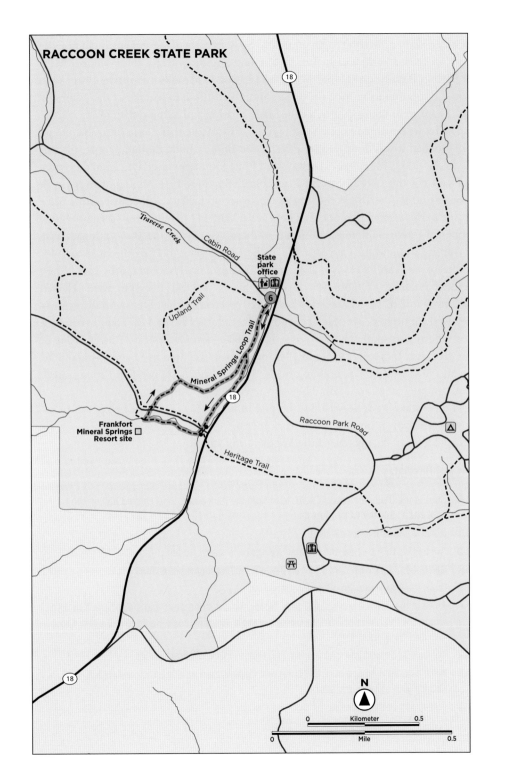

RACCOON CREEK STATE PARK

Edward McGinnis noticed the health benefits of the water, too. He said the mineral water seemed "healing to his ailments." So he bought 12 acres here, including the spring, in 1827. He then cashed in by building a resort and spa, the Frankfort Mineral Springs Resort, on the site in the mid-1800s. It became instantly popular, with wealthy Pittsburghers visiting for up to a month at a time to partake of the water and relax. There were tennis courts, a dance hall, a parlor, and a fine restaurant.

The resort remained popular through the early 1920s, then came to an abrupt end in 1930 when it was destroyed by a fire. It was never rebuilt, though people still visit here to check out the ruins—stairways and stone foundations remain—and the water.

That's not the only history in Raccoon Creek State Park, though. Kings Creek Cemetery, off Route 168 in the southwest corner of the park, is the final resting place of some of the area's first pioneers. There are at least 142 people here—that's the total number of tombstones anyway—some of them veterans of the Revolutionary War, the War of 1812, and the Civil War. The earliest stone dates to 1810, the latest to 1906.

The park—like so many—also has a Civilian Conservation Corps past. When President Franklin D. Roosevelt launched his New Deal, five sites were selected in Pennsylvania to be rehabilitated as RDAs, or Recreational Demonstration Areas. They were deforested, over-farmed lands—worthless, in the eyes of many—that were to be reborn as natural, outdoor playgrounds. Raccoon Creek State Park was one of those five sites. Between 1935 and 1941 more than 700 men lived and worked here, in camps SP-6 and SP-16, building roads, the dam for the upper pond, picnic areas, group camping areas, and trails. They also replanted thousands of trees.

The National Park Service ran the park until 1945, when ownership was transferred to the state. It became a state park in 1967.

That's a lot of change over time. Yet the water still flows.

Miles and Directions

0.0 Start at the trailhead across Cabin Road from the park office. Pass Upland Trail on the right and follow the white blazes.

0.1 Notice a power line on the right.

0.2 The trail Ys. This is where the Mineral Springs Loop starts. Go left.

0.4 Go straight, passing a parking lot on the left and crossing Heritage Trail.

0.5 Cross the bridge over an often dry streambed.

0.6 Arrive at the mineral springs and cave. Notice the old stone walls and steps here. Turn right and follow the path uphill. At the top of the stairs, the trail meets Heritage Trail again. Cross over and continue straight.

0.7 The trail Ts. Upland Trail is to the left. Turn right to follow Mineral Springs.

0.9 Make a sharp right at a spot that's not well marked, then an almost immediate left. Retrace your steps to the start.

1.1 Arrive back at the trailhead.

7 Fort Pitt Museum and Point State Park

Start: At the reflecting pool
Distance: 0.8 mile
Type: Loop
Hiking time: 1 hour
Difficulty: Easy
Best season: April to October
Traffic: Hikers, bicyclists, runners, in-line skaters
Fees and permits: None for the trail. Admission to Fort Pitt Museum is $8 adults, $7 seniors 62 and older, $4.50 children 6–17 and students with a valid ID. There are fees for parking, too.
Maps: Available at www.docs.dcnr.pa.gov/cs/groups/public/documents/document/dcnr_003297.pdf
Trail contacts: Fort Pitt Museum, 601 Commonwealth Place, Bldg. B, Pittsburgh 15222; (412) 281-9284; www.heinzhistorycenter.org/fort-pitt/. Point State Park, 601 Commonwealth Place, Bldg. A, Pittsburgh 15222-1212; (412) 565-2850; www.dcnr.pa.gov/StateParks/FindAPark/PointStatePark/Pages/default.aspx.

Finding the trailhead: From Monroeville, take I-376 West to the Stanwix Street exit. Turn left at the light onto Fort Pitt Boulevard and bear right onto Commonwealth Place. Fort Pitt Museum is located in Point State Park just beyond and to the left of the portal bridge. Parking is available in nearby garages (listed on the Fort Pitt Museum website). GPS: N40 26.486' / W80 00.556'

The Hike

Before there were airplanes, before there were trains, before there were vehicles, water was king. Nations looking to move goods and people used ships and rivers. It's no wonder then that the "point" at Pittsburgh was so desirable that armies were willing to fight to control it. Here, the Allegheny and Monongahela Rivers meet to form the Ohio, which in turn flows into the Mississippi.

That's not changed. Nor has how this arrowhead-shaped piece of land is valued. But the reason for its popularity has.

Today people flock to Point State Park for its scenic beauty—a wedge of green space in the downtown of Pennsylvania's second-largest city—and the chance to frolic and play. People spread out blankets and soak up the sun in the grass where Fort Duquesne and later Fort Pitt stood. They walk the rivers' edges, talking with boaters who gather here to relax and maybe catch a home run hit out of PNC Park. They dangle their feet in the Point's famous fountain, which shoots a geyser of water 150 feet into the air.

This hike allows you to do those same things while also exploring the history of the location. You'll enter the park via the reflecting pool portal, with the city at your back and the park in front. It's the pedestrian version of entering the city via the Fort Pitt Tunnels. In the blink of an eye, the city skyline opens before you.

From there the hike includes a stop at the Fort Pitt Museum, a 12,000-square-foot, two-story affair. It's built on the footprint of what was the original fort's

Fort Duquesne is marked by a granite tracery, or outline, in Point State Park.

Monongahela Bastion, or projecting corner. Its façade reflects what the fort would have looked like, size-wise.

This hike also allows you to visit the Fort Pitt Block House. Built in 1764, it still retains much of its original character, including some original timber, bricks, and stone foundation. Once a part of the fort, then later a trading post, then later still a multi-family private residence, the blockhouse was finally donated to the local chapter of the Daughters of the American Revolution in 1894. They've kept it open for free tours since 1895.

Once you've taken all that in, the hike follows the park edges so that you can see all three of Pittsburgh's rivers. There are a number of historical markers in Point State Park, and this hike takes you past several of them. You'll see markers for the Ohio Bastion, Forbes Road marker and map, and a Forks of the Ohio plaque. Others are here, too, all easily seen by doing little mini-detours.

A concrete outline of Fort Duquesne and a marker showing the original "point" where the rivers came together—it's not where things are now—are found in the grassy area around the Point known as the "Great Lawn." They're worth seeing (though something special is to see them from above; the outline of Fort Duquesne and Fort Pitt are lit by LED lights so as to be visible from the sky). The Venango Path plaque and Forks of the Ohio plaque are both located at the entrance to the Great Lawn, too.

Meanwhile, by walking to the city side of the park entrance, it's possible to see the Music Bastion of Fort Pitt, while a trip in the direction of the parking lot off Commonwealth Place leads to the Flag Bastion marker.

None of the markers are necessarily immediately obvious—countless people undoubtedly walk past them every day without realizing they're there. But take a map and walk the park. You'll get a feel for how massive Fort Pitt was. Maybe that's how things should be. This is a majestic site, so it deserved a majestic fort, and it got one.

The History

Even as a young man, George Washington knew a good piece of real estate when he saw it.

In 1753 he was a raw lieutenant with the Virginia militia. His task was to travel to what would later become Pittsburgh to negotiate with the French forces there. He took one look at what's known today as the "Point"—the triangular-shaped piece of land where the Allegheny and Monongahela Rivers meet to form the Ohio—and recognized its value strategically. "As I got down before the canoe, I spent some time in viewing the rivers, and the land in the fork; which I think extremely well situated for a fort, as it has the absolute command of both rivers," Washington wrote in a report.

He continued, "The land at the point is 20 or 25 feet above the common surface of the water; and a considerable bottom of flat, well-timbered land all around it, very convenient for building: The rivers are each a quarter of a mile, or more, across, and

A cyclist stands near a rainbow at the fountain at Point State Park.

run here very near at right angles: Aligany bearing N. E. and Monongahela S. E. The former of these two is a very rapid and swift running water; the other deep and still, without any perceptible fall."

All that made it desirable to both sides. Great Britain and France spent years vying for control of the Ohio Valley, and this spot was considered crucial to those efforts. The irony is that relatively little actual fighting ever took place here.

In February 1754, following up on Washington's advice, the British sent Capt. William Trent to the Point. He built Fort Prince George—more commonly called Trent's Fort—on the site. It didn't last. Just months later, in April, the French floated down the Allegheny, arrived at the same spot, and, with superior numbers, demanded the British leave. They did, and the French built Fort Duquesne.

The British sent a force to recapture it in July 1755, but it was defeated before arriving, losing the Battle of Monongahela 8 miles away. They tried again in September 1758 and actually reached Fort Duquesne, but were defeated by the French and their Indian allies. The British finally regained control of the area in November 1758,

The Fort Pitt Block House is the oldest building standing in western Pennsylvania.

but did it without firing a shot. The French, aware that they were about to be attacked by a much larger force, burned Fort Duquesne down and left ahead of the fight.

Gen. John Forbes—with a young Washington by his side—arrived two days later and named the area Pittsburgh in honor of William Pitt, secretary of state to Great Britain. The British then built the temporary Fort Mercer, with designs on quickly replacing it with a bigger, better structure. Fort Pitt was the result. It was the most state-of-the-art fort in North America at that time, with "bombproofs"—areas deep within the fort's walls able to withstand an artillery attack—as part of the design. It was the second-largest fort on the continent, too.

It never got put to the test, though.

Native Americans besieged the fort in 1763 as part of the uprising known as Pontiac's Rebellion. But the arrival of Col. Henry Bouquet's force for Bushy Run put an end to that threat. The Fort Pitt Block House—the oldest authenticated pre–Revolutionary War structure in western Pennsylvania—was built a year later, in 1764. In 1772, the British abandoned the fort. They reclaimed it in 1774 and

FORT PITT MUSEUM AND POINT STATE PARK

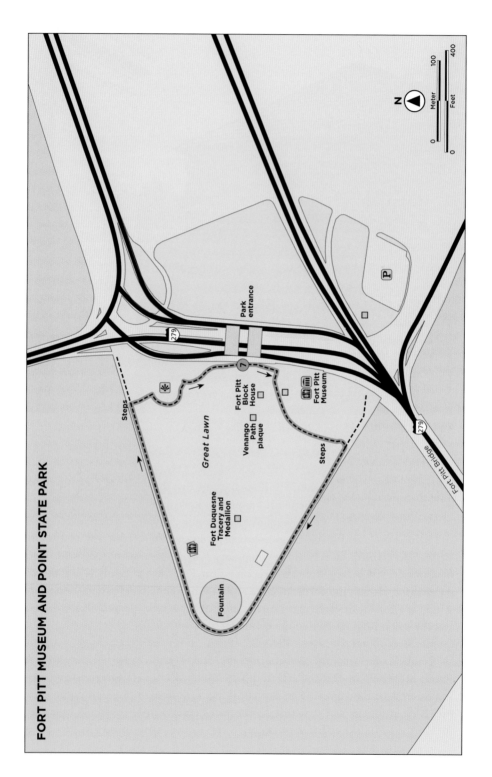

renamed it Fort Dunmore, with designs on using it during the Revolutionary War. But they didn't stick around, and by 1777 the Continental Army was using it as a western headquarters. It kept it for a while—the first-ever peace treaty between the United States and American Indians was signed here in 1778—but by 1792 it had been torn down, its pieces used by locals to build homes.

Taking its place initially was a busy industrial zone. It deteriorated over time, though, and by the early 1940s the Point was a commercial slum. The state stepped in and bought 36 acres here in 1945 with the goal of establishing a state park on the site. It was completed in 1974, and the park was designated a National Historic Landmark a year later. Today it's a popular spot for history buffs, walkers, joggers, cyclists, anglers, and others, with its beautiful fountain a landmark at what is one of Pittsburgh's grandest spots.

Miles and Directions

0.0 Start at the reflecting pool at the main entrance to Point State Park. Go left to Fort Pitt Museum. After a couple hundred feet you will arrive at the front door of the museum. When exiting, go straight across the paved walkway to the Fort Pitt Block House. It's open for tours at certain times. Tour it, then exit and go right.

0.1 Go down the steps to Three Rivers Heritage Trail on the Monongahela River. Go right.

0.3 Come to the fountain. Go left to circle it. Follow the Allegheny River upstream via Three Rivers Heritage Trail.

0.7 Climbs two sets of stairs on the right. At the top, at a roundabout, go right.

0.8 Arrive back at the reflecting pool to close the loop.

8 Bushy Run Battlefield

Start: At the main parking lot, by the pavilion

Distance: 1.7 miles

Type: Loop

Hiking time: 1.5 hours

Difficulty: Easy

Best season: April to October

Traffic: Hikers only

Fees and permits: None to hike; museum admission is $5 adults, $4.50 seniors 65 and older, $3 children 3–12

Maps: Available at http://bushyrun battlefield.com

Trail contact: Bushy Run Battlefield Heritage Society, 1253 Bushy Run Rd., Jeannette 15644; (724) 527-5584; http://bushy runbattlefield.com

Finding the trailhead: From Delmont, follow Route 66 South. Turn right onto Route 993. Go about 3 miles; the battlefield entrance is on the right. GPS: N40 21.497' / W79 37.579'

The Hike

The most vibrant time to hike through Bushy Run Battlefield is the first weekend of August. That's when it plays host to its annual reenactment of the battle that made the site famous. People dressed as colonial soldiers and painted to look like Native American warriors roam the fields and woods, with muskets and other accouterments in hand. They bring the scene to life so that visitors can not only see, but also smell and hear, what the men who fought here centuries ago might have.

If you can't get here then, though, this is still a pleasant walk at any time.

The hike begins from the main parking lot. There's a small but interesting museum and visitor center here, so check it out either before or after your walk. Then go uphill between twin rows of oaks, following what remains of some long-ago stone steps. You'll pass the flagpole and angle toward a little grassy opening's far right corner. There's a trail there that leads right, downhill into the woods.

There are some small signs along the way, explaining a bit about the vegetation. If you're into wildlife, though, spend some time looking at the base of the pine trees that line the trail to the left. They're often used by owls. Below the trees it's sometimes possible to find pellets—balls of dry fur and bone they can't digest and spit back up—on the ground. Schoolkids at nature centers all over dissect these sorts of things.

The trail then winds around until it comes very near the visitor center. You can stop the hike here if you want, but you'll miss some cool things yet to come.

Turn left on the trail, go down some stairs, and double back on a wide path. In time, you'll come to the road you drove in on. Turn right just before it and enter another field, this one home to the "flour bag fort" monument.

You'll then walk to an amphitheater in the park. For years this was little more than a stage—looking like a mini-clay tennis court, really—with some benches around it.

This monument was erected to mark the 250th anniversary of the Battle of Bushy Run.

Today it's much more impressive. The seating remains, but there's a brick walkway here, informational panels that help explain the battle, and, most impressively, a bronze monument. Dedicated in 2013 to mark the 250th anniversary of the battle, and the first monument added to the park in more than one hundred years, it features a British soldier and Native American warrior squaring off. Below them, a colonial Ranger lies slumped against flour bags. Note the shape formed by the bricks here. They form an eight-point star—mimicking the outline common to colonial-era forts, like Fort Pitt.

Check it all out and then turn and cut through the grass to return to the main parking lot and the starting point, thereby closing the loop. There's a pavilion at that lot, one that doesn't get used nearly enough, so if you pack a lunch you can make an afternoon of things.

The History

How'd you like to be behind nothing but a stack of canvas bags filled with flour, wounded, parched, and assuredly scared, with whistling arrows and angry musket balls flying your way? Doesn't sound like much protection, does it? But that was the extent of Bushy Run's "flour bag fort."

Desperate times, desperate measures, I suppose.

It all began with a fight over a broken promise far away, at Fort Detroit. At the height of the French and Indian War, the British were eager to keep the Native Americans from aiding their enemies. They made an offer: Stay out of the fight, they told the natives living in the Ohio Valley, and when the war was over they'd leave the land west of the Allegheny Mountains to them. The Native Americans complied, the British won the war . . . and then they inevitably stayed. What's more, they built forts—including Fort Pitt—and sent settlers into the region, all while limiting trade with the natives. That left the tribes short on things like firearms and gunpowder.

Finally, a Delaware prophet named Neolin said he'd had a vision suggesting the native tribes should drive the British out and return to their traditional lifestyle. An attack on Fort Detroit followed in May 1763. The fighting spread, with a chain of forts—Sandusky, St. Joseph, Miami, Quiatenon, and Michilimackinac—falling. A siege of Fort Pitt began on May 29, with an attack on nearby Fort Ligonier following just days later.

It was too much.

British general Jeffrey Amherst sent Col. Henry Bouquet marching west to what is now Pittsburgh with a relief force. Bouquet set off with 500 soldiers—the men of the 42nd and 77th Highlanders, 60th Royal Americans, Royal Artillery gunners and frontiersman—and 50 civilians. They had with them 60,000 pounds of flour, 100 cattle, and 200 sheep. All that made for predictably slow going along wet, muddy, often nearly impassable roads. Bouquet eventually decided to leave the livestock and wagons behind and press on, headed for Bushy Run Station. The plan was to rest there, then head for Fort Pitt under cover of darkness.

The Native Americans had other ideas. On August 5 they attacked the British in what was described as their usual style. That is to say, it was a running battle, with native warriors darting in and out among the trees so as to never present a unified, attackable front.

The British suffered immensely. Bouquet moved his pack animals and wounded to the top of "Edge Hill," then built a circular fort around them with flour bags. It made for a long, frightful, brutal night. "In an American campaign everything is horrible; the face of the country, the climate, the enemy," wrote one officer who survived the fight. "There is no refreshment for the healthy, nor relief for the sick. A vast inhospitable desert, unsafe and treacherous surrounds them, where victories are not decisive, but defeats are ruinous; and simple death is the least misfortune which can happen to them."

Things looked bleak for the British. On the second day, August 6, after suffering several attacks early, surrounded on three sides and desperate for a breakout, Bouquet tricked the natives. He feigned a retreat, then counterattacked when his enemies thought they were moving in for the kill.

Hit hard, suffering more casualties than usual, the native tribes retreated, and Bouquet was able to limp to Fort Pitt by August 10. The siege was soon ended, and so too

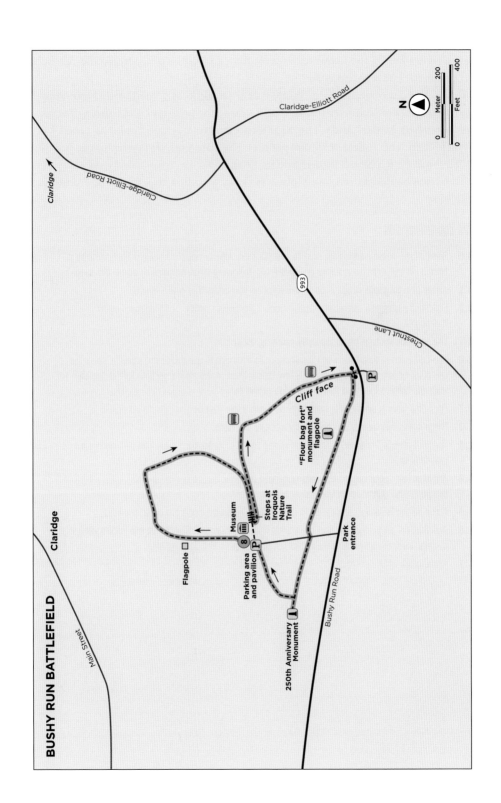

BUSHY RUN BATTLEFIELD

Claridge

Main Street

Claridge

Claridge-Elliott Road

Claridge-Elliott Road

993

Chestnut Lane

Cliff face

"Flour bag fort" monument and flagpole

P

Steps at Iroquois Nature Trail

Museum

Flagpole

Parking area and pavilion

P

Park entrance

Bushy Run Road

250th Anniversary Monument

N

Meter   0   200

Feet   0   400

was the brief war. On October 3 the British left Fort Pitt and continued west into Ohio. By October 25 the native tribes were forced to sign a peace treaty and release their prisoners. The war had ended.

Bushy Run, though, was not immediately set aside as a memorial. Numerous families farmed the land over the next 150 years. It wasn't until 1921 that 6.5 acres were purchased and set aside. The $7,000 needed to buy the land was raised by schoolchildren who collected 70,000 pennies. The state took ownership of the site in 1927 and named it a State Historic Site in 1963.

Today the battlefield is a lovely place to walk, with flowers—not flour—dotting the hillsides.

Miles and Directions

0.0 Start at the main parking lot next to the pavilion. After a couple hundred feet come to a bench on the right; turn left to go up the hill, following what remains of some old steps.

0.1 Arrive at a flagpole. Angle a bit to the right as you cross this open space.

0.2 Follow the trail into the woods at the back right corner of the open space. Follow it downhill.

0.4 The trail comes to a bit of a grassy opening. Bear left.

0.6 The trail comes to a four-way intersection. To the right is the museum; straight ahead is the parking lot. Turn left, go down a few steps, then make an immediate left at the sign for Iroquois Nature Trail and follow the wide gravel trail.

0.7 There's a bench on the left, immediately before the trail bends right to go uphill.

1.0 There's another bench on the left, by a rocky cliff face.

1.1 The trail meets Route 993. Don't cross the road. Instead, turn right. The trail enters a grassy field.

1.2 Arrive at the "flour bag fort" monument and another flagpole. Check it out, then return to the path and continue on the trail.

1.4 Arrive at the driveway you came in on. Cross over it and continue down the hill.

1.5 Arrive at an amphitheater and the park's main monument. Check out the informational panels here, then turn and walk through the grass to the parking lot.

1.7 Arrive back at the start.

9 Friendship Hill National Historic Site

Start: At the main parking lot
Distance: 4 miles
Type: Loop
Hiking time: 2 to 3 hours
Difficulty: Moderate to difficult
Best season: April to October
Traffic: Hikers only

Fees and permits: None
Maps: Available at www.nps.gov/frhi/plan yourvisit/maps.htm
Trail contact: Friendship Hill National Historic Site, c/o Fort Necessity National Battlefield, 1 Washington Pkwy., Farmington 15437; (724) 329-2500; www.nps.gov/frhi/index.htm

Finding the trailhead: From Uniontown, take Route 119 South to Route 43 South. Go about 4 miles, then exit onto Route 857 toward Fairchance. Go right on Big Sixx Road for 0.2 miles, then left back onto Route 119 for 2 miles more. Turn right on Church Street and go 0.2 miles, and then left onto New Geneva Road, which becomes Route 166. After 7 miles, Friendship Hill is on the right. GPS: N39 46.645' / W79 55.858'

The Hike

Friendship Hill National Historic Site is home to about 10 miles of trails overall, so this particular hike takes in almost half of them. They're some of the more relevant, too.

It begins by delivering hikers to Albert Gallatin's home, for starters. It's a house that's seen a lot of changes. The home, as it originally existed, was a two-story brick structure, built in 1789 for Gallatin's first wife, Sophia. For his second wife, with whom he had children, he added on in 1798 and 1823. At various times in between, he had a barn, well, orchard, vegetable and pleasure gardens, and a gardener's cottage added. Visitors can tour portions of the house—those that existed in the Gallatin era—at the start of this hike. Rooms showcase period furnishings and other exhibits.

From there the hike leads to an overlook of the Monongahela River and, later, a walk alongside the river. It was originally meant to play a large part in Gallatin's life, as he hoped to build an industrial center along it. Before decent roads, and before railroads, rivers were key to moving goods, especially from the undeveloped frontier. It's clear that notion persisted long after Gallatin. There are still obvious signs of industry along the river, as well as a rail line that follows its banks.

Farther along on this hike you'll pass a small but old cemetery. Some of the stones date to the early 1800s.

Expect to see lots of wildlife here, too. White-tailed deer, turkeys, and squirrels are common neighbors. They're often most visible early and late in the day.

As for when to hike here, there's really not a bad time. But if you want to add something different to your walk, plan to be here for FestiFall, typically held the last full weekend of September. The event, a celebration of the life and times of Albert Gallatin, includes demonstrations of historical trades and crafts—think soap making,

A statue of Albert Gallatin as a young surveyor stands at Friendship Hill National Historic Site.

quilting, leatherworking, furniture making, and the like—along with historical toys, live period music, eighteenth-century foods, and more.

The History

George Washington. Thomas Jefferson. Benjamin Franklin. Patrick Henry. Alexander Hamilton. Those are all names even the most casual person can connect with the birth of America. But Albert Gallatin? Don't be fooled. He's right up there, too. The man played a large role in shaping the nation.

And it all began with tragedy.

Born in Geneva, Switzerland, he traveled to America and settled in western Pennsylvania, on the banks of the Monongahela River. That then qualified as the leading edge of the western frontier. The idea was to live there with his new bride, Sophia, manufacturing firearms, glass, and other goods. Perhaps he might have, if things had gone according to plan.

They didn't. Shortly after arriving in what they called "New Geneva" in 1789, Sophia died. Maybe it was during childbirth. Maybe it was disease, maybe something else claimed her. No one seems to know for sure. Whatever the cause of her death, Gallatin left, turning to politics to occupy his time. He was named a senator for Pennsylvania in 1794, removed on a technicality, then appointed to the House of Representatives in 1795.

During that time, he also remarried. His new wife, Hannah Nicholson, a New York native, wanted no part of the frontier. That, combined with his growing reputation as a financial watchdog—he created the still powerful ways and means committee in Congress—determined his path.

When Thomas Jefferson was elected president in 1800, he named Gallatin his Secretary of the Treasury. His charge: reduce the national debt. It stood at more than $80 million. Gallatin tackled that on two main fronts: cutting government spending, particularly on the military, and increasing revenue through import taxes. He was also a big believer in selling public land to raise cash.

Gallatin was not totally opposed to spending, though. He arranged for the country to buy the Louisiana Territory from France for $15 million—about 3 cents an acre—without having to borrow. Then he helped fund the Lewis and Clark expedition.

Those explorers recognized his importance. Lewis and Clark explored the headwaters of the Missouri River, determining that it came from three sources. They named one the Jefferson River, for Thomas Jefferson, another the Madison River, for James Madison, and the third the Gallatin River, for Albert Gallatin. That's lofty company.

Gallatin also arranged for funding to build the National Road. Known today as Route 40, the road was America's first federally funded highway. It ran, not coincidentally, very near Friendship Hill, giving him a better route to travel between home and the nation's capital. If it helped him, though, it also helped his neighbors throughout western Pennsylvania. They suddenly had a way to move goods around.

The hike through Friendship Hill National Historic Site goes past the Thomas Clare Cemetery. Clare was an early settler in the area, who leased the land where Albert Gallatin put his first store. Clare died in 1814.

The road cost about $13,000 a mile to build. Under Gallatin's stewardship, though, the government did it without falling any deeper into debt. In fact, by the time he left office in 1814, he'd cut the national debt from $80 million to $45 million. His successors eliminated it completely by 1833.

Makes you think we could use another Albert Gallatin today, doesn't it?

His life of service wasn't over, though. In the ensuing years, Gallatin helped negotiate the treaty that ended the War of 1812, served as US ambassador to France and then Great Britain, helped establish New York University, and, finally, was president of National Bank of New York.

All that kept him away from Friendship Hill for years at a time. That's why he sold it in 1832. It would go through six owners thereafter before finally becoming a National Historic Site in 1978.

Gallatin never lived to see that, of course. He died in 1849 in Long Island, having been married fifty-five years. But by then, his legacy as a vital part of American success was secured.

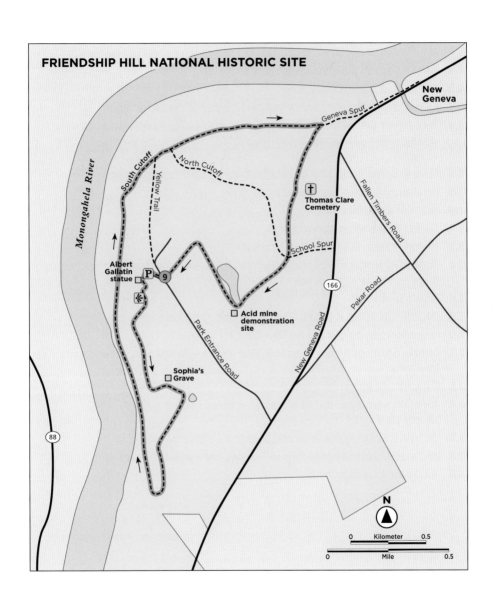

FRIENDSHIP HILL NATIONAL HISTORIC SITE

New Geneva

Geneva Spur

Monongahela River

South Cutoff

North Cutoff

Yellow Trail

Thomas Clare Cemetery

School Spur

Fallen Timbers Road

Pekar Road

Albert Gallatin statue

P

9

166

Acid mine demonstration site

Park Entrance Road

New Geneva Road

Sophia's Grave

88

N

Kilometer
0   0.5

Mile
0   0.5

Miles and Directions

0.0 Start at the main parking lot, where the sidewalk leads up to Albert Gallatin's Friendship Hill home. After a few hundred feet, come to a statue of Albert Gallatin as a surveyor.

0.2 The sidewalk Ts by a sign for Gallatin's "Wilderness Home." Turn right and walk toward the house. Back on the trail you soon come to an overlook of the Monongahela River. Take in the view, then follow the edge of the grass to the left.

0.3 At the bottom of the hill, by a bench, turn right and enter the woods on Main Loop Trail.

0.5 Come to Sophia's Grave, then pass a pond on the left.

0.6 The trail Ys. Go right, across a bridge.

0.9 Cross another bridge and continue straight. Soon the trail Ys again. Go right.

1.0 Near a bench the trail wraps around to the right and switchbacks steeply downhill on wooden, unevenly spaced stairs. Soon the trail Ts. Go right. Note the Monongahela River on the left.

1.3 Come to a small bridge. Note the waterfall to the right, then continue straight.

1.5 Pass some interesting large boulders.

1.6 Pass a bench on the right.

2.0 The trail Ys. Stay left on Main Loop Trail.

2.1 The trail Ys again. Stay left on Main Loop Trail.

2.2 Come to yet another Y. To the right is North Cutoff Trail. Stay left on Main Loop Trail. Note the railroad tracks to the left here.

2.6 Cross a small bridge.

2.8 The trail Ys. To the left is Geneva Spur Trail. Go right, up the hill, on Main Loop Trail.

3.0 Note a bench on the right and the Clare Cemetery on the left.

3.3 Come to a four-way junction where Main Loop Trail meets School Spur. Go straight on Main Loop.

3.5 The trail Ys. Go left.

3.6 The trail Ys again, by an acid mine drainage treatment site. Turn right onto North Meadow Loop.

3.8 The trail Ys. Turn left and walk the field edge, past a maintenance building.

3.9 Hit the main road leading into the park. Turn right and walk to the parking lot.

4.0 Arrive back at the start.

10 Fort Necessity National Battlefield

Start: At the visitor center
Distance: 2.2 miles
Type: Loop
Hiking time: 1.5 to 2 hours
Difficulty: Moderate to difficult
Best season: April to October
Traffic: Hikers only

Fees and permits: None
Maps: Available at www.nps.gov/fone/planyourvisit/maps.htm
Trail contact: Fort Necessity National Battlefield, 1 Washington Pkwy., Farmington 15437; (724) 329-5512; www.nps.gov/fone/index.htm

Finding the trailhead: From Uniontown, travel east on Route 40 for about 11 miles. The entrance to the battlefield is on the right. GPS: N39 48.888' / W79 35.313'

The Hike

Most historic sites offer the chance to "step back in time," as it were. At Fort Necessity, you can step back in time on roads that actually date to the ancient past.

Gen. Edward Braddock and George Washington led British forces in building what was then known as the Braddock Road. It was designed to be a path of destruction, in one sense. The idea was to hack a substantial enough way through the forested mountains to allow for the passage of artillery and baggage wagons headed to forts in and around Pittsburgh. Walking this loop around the National Battlefield puts you on what remains of that road, at least for a little bit.

This hike also provides some perspective.

The "Great Meadows" area around the re-creation of Fort Necessity is largely that, open green space. So while the fort seems shockingly small—suitable for keeping sheep penned up temporarily perhaps, but not men—it doesn't necessarily seem exposed either.

This hike shows otherwise. All around the fort are markers showing where the tree line existed when the French and their Indian allies were attacking. They're uncomfortably close. To be in the fort, in the middle of a rainstorm, partially submerged in a rain-filled trench, surrounded by sick, dying, and dead men? With enemies that close? It had to be brutal.

This hike offers plenty of beauty, too, though. Expect to see lots of wildflowers. Wildlife is abundant, as well, from all manner of songbirds to white-tailed deer. And there's a very nice overlook along the Outer Meadow Loop portion of the trail that offers some really nice views, especially in fall when the leaves have changed colors. A bench there makes it a wonderful spot to just sit and relax.

You'll have one decision to make, though. This hike leads from the visitor center to the fort, makes a loop that returns to the fort, then goes back to the visitor center. If you want to visit Mount Washington Tavern—and you definitely should—you have

Fort Necessity more closely resembles a small stockade for holding livestock than a fort.

to choose between walking and driving. As devised, this hike takes you back to your car so you can drive there. If you prefer to walk, there's a side trail leading from the fort to the tavern. It's about 500 yards long, some of it steeply uphill, though always on paved ground.

The History

It is not much to look at, that's for sure. But then, what would you expect? It is, after all, the Fort of Necessity.

George Washington led a successful revolution unlike any the world had ever seen, piloted it in peace, then stepped aside when he could have been king. It's quite literally the stuff legends are made of. But his first foray into battle as a commander was an experience to forget.

It all started on May 24, 1754. Washington, at the head of a regiment of Virginia frontiersmen, was traveling west, having been sent months earlier to help guard a fort being built at the "point" in Pittsburgh where the Allegheny and Monongahela Rivers meet to form the Ohio.

He never made it.

The fort had been taken over and enlarged by the French almost as soon as the British finished it. They renamed it Fort Duquesne.

Reenactors tell the story of Fort Necessity and soldierly life in the 1700s at the national battlefield.

Washington, having learned of the situation en route, stopped in the "Great Meadows," as the Fort Necessity area was called, and set up camp. He labeled it, in his innocence, "a charming field for an encounter." He'd been there three days when he got word of a French encampment about 7 miles away on Chestnut Ridge. He took forty men—along with some warriors from the Iroquois tribe—and went to find them.

They surrounded the camp and, before long, shooting started. No one knows who fired the first shot. But in the end, after just 15 minutes, thirteen French were dead, including their commander, Ensign Coulon de Jumonville. Washington lost only one man. It wasn't long, though, before the tables turned.

The British and French had been sparring, verbally at least, for control of North America for a while. But they were not technically at war. Washington's encounter changed that. Indeed, English author Horace Walpole later wrote of Washington's actions: "The volley fired by a young Virginian in the backwoods of America set the world on fire."

Washington returned to Great Meadows, where he soon took top command upon the death of Col. Joshua Fry. His force swelled to 293 when reinforcements arrived on June 9. Another 100 men showed up a few days later. They were working to build a road when they got news that a French force from Fort Duquesne was approaching. The French were outraged over the prior skirmish, convinced that their troops—on a peaceful mission to ask the British to leave land that they claimed—had been ambushed and massacred.

Washington set about solidifying his position. The result was Fort Necessity. It was little more than a stockade really, just 53 feet across with rough-cut logs stuck in the ground vertically for walls. A small storehouse inside held food and supplies. The entire thing was surrounded by a trench. It proved wholly inadequate.

When 700 or so French troops arrived, with their own Native American allies, Washington sent his force out in classic lines to do battle. The French would have none of it. They disappeared into the surrounding forest—young Washington had miscalculated in building the fort too close to the trees—and fired from under cover. The British retreated into their fort, but when heavy rains started to fall, wetting their powder and leaving them virtually unable to fight back, their fate was sealed. After 8 hours of fighting, perhaps half of Washington's 400 troops were sick, wounded, or dead, and most were lying in water-filled trenches.

The French offered him the chance to surrender, something he had no choice but to do. But even that didn't go well. The terms allowed Washington and his men to leave with their arms and supplies. But, unbeknownst to Washington, the surrender document—negotiated with the help of a Virginian of Dutch descent who spoke some French—also included an admission that he had "assassinated" de Jumonville.

It was the only time Washington ever surrendered on a battlefield.

That wasn't the worst of it, though. The skirmish and following battle essentially started the French and Indian War. The British would prevail, but only after seven years of global conflict.

Mount Washington Tavern was an important and busy stop for travelers along the National Road.

Washington would get a taste of battle again later. That time, though, he would emerge victorious, as leader of the new American armies.

More History to See

Visitors to Fort Necessity can check out three other historic areas.

Just west of Fort Necessity, on Route 40, sits a monument known as Braddock's Grave. It's the final resting place of British general Edward Braddock.

The French had hoped the battle at Fort Necessity would convince the British to give up any claims to western Pennsylvania. That wasn't to be. In April 1755, at 60 years old, Braddock headed for Fort Duquesne, to engage the enemy. By July 9 he was within 8 miles of the fort. There his forces clashed with the French and were roundly defeated. Braddock was among the wounded and died during the retreat. He was buried in the road his troops had built on their way to Pittsburgh.

Farther west still, on Jumonville Road, is what's known as Jumonville Glen. This is where Washington's troops engaged in the skirmish that started the battle of Fort Necessity.

Finally, right next to Fort Necessity National Battlefield—you can walk to it or drive up—is Mount Washington Tavern. Its significance is tied to the road it sits along.

For years and years, the Appalachian Mountains were a giant—literally—hindrance to travel from American cities along the East Coast to the western frontier. None

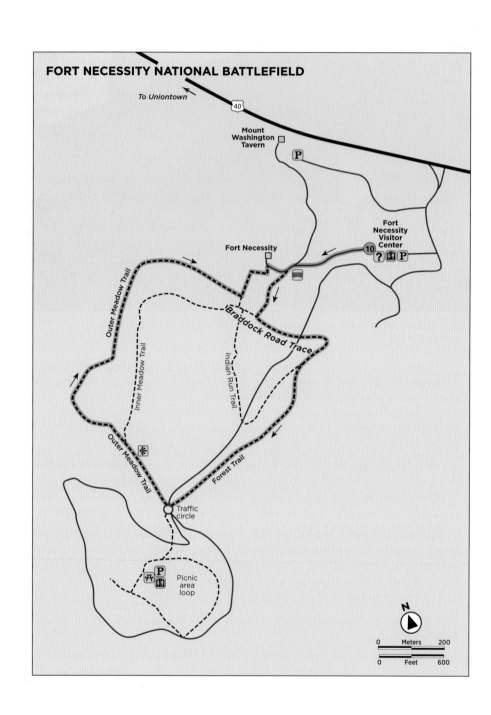

FORT NECESSITY NATIONAL BATTLEFIELD

To Uniontown

40

Mount
Washington
Tavern

P

Fort
Necessity
Visitor
Center

Fort Necessity

10 ? 🏛 P

Outer Meadow Trail

Braddock Road Trace

Inner Meadow Trail

Indian Run Trail

Outer Meadow Trail

Forest Trail

Traffic
circle

P

Picnic
area
loop

N

0	Meters	200
0	Feet	600

other than George Washington himself, while visiting some properties he owned in Pennsylvania in 1784, called for creation of an east–west road that would "open a wide door, and make a smooth way" for travelers.

Congress authorized such a road in 1806. The National Road—today Route 40—was the result, becoming America's first federally funded highway. Work began in 1811. By 1839 the road stretched more than 600 miles, to Illinois.

Around 1830 or so, Mount Washington Tavern was built to service Good Intent Stage Line travelers on the road. It offered meals, conversation, and rest, though how comfortable it was varied. Passengers sometimes could share a bed, men with men and women with women, usually fully clothed. At other times, when crowds were heavy, they paid to sleep on a hall floor. Still, the tavern was considered upscale for its time.

Today visitors can walk through portions of the building and see how it was furnished. There's a parlor, dining room, attic, and bedrooms. What's perhaps most interesting, though, is the graffiti. At one point, as part of a restoration, non-historic wallpaper was removed from the tavern. Underneath was discovered signatures and numeric equations, the doodling of workmen who constructed the house. One signature dates to July 28, 1839.

Miles and Directions

0.0 Start at the visitor center, going out the back door to the playground area. Go left on the sidewalk, past the pavilion.

0.1 The trail Ts. Going right leads to Mount Washington Tavern. Go left, toward Fort Necessity.

0.2 Arrive at the fort. Explore it, then turn around and retrace your steps.

0.3 With the fort to your back, cross a tiny bridge and then take the first right, just at the tree line.

0.4 The trail Ts at Braddock Road Trail. Turn left and go up the hill.

0.5 Cross the road and reenter the woods via the steps on the far side.

0.6 The trail Ys. Indian Run Trail goes to the right, toward the road. Go left on Forest Trail, which angles along the side of the hill.

0.9 Arrive at a roundabout. The road leading to the picnic area is to the left. Turn right, cross the road, go through the gap in the fence, and start downhill into a meadow on Outer Meadow Trail.

1.1 On the right is a short trail leading to an overlook. Take in the view, then return to the trail, continuing straight.

1.3 The trail Ys. Inner Meadow Trail is to the right. Go left, on Outer Meadow Trail.

1.6 The trail Ys again. Go left again.

1.9 Another Y in the trail, requiring another left turn. The trail Ts. Go left, into the field leading toward the fort.

2.0 Arrive at the sidewalk by the fort. Follow the walkway back to the start.

2.2 Arrive back at the visitor center.

11 Fallingwater

Start: At the visitor center
Distance: 1.3 miles (not including the house tour)
Type: Loop
Hiking time: 3 hours
Difficulty: Easy to moderate
Best season: March to December
Traffic: Hikers only
Fees and permits: Tickets are required to get on the grounds. Cost is $30 adults, $18 youth. Special in-depth, brunch, and sunset tours are available for additional fees, as is a landscape hike. Group rates are available. Note that there are restrictions on backpack and purse sizes, photography, and more. Check the website for up-to-date rules.
Maps: Available at the registration desk
Trail contact: Fallingwater, c/o Western Pennsylvania Conservancy, 1491 Mill Run Rd., Mill Run 15464; (724) 329-8501; www.fallingwater.org

Finding the trailhead: From Connellsville, follow Route 711 north for 8 miles to Normalville. Turn onto Route 381 and head south for about 7.2 miles, then turn right onto Fallingwater Road. GPS: N39 54.348' / W79 27.989'

The Hike

Imagine a wheel with four spokes emanating from its hub. That's the visitor center at Fallingwater.

Rather than being one building, it's a reception desk with four buildings spinning off from it. There's the Speyer Art Gallery, a cafe, a gift shop, and a set of restrooms, all connected by beautiful planking overhead and underfoot. That will get your attention. So, too, will the variety of languages you hear spoken. Fallingwater draws an international crowd. If the license plates from a multitude of different states on cars and buses in the parking lot don't tell that tale, the voices will.

Your hike here will be partially guided, partially on your own. When you schedule a visit, you pick a start time. Tours are held every 15 minutes. When your group is called, a host will give you a quick, 5-minute lay-of-the-land welcome, then you'll enter the grounds. Right away, on your right, you'll encounter the rocks that are so much a part of the landscape here. Keep them in mind for later.

The trail winds past a small garden, and, on the right, heard but largely unseen, Bear Run. If you want to check it out, there is a spot on the right—like a small spur— where you can get a peek at the stream.

Shortly after, you'll come to the bridge leading to Fallingwater itself, the magnificent home built by famous architect Frank Lloyd Wright. Here's where you'll meet your guide. He or she will lead you on a tour of the home. It's fascinating, but be prepared for a fair number of steps. The house tour probably adds a quarter mile to

This is a look at Fallingwater from "The View," downstream on Bear Run. Note how the home is built on top of the waterfall.

your walk, as well. And once you start, there are no opportunities to sit down and no public restrooms.

At tour's end, you'll leave the home at what once was the garage, then follow the driveway back to the bridge. Turn right and follow the path to a right-hand turn. It leads to an overlook, called "The View," that offers a chance to see Wright's creation from downstream. It is, I think, the best way to get a feel for the majesty of the home.

When you're done, retrace your steps to the main trail, then turn right at the four-way intersection and follow the sign for Lower Bear Run Trail. The sign says the walk is .089 mile. That, though, is round-trip.

Follow the trail—it goes downhill consistently but slightly—paying attention to the several spots in the trail where in-ground gutters, made from stone, allow runoff water from uphill to flow across the trail without causing any erosion. It's pretty ingenious, and definitely more attractive than your standard culvert pipe.

The path is one the Kaufmans, the original owners of the home, used to enjoy walking. There are some views of Bear Run here, too, though they can be obscured by trees. There's also mountain laurel and rhododendron on both sides of the trail, something that makes this a pretty walk in June.

When you reach the railroad tracks at the bottom of the hill, turn around and go back. At the four-way intersection, turn right and climb the stairs. There's quite a few, but they're well maintained and not steep. It's not as difficult a walk as it might be otherwise.

Eventually, the hike will pass a sign for Nature Walk Trail and a maintenance building, then you return to the visitor center, on the opposite side from where you started.

And then? If you still want to hike, Bear Run Nature Reserve—the Western Pennsylvania Conservancy's showcase property here—offers miles and miles of beautiful hiking trails. You might also consider a visit to Kentuck Knob, another Wright house built in the area, this one of the "Usonian" variety. That means it was meant to be affordable to the common man. Details are at http://kentuckknob.com.

The History

Have you ever wanted a house on the water? Edgar J. Kaufman Sr. did, and he got one more unusual than he could have ever imagined.

Kaufman was a famous, beloved, and hugely successful department store owner, one who ran what was for a long while the most famous department store in the Pittsburgh area. By 1920, when he was in his mid-thirties, the family business was doing more than $30 million a year in sales.

He and his wife, Liliane, loved to travel the world, but one of their favorite places to visit were the mountains of southwestern Pennsylvania. Edgar, a hiker, fisherman, and horseback rider, had gotten to know the countryside when apprenticing in nearby Connellsville and maintained his love of the area forever. So in 1935, when

A view of Fallingwater from upstream on Bear Run. Note the steps leading down from the terrace that holds the main living area. Guests could dangle their feet in the creek without technically leaving the house.

he wanted a summer cabin in the area, he bought land and turned to architect Frank Lloyd Wright to build it.

Wright's charge? Build the home overlooking Bear Run, the classic southwestern Pennsylvania mountain stream—full of water rushing over giant boulders, all surrounded by mountain laurel and rhododendron, hemlock and hardwoods—that the Kaufmans so treasured. The family was expecting a house near the creek, one that would allow them to see its waterfalls while sitting on the porch, perhaps.

Instead, Wright crafted a masterpiece.

A proponent of "organic architecture," where homes blend into the landscape and vice versa, he was not content merely to build the Kaufmans a retreat next to the stream. He built it directly over the water and folded it onto the hillside. The home and surrounding countryside became one.

Fallingwater—as Wright named the design, almost in an offhand matter—features numerous patios that extend out over Bear Run, cantilevered over the stream, for

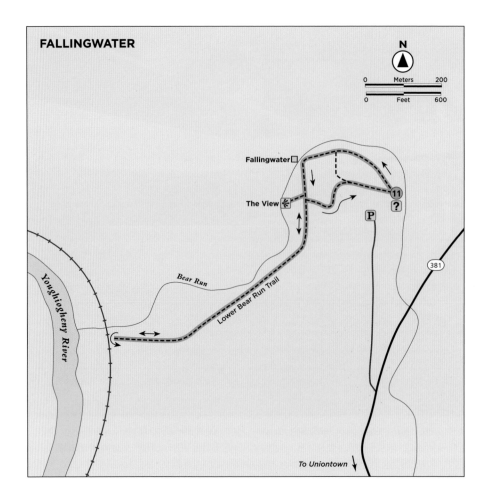

FALLINGWATER

N

| 0 | Meters | 200 |
| 0 | Feet | 600 |

Fallingwater

The View

11
?

P

Youghiogheny River

Bear Run

Lower Bear Run Trail

381

To Uniontown

example. From one—housing the home's main room—the Kaufmans could go down a set of steps and sit with their feet dangling in the water.

Then there's the structure of the home itself. Rather than remove things like the huge boulders that dotted the hillsides here, Wright used them. The fireplace in that main room? It sits atop a boulder that not only rises up from the floor to create a natural lead-in to the hearth, but anchors it to the ground, too. Another giant rock sits in the corner of a hallway connecting the main house with the guest house, like a giant rustic ornament. When it rains, water from the hillside naturally runs over the rock into the home and then back out to the stream through the floor. All of the home's staircases, meanwhile, feature handrails built into the walls using native stone quarried on-site.

The house is full of oddities like that, and some interesting stories, too. In one room, for example, Kaufman has a desk. Wright wanted it to be small; Kaufman wanted it larger. They debated the issue, neither wanting to budge, until Kaufman said he didn't think the desk offered enough space to write out a check paying Wright. The desk was made bigger, but in such a way as to still fit into the design of the home.

Visitors today get to see and hear all the stories, plus get a look at the original furnishings of the home. There are original paintings from around the world, assorted styles of furniture—from Japanese "zabutons" to "slipper" chairs—and all manner of sculptures, some of them dating back to AD 750.

The Kaufmans used this as their weekend home from 1937 to 1963. Then Edgar Kaufman Jr. donated the home and everything in it to the Western Pennsylvania Conservancy, which has maintained it ever since. It remains, to this day, the only one of 1,100 structures designed by Wright, and one of only 500 he saw through to completion, to come into the public domain with its setting, original furnishings, and artwork intact.

So it really is as one of a kind as it seems, after all.

Miles and Directions

0.0 Start at the visitor center. A guide will direct you down a plank walkway.

0.1 Turn left onto a gravel road. Pass a cuttings garden on the right.

0.2 A small spur on the right leads to a view of Bear Run. Soon turn right on the road toward Fallingwater.

0.3 Arrive at the bridge over Bear Run that leads to the home. A guide will take you on from here. Tour the house, then walk back down the hill to this bridge again. Turn right and follow signs to "The View." Soon the trail hits a four-way intersection. Turn right, visit The View, then return to this spot. Back at the four-way intersection, turn right onto Lower Bear Run Trail. This is especially colorful from June through early July when the laurel blooms.

0.6 Cross a rocky cut—think of a stone gutter level with the ground—that allows water to cross the trail without washing it out. There are several of these here.

0.7 A small overlook is on the right. Soon the trail dead-ends at a set of railroad tracks. Turn around here and retrace your steps up the hill.

1.2 Back at the four-way intersection one more time, turn right and go up the steps, following the sign for the visitor center. You will see the Nature Walk Trail on the left and a maintenance building on the right. Continue straight.

1.3 Arrive back at the visitor center.

12 Allegheny Portage Railroad National Historic Site

Start: At the trailhead near the town of Mineral Point

Distance: 4.2 miles

Type: Out and back

Hiking time: 2.5 hours

Difficulty: Easy

Best season: May to October

Traffic: Hikers and bicyclists

Fees and permits: None

Maps: Available at www.nps.gov/alpo/planyourvisit/maps.htm

Trail contact: Allegheny Portage Railroad National Historic Site, 110 Federal Park Rd., Gallitzin 16641; (814) 886-6150; www.nps.gov/alpo/index.htm

Finding the trailhead: From Blairsville, take Route 22 West for 20 miles to the Mundy's Corner/Nanty Glo exit. Turn right onto Route 271 South. Go about 5 miles, then turn left at the sign onto Mineral Point Road. Continue for 2 miles, then turn right at the sign onto Beech Hill Road. Cross the bridge. Go through the railroad underpass; the paved parking lot for Staple Bend Tunnel is on the right. GPS: N40 22.584' / W78 50.170'

The Hike

It seems almost unfair, really. The Staple Bend Tunnel is about 901 feet long: That's three football fields laid end to end, plus another 12 inches. It has no lights. Sun enters from each side, but to be in the middle is to be in some serious darkness. What it does have is water. Droplets fall from the ceiling like rain, and while it's not uncommon, to get splashed by one is always a small, if sudden and chilly, surprise. Yet, despite all that, to walk the tunnel end to end takes a matter of minutes.

Building it certainly wasn't so easy.

Staple Bend Tunnel is the oldest railroad tunnel in America, and the nation's third-oldest tunnel overall (the two that preceded it were for canals). It was a vital piece of the Allegheny Portage Railroad, itself a technological marvel that changed the world, then disappeared from it almost overnight. Without the tunnel, the railroad couldn't have succeeded.

Constructing it was a job, though. Irish and Welsh miners dug it by hand, earning $13 a month in return for six-day, 72-hour workweeks. They crawled into the hole each morning to hack away at the rock, placed explosive charges, blew things up, ate lunch while the dust and smoke cleared, then "mucked" out what had crumbled. Progress? If they made 18 inches a day—18 inches, mind you—that was considered a success. It took workers digging from each end thirteen months to meet in the middle, then another four to finish excavation. To walk the trail today reveals their handiwork.

The tunnel itself is a wonder. Notice its two faces. The one you'll see first coming from the trailhead is a simple, if well-constructed, stone arch. Look back at the tunnel

A hiker walks into Staple Bend Tunnel. The fancy stonework here once existed at both ends of the tunnel and was meant to impress visitors traveling between Philadelphia and Pittsburgh.

when exiting the other end, though, and you'll see much fancier decorative stone-work. Both ends of the tunnel had such a façade once—building them accounted for nearly half of the tunnel's final price tag of $37,498.85—but one was cannibalized for use elsewhere after the railroad went out of business.

Notice, too, the flat stones on the left side of the trail as you approach the tunnel. Those are "sleepers." They're hand-cut blocks of stone that measure 1 foot deep, 2 feet long, and 4 feet, 9 inches apart. The rail's tracks were laid on them rather than on wood.

Also note the trail's culverts. At one time there were seventy-three culverts and eighty-five drains along the path of the railroad, to channel rain and winter snows away from the tracks. A few remain, preserved for history's sake.

You won't work nearly as hard as the miners to see any of it. The trail is wide and flat along its entire length.

One word of advice? Though a part of the Allegheny Portage Railroad National Historic Site, the Staple Bend Tunnel is not on the same grounds as the main visitor center. It's a separate property, a roughly 40-minute drive to the northeast in Cresson.

The underground system that was used to haul trains carrying canal boats over the mountains

There are some informational kiosks along the trail, but to really understand what you're looking at, start at the visitor center. It shows a nice 20-minute movie on the railroad and has additional displays.

Do the 0.7-mile round-trip walk to see Plane and Engine House No. 6, with its underground steam engine, and the historic Lemon House, which catered to travelers along the rail line. Then drive to the Tunnel Trail and take the hike.

The History

Five hours. That's about how long it takes to drive the Turnpike from Philadelphia on Pennsylvania's eastern edge to Pittsburgh on its western edge. Things weren't always so easy.

Prior to 1834, the same trip took twenty-three days. It's no surprise, then, that it was costly to move people or goods between the state's two largest cities. There had to be a better way, right?

There was. And as is often the case, economics powered invention.

New York, to the north, was at that time developing an east–west canal system. So, too, was Maryland, to the south. Fearful of being shut out of the freight and people-moving businesses, Pennsylvania's elected officials decided to build their own canal, to be called the "Main Line." There was just one problem.

Between the two cities stood the rugged Allegheny Mountains. Canal boats coming from the east could go only as far as Hollidaysburg, which sits at 910 feet above sea level. Boats coming from the west could go only as far as Johnstown, at 1,154 feet. In between—roughly 37 miles across, but more importantly, rising to 2,348 feet—stood the Alleghenies. They were too steep for locomotives of the day to traverse, and too wide to dig a canal through. How to get over that barrier?

The Allegheny Portage Railroad was the answer.

It was built utilizing a series of inclined planes. Flat rail cars holding canal boats would be pulled partially up the mountain, in stair-step fashion. The power to drag them would come from stationary, underground steam engines (you can tour the remains of one of these, Engine House No. 6, near the visitor center). At each of eleven "levels" between steps, horses would take over. They'd haul the cars to the next hill, or incline, where additional underground engines would take over again. Once at the top, the cars would be slowly lowered the same way. It was slow going at best. Traversing the mountains took 6 to 8 hours.

It could be alternately thrilling and dangerous, too. Until John Roebling—builder of the Brooklyn Bridge—invented wire rope, hemp was often used to connect cars to horses and engines. Occasionally, it broke. That would send rail cars plummeting back downhill.

One passenger, Wilford Woodruff, called the experience of riding the train up the inclines "one of the most awful, fearful, dangerous, exciting, affecting, grand, sublime and interesting day's journey I ever took in my life."

The famous author, Charles Dickens, a passenger in 1843, was likewise impacted. The ride seemed safe, he said, undertaken with care. And the views? "Occasionally, the rails are laid on the extreme verge of a giddy precipice; and looking from the carriage window, the traveler gazes sheer down, without a stone or scrap of fence between, into the mountain depths below," Dickens wrote in an 1842 account.

For all that, the railroad shortened the trip between Philadelphia and Pittsburgh to a remarkable five days, thereby not only making it easier for people to get around, but opening up markets for all kinds of goods, as well.

A lot of people prospered. Samuel Lemon was one. His home—which still stands near the Allegheny Portage visitor center and can be toured—served as a way station for travelers. The prices charged seem quaint today. Twenty-five cents a night each for a room, a meal, a deck of cards or stable space for up to four horses; 12.5 cents for a whiskey "punch," 31.25 cents for a bottle. Those prices ultimately made Lemon the richest man in Cambria County, though.

And yet it didn't last. The development of more powerful steam engines, which could climb steep mountains on their own, doomed the Allegheny Portage Railroad.

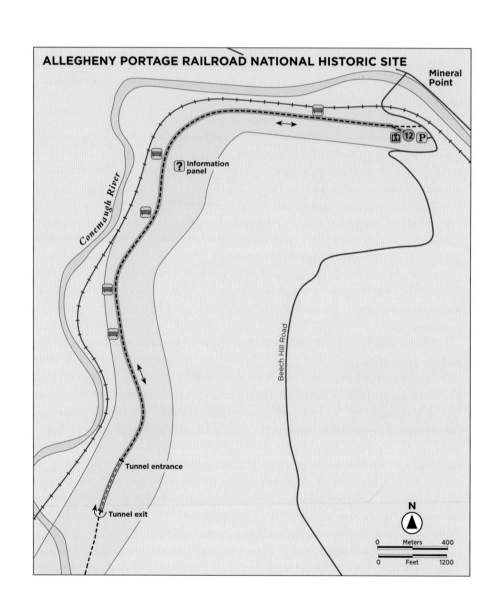

ALLEGHENY PORTAGE RAILROAD NATIONAL HISTORIC SITE

Mineral Point

Information panel

Conemaugh River

Beech Hill Road

Tunnel entrance

Tunnel exit

N

| 0 | Meters | 400 |
| 0 | Feet | 1200 |

Though hailed as a marvel of the age when first constructed, the railroad lasted only about twenty years. Put into operation in 1834, it was already being phased out in 1853 and was done by 1854.

"The old Portage," wrote surveyors who ultimately recommended that state officials quit operating it, "once the wonder of the age in which it was constructed, has done its work."

Miles and Directions

0.0 Start at the Staple Bend Tunnel trailhead, off Beech Hill Road (note that this also serves as one of four trailheads for the Path of the Flood Trail).

0.3 Notice a bench on the right, one of many where hikers can stop and rest or just enjoy the scenery.

0.4 On the left is an informational panel, one of many along the trail explaining the history of the tunnel on the Allegheny Portage Railroad and of the people who built and used it.

0.5 Small waterfall on the left. Notice on the right evidence of a culvert and, through the trees, trains running on parallel tracks even today. They show the wisdom of engineers who originally picked this route.

0.8 A bench and informational panel are on the right.

0.9 Pass another bench on the right.

1.0 Another waterfall is on the left. These seeps, most noticeable in spring and during times of high water, were a constant maintenance issue for the railroad. Water often moved tracks, which had to be re-spaced so the rails were always 4 feet, 9 inches apart.

1.3 Waterfall on the left.

1.5 Bench and informational panel on the right. Look left here to see "sleepers."

1.6 Bench on the right.

2.1 Entrance to the Staple Bend Tunnel. There are picnic tables here, too, as well as informational panels. Here or nearby once stood a blacksmith shop, a store, and more. Soon you emerge from the tunnel. To continue on goes to Johnstown. Turn around and retrace your steps back to the start.

4.2 Arrive back at the trailhead.

13 Johnstown Flood National Memorial

Start: At the south abutment of South Fork Dam
Distance: 0.4 mile
Type: Loop
Hiking time: 1 hour
Difficulty: Moderate to difficult
Best season: April to October

Traffic: Hikers only
Fees and permits: None
Maps: Available at www.nps.gov/jofl/plan yourvisit/maps.htm
Trail contact: Johnstown Flood National Memorial, 733 Lake Rd., South Fork 15956; (814) 886-6170; www.nps.gov/jofl/index.htm

Finding the trailhead: To get to the visitor center from Johnstown, follow Route 56 East for 5.3 miles to Route 219 North. Go 5.2 miles and take the Route 869 East exit. Go 1 mile, then turn left onto Pine Street, which becomes Frankstown Road. Go 1 mile and turn onto Lake Road. To reach the trailhead, take Lake Road for 1.4 miles. Turn right onto Route 869 and go 1.2 miles. Turn right at the sign for the picnic area. GPS: N40 20.888' / W78 46.603'

The Hike

There are parks and historic sites that just seem made for hiking. Johnstown Flood National Memorial is not necessarily one of them. That's not to say there's not good hiking here. There assuredly is. It's just not overly convenient in some ways.

Take the Path of the Flood hike, for example. It's an 8- to 10-mile walk rich in detail and history. But it's usually done in two legs, and even then requires shuttles and walking through towns where, without a park ranger serving as a guide, it's hard to know what you should be looking for.

So while it's worthwhile to find out when those hikes are (limited tours are available) and preregister for one or both, we're focusing on a short but interesting self-guided walk. It's the South Fork Dam Trail. Less than half a mile long, it can still be challenging.

Before starting, though, make a point of visiting the memorial's visitor center. It features two floors of exhibits that put in perspective what happened here and why it happened. The center shows a 35-minute movie, at 15 minutes past the hour, continuously from 9:15 a.m. to 4:15 p.m. Titled *Black Friday*, it's a riveting documentary that outlines how Johnstown came to be, why it's location made if perfect for such a disaster, and what—if anything—could have been done to prevent the tragedy.

Afterward, visit the 1889 historic district, on the National Register of Historic Places. It's south of the visitor center, off the St. Michael/Sidman exit of Route 219 (near the South Abutment picnic area). This is where the lodge and some of the cottages still remain. In between, drive over to the South Abutment picnic area to get started.

A set of stairs leads down from the top of one end of the old dam through the woods to the South Fork Little Conemaugh River. It's a relative trickle—you can

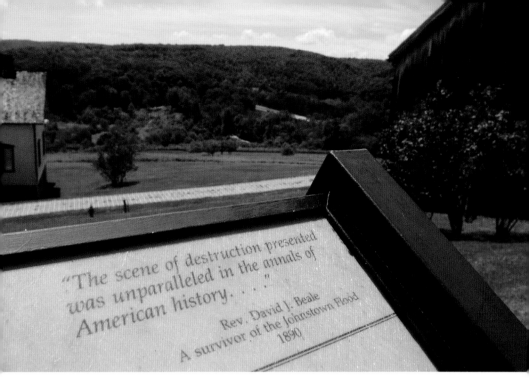

"The scene of destruction presented was unparalleled in the annals of American history...."

Rev. David J. Beale
A survivor of the Johnstown Flood 1890

The view looking from the Johnstown Flood visitor center toward what was the site of South Fork Dam. Just to the left, partially out of the photo, is the home of Elias Unger, which serves as the park office today.

imagine wading it—that unfortunately has a tint of orange to it from acid mine drainage, a sad and harmful leftover of the region's coal mining past.

Here along the creek you're walking on what would have been, in 1889, the floor of Lake Conemaugh. Remnants of the old dam walls, visible here from below, give some sense of just how large the dam was, how much water it held back, and how powerful the rush must have been when it all let loose.

You really want a feel for how much water was here, though?

That comes near the end of the hike. Climbing up from the lakebed—steep, but not as bad coming from this direction—brings you to the South Abutment overlook. Take a look from there, across the gulf between where you're standing and the North Abutment and, beyond that, to the visitor center. Now imagine that whole divide filled with water—and then that water pouring forth, all at once, in an uncontrollable flood.

The wonder is not that so many people died. It's that not more did.

The History

It remains one of the deadliest calamities in American history.

The Great Johnstown Flood of May 31, 1899, claimed the lives of at least 2,209 people: 99 entire families were wiped out; 124 wives lost husbands; 198 husbands

Visitors at the Johnstown Flood National Memorial stand below a three-dimensional display meant to capture the size and terror of the flood.

lost their wives; 396 children younger than age 10 died; another 568 lost one or both parents. The death toll was greater than that of Hurricane Katrina, one of the twenty-first century's greatest natural disasters.

So what caused it? Greed? Neglect? Apathy? A freakishly powerful storm? The answer is probably all those things together.

It all goes back to the birth of South Fork Dam in 1853. The Commonwealth of Pennsylvania built it to form Lake Conemaugh and provide water for its canal system. The dam—72 feet high, 10 feet across at the top and 931 feet long—was well constructed, according to reports. It was made of packed earth to be watertight. Just to be sure, though, it also had a water control tower, discharge pipes that could be used to regulate water levels, and a large, unobstructed spillway.

It wasn't foolproof, though. With the canal system giving way to railroads not long after the dam was built, it was neglected a bit, and failed in 1862. The controls in place mitigated the flow of water, though. The flood gave people a good scare, but no real damage resulted. That's perhaps the worst thing that could have happened.

In 1881 a group of wealthy Pittsburgh industrialists—Andrew Carnegie, Henry Clay Fisk, and Andrew Mellon, among others—bought the lake and the surrounding countryside to create the South Fork Hunting and Fishing Club, a mountain retreat. Members built a forty-seven-room clubhouse and sixteen elegant cottages, all connected by a boardwalk and each with its own boathouse and dock. They also paid $1 a fish to have 1,000 live bass shipped from Lake Erie by train to stock in the lake.

No money went into the dam, though. And, having been abandoned by then for seventeen years, it was failing. By 1889 the water control tower had burned down. The iron outlet pipes had been removed, making it impossible to control the water level. Breaches in the dam had been filled with stones, dirt, brush, and even manure. The dam was already sagging in the middle when club members had the dam lowered a bit to better accommodate the carriages that often stopped halfway across to offer passengers a view of the area.

The result was a lower, weaker, flimsier dam holding back much more water—500 to 600 million cubic feet—which rose to within 7 or 8 feet of the top, all with no safety valves.

Still, people downstream in Johnstown didn't worry too much. "Nobody seemed particularly concerned at the time over the dam which rich Pittsburghers had maintained high up on the South Fork," said 16-year-old Victor Heiser, a survivor of the flood, after the tragedy. "When the earthen dam had first been constructed, there had been some apprehension. But the dam had never burst and, with the passage of time, the townspeople . . . grew callous to the possibility of danger. 'Sometime,' they thought, 'that dam will give way, but it won't ever happen to us.'"

But in fact, it did.

By 9 a.m. on May 31, after a day and night of heavy rains, Elias Unger, manager of the club, noticed the waters rising dangerously. He put thirteen Italian immigrants, already on-site to dig a sewer system, to work digging an auxiliary spillway. When it

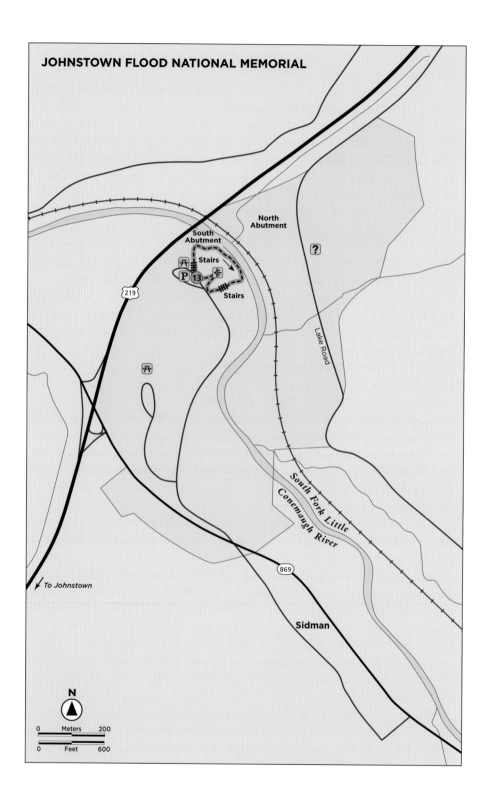

JOHNSTOWN FLOOD NATIONAL MEMORIAL

North
Abutment

South
Abutment

Stairs

🅿 13

Stairs

219

?

Lake Road

South Fork Little
Conemaugh River

869

To Johnstown

Sidman

N

0   Meters   200
0   Feet   600

was clear that wasn't working, he had them try to make the dam higher by plowing its crest and piling the dirt up. But that didn't work either.

At 3:15 p.m., the center of the dam gave way, sending 20 million tons of water—roughly equivalent to the output of Niagara Falls—downstream, sometimes traveling as fast as 40 miles per hour. The wall of water stood as much as 60 feet tall. On its way to Johnstown it picked up trees 4 feet in diameter, took houses off their foundations, and even swept multi-ton railroad cars along like toy boats.

Three telegraph messages raced it, trying to warn people of what was coming. It was to no avail. In less than an hour, the water hit the town. "The scene of destruction presented was unparalleled in the annals of American history," wrote Rev. David Beale, another survivor, afterward.

Pleas for help went out, seeking food, clothing, shelter, and hundreds of coffins, as the city had been left without an undertaker. The Red Cross moved in, too, led by then 67-year-old founder Clara Barton, and stayed five months. So bad was the wreckage that experts in explosives had to be called in to dynamite areas.

A total of 2,142 bodies were recovered, though some weren't found until 1911, a full twenty-two years after the flood. Some turned up as far away as Cincinnati, Ohio.

People on both sides of the issue—one blaming the wealthy industrialists for neglecting the dam, the other saying the flood was no one's fault, but an act of nature—would debate the flood for years. The reality, though, was that the flood would impact people for generations. It took years to rebuild—4 square miles of the city had been destroyed—and simultaneously spawned several major journalistic careers.

Amazingly, two more major floods would follow. About 24 people died in the Johnstown flood of 1936, while another 85 died in a 1977 flood.

Miles and Directions

0.0 Start at the South Abutment of South Fork Dam, at the South Abutment picnic area. Go down the steep steps—left of the overlook—marked "no winter maintenance." After 300 feet you come to the first of many informational panels, this one referencing how the flood carried along 20 million tons of water. You'll learn how twenty-two passengers in a train died when the water swept the entire locomotive away. There is another panel about 200 feet farther.

0.1 Arrive at a "you are here" panel. Soon the trail offers views of the South Fork Little Conemaugh River.

0.2 A panel here describes how some believed human lives were sacrificed for good fishing. Then the trail starts back uphill to the parking area. Start up the wooden stairs. At the top, turn right to go to the overlook.

0.3 Reach the overlook. It shows just how deep the dam was and how wide; the North Abutment and, beyond it, the visitor center, are in the distance. Take in the view, then retrace your steps toward the parking lot.

0.4 Arrive back at the parking lot to close the loop.

14 Flight 93 National Memorial

Start: At the parking lot by the visitor center

Distance: 2.4 miles

Type: Loop

Hiking time: 2 hours

Difficulty: Easy to moderate

Best season: April to October

Traffic: Hikers only

Fees and permits: None

Maps: Available at www.nps.gov/flni/plan yourvisit/maps.htm

Trail contact: Flight 93 National Memorial, PO Box 911, Shanksville 15560; (814) 893-6322; www.nps.gov/flni/index.htm

Finding the trailhead: From Bedford, follow Route 30 west for about 22 miles. Turn left into the memorial on Skyline Road. GPS: N40 03.421' / W78 54.387'

The Hike

The Flight 93 National Memorial is a sprawling facility, as you'd expect. A plane traveling in excess of 500 miles per hour covers a lot of ground in a hurry.

That makes it surprisingly peaceful, though.

The facilities here—the visitor center, Memorial Plaza, walkway, and more—are surrounded by meadows full of tall grasses and wildflowers and birds and butterflies. White-tailed deer occasionally wander by, and Canada geese and assorted ducks dot the ponds. It all serves to show the unquenchable nature of life, even in the face of hate and terror.

You'll start near the visitor center. Before going in, though, follow from the parking lot the "flight path" walkway, which not only traces the course the plane took in its final moments, but also highlights what else was going on in the country and when. It leads to an overlook of the debris field where the plane crashed. Haunting is the writing on the glass there: "A common field one day. A field of honor forever."

Next check out the visitor center, then follow the Allee, or formal walkway. A big loop, it takes you to the Memorial Plaza, the wall of names identifying all the passengers and crew on the plane, and past a giant boulder. Visible to the left, in the area where the plane crashed, it marks the site of impact. You can then continue up the hill to return to the start. (There are plenty of benches along the way so you can stop and rest if needed.)

When you're done, if you're up for more walking, there's another opportunity here. Across Route 30 from the memorial is State Game Land 93. It's a piece of public property owned by the Pennsylvania Game Commission. Game lands are managed for hunting and wildlife. This one, though, is also home to a wetland and hiking trail dedicated to Richard Guadagno. One of the passengers aboard Flight 93, Guadagno was an eighteen-year veteran of the US Fish and Wildlife Service, someone who had devoted his life to conserving and protecting the outdoors and its natural resources.

Visitors at the Wall of Names, which lists all the passengers and crew aboard Flight 93

There's a marker and some benches at the wetland, located just off Johnson Bottom Road. You can pick up the hiking trail there, too. It heads uphill through open fields presenting opportunities to see songbirds—birdhouses line the trail—and deer and turkeys, among other things. There's a scenic overlook at about the half-mile mark, complete with a bench. It's a fabulous place to take in the view, especially in fall, when the leaves have changed colors.

The trail cuts just inside the tree line when starting downhill at about the halfway point, then makes a loop around another, much larger wetland. You have to do just a bit of bushwhacking here. There's no bridge over that wetland's spillway; you have to step off the trail and go down the bank. The choices there are to either walk across the stair-step concrete outflow or go a few more steps and cross the trickle of a creek, something you can do in a step or two without so much as getting your feet wet. From there you walk back the way you came to the start. The hike, round-trip, covers about 3 miles.

This site sees lots of hunters from October through December and in May. There's no hunting on Sunday, though, so then and much of the rest of the year it's hike friendly.

A bridge over wetlands along the Allee and 40 Memorial Groves

The History

It was nothing less than twenty-first-century America's version of Pearl Harbor.

On September 11, 2001, the nation came under attack. Islamic terrorists—some of whom had been living in the country for more than a year, taking flight lessons—hijacked four commercial airliners each filled with roughly 20,000 gallons of jet fuel.

The first plane crashed into the north tower of the World Trade Center in New York City at 8:45 a.m., leaving a gaping, fiery hole near the 80th floor of the 110-floor building. It seemed a horrific, yet random, accident. But then another plane crashed into the south tower. Striking at 9:03 a.m., it hit the 60th floor. Together, those planes claimed the lives of nearly 3,000 people, including 343 firefighters and paramedics, 23 New York City police officers, and 37 Port Authority police officers who were trying to rescue people.

The attack wasn't over, though. At 9:45 a.m., another plane was intentionally crashed into the Pentagon in Washington, DC. That killed all 64 people aboard, plus 125 military personnel and civilians in the building.

And then there was Flight 93.

It, too, was a transcontinental flight bound for California. It was delayed, though. That allowed passengers to learn of what was going on elsewhere in the country. So when, shortly after takeoff, it was hijacked, they knew better than to believe the claims of the terrorists, who said they were being rerouted to another airport.

So they fought back.

"I know we're all going to die," one passenger, Thomas Burnett Jr., told his wife over the phone. "There's three of us who are going to do something about it. I love you honey."

Todd Beamer, another passenger, was famously heard to say over an open line: "Are you guys ready? OK. Let's roll."

A flight attendant on the crew, Sandy Bradshaw, was in a galley filling pitchers with boiling water for the passengers to use against the terrorists when she called her husband. She had just seconds to talk. "Everyone's running to first class. I've got to go. Bye," she said. They never spoke again.

Where the plane was headed exactly remains a mystery. Some have speculated its target was the White House. Others think it might have been the US Capitol or perhaps a nuclear power plant along the East Coast. In any case, it was just 18 minutes from reaching Washington. It never made it.

The passengers stormed the cockpit and the terrorists, who were armed with box cutters and other weapons. The plane flipped over in midair and, traveling at 563 miles per hour, crashed upside down in a field near Shanksville, in Somerset County. The resulting blast and explosion could be felt in a nearby elementary school. All forty-four people aboard the plane died instantly.

But the thirty-three passengers and seven crew members prevented what would surely have been an even worse disaster.

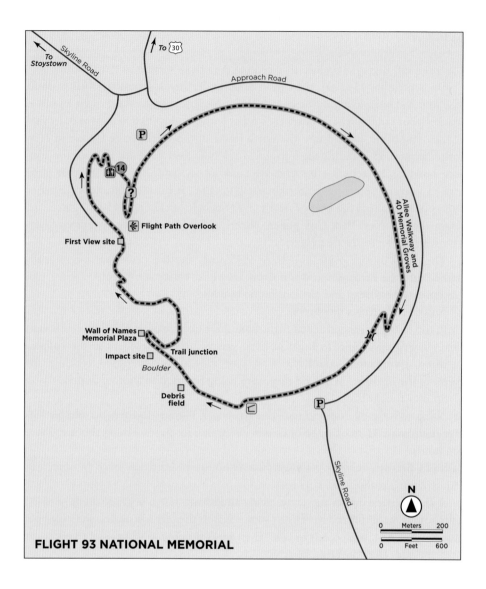

FLIGHT 93 NATIONAL MEMORIAL

Today that heroism is honored at the Flight 93 National Memorial, which continues to evolve. It's home to a "flight path" walkway that traces the plane's final route, with an overlook of the debris field at the end. There's a visitor center, too, and a visitor shelter and Memorial Plaza, with a "Wall of Names" for the forty passengers and crew. A formal walkway, called the Allee, connects everything.

Scheduled to debut in late 2018, meanwhile, is the Memorial Tower of Voices. A 93-foot-tall tower containing forty wind chimes, it will represent the voices of those on board who called loved ones in their final moments.

This site—what was before the crash a strip mine—is often quiet, as a place of reverence should be. The chimes, perhaps, will show that the voices of those who fought for what they believed in can never be silenced.

Miles and Directions

0.0 Start at the parking lot by the visitor center. Follow the sidewalk, which indicates the flight path of Flight 93. Soon you will reach the visitor center on the left. Before going in, though, continue straight to the overlook.

0.1 Reach the Flight Path Overlook. Take in the view, then retrace your steps to the visitor center.

0.2 Exit the visitor center and follow the gravel path. This is the Allee and 40 Memorial Groves walkway.

0.5 Notice a bench and overlook on the right.

0.7 See the first wetland pond on the right.

0.8 Pass another bench on the right.

1.1 Cross a bridge over the wetland. Follow the gravel path up the hill, toward the visitor shelter.

1.4 Reach the Memorial Plaza building, with benches and a flagpole. Check out the informational panels, then continue along the walkway.

1.5 Visible to the left is a giant boulder. It marks the spot of impact for Flight 93.

1.6 The path to the visitor center is on the right. Pass it for now and continue on to the Wall of Names.

1.7 Spend some time at the wall, then return the way you came. Turn left onto the trail you passed earlier. The trail goes uphill here, but there are benches at several points along the way if you need a break.

2.1 The trail crosses over a service road. This is the area known as the "first view." It's where family members of the victims were first brought after the crash. The makeshift memorial that appeared on televisions the world over was located on this spot.

2.3 The last of the multiple benches along the trail is located here.

2.4 Arrive back at the parking lot to close the loop.

Central

15 Kinzua Bridge State Park

Start: At the back entrance to the visitor center
Distance: 1 mile
Type: Out and back
Hiking time: 2 hours
Difficulty: Moderate to difficult
Best season: April to October
Traffic: Hikers only
Fees and permits: None

Maps: Available at www.dcnr.pa.gov/
StateParks/FindAPark/KinzuaBridgeStatePark/
Pages/Maps.aspx
Trail contact: Kinzua Bridge State Park, 296
Viaduct Rd., Kane 16735; (814) 778-5467;
www.dcnr.pa.gov/StateParks/FindAPark/
KinzuaBridgeStatePark/Pages/default.aspx

Finding the trailhead: From Kane, follow Route 6 east for about 12 miles. Turn left onto Route 3011/Lindholm Road and go 2.7 miles. Turn left into the park at the sign. GPS: N41 45.609' / W78 35.226'

The Hike

Please understand, this hike is every bit as challenging as the signs at the trailhead warn. "Hikers on the Kinzua Creek Trail," the sign reads, "should be in good physical condition, wear sturdy boots, and use caution due to steep trail sections."

You don't have to be some cross between Daniel Boone, a mountain climber, and a marathon runner to do this hike. The whole trip, total, counting both directions, is only about a mile. But use common sense. Every time I hike this, I encounter people in flip-flops trying to negotiate the steep grade, sometimes, unbelievably, carrying babies or even pushing strollers. Strollers, for Pete's sake! The pathway is gravel in spots, so it's not like you're climbing over boulders and slogging through mud, but you're walking from the top of a ridge to the valley below. It's a long way down in a short space of time.

It's that deep gorge that made the bridge here special in the first place. But if you dress properly, pack some water, and take your time, this is a hike that's impressive all out of proportion to its length.

You'll surely at some point—before or after checking out the visitor center—walk out on the skywalk and get a look at Kinzua Creek far below. In fact, make sure to do that. But as impressive as that view is—and there's a reason people once walked out here even during the era when it routinely hosted trains—the view from the bottom is just as jaw-dropping. You think the platform at the end of the skywalk seems high when you're on it. Get a look at it from the bottom. You'll be surprised at just how high up you were.

The trail that leads to the bottom does so via a series of switchbacks, so it's a little less strenuous than it might be otherwise. There are a couple of benches along the way, too, so don't be afraid to take a break if you need it. Just don't wander into the "debris field" at the very bottom of the hike. The twisted metal and old concrete scattered on the forest floor can be hazardous. There are on occasion rattlesnakes sunning here, too. Best to leave them alone. Besides, there's enough to see here without wandering into zones park officials have placed off-limits.

Note that this hike description doesn't include walking out on the skywalk. That's not because it's not worthwhile. Quite the opposite is true. The skywalk is not part of the "official" trail, but don't leave here without taking the stroll out onto it. The views are magnificent, both from the observation deck and from looking through the partial glass floor. You can walk on the old railroad tracks on the way out and back or on plank sidewalks on their edges. Once you factor it in, you'll end up walking about 1.6 miles or so total while here.

The History

It was at one time labeled "the eighth wonder of the world." Not surprisingly, it was born of bold thinking and innovation.

Thomas Kane was a fighter. A Civil War veteran—he walked with a limp because of one injury and wore a full beard to hide some disfiguration from another—abolitionist, and advocate for women's rights, he was also in 1881 president of the New York, Lake Erie and Western Railroad Coal Company. And he had a problem.

His company had natural resources to sell in the form of coal, oil, and timber. They originated in Pennsylvania's McKean County and areas south. He had markets eager to buy, too. They were located in Buffalo, New York.

The trouble was the Kinzua Creek valley in between. It was 300 feet deep and half a mile wide.

Kane had three choices. Option one was to detour his railroad 8 miles around the valley, through rugged terrain. Option two was to descend the valley slopes in a slow zigzag pattern, then climb the opposite side the same way. And option three? Why, that was to build the tallest and longest railroad bridge the world had ever seen, that's all.

Kane chose option three.

The job of building the bridge fell to two men, Adolphus Bonzano and Octave Chanute. They proved brilliant. Bonzano developed what came to be known as "Phoenix columns." Hollow, wrought-iron columns held together with rivets, they proved capable of withstanding strong winds, which was critical to allowing such a tall structure to stand. Chanute, meanwhile, when not designing gliders for the Wright brothers, figured out how fast trains could cross the bridge—5 miles per hour, was the answer—and still have it stand.

Their plans in hand, workers started construction in 1882, from the bottom up. Ready-made Phoenix towers were sent to the valley floor using chutes. Workers then erected them, one after the other, until the valley was spanned. Amazingly, despite a crew of just 125 men working 10-hour days, everything was done in ninety-four days.

Hikers walk out on the Kinzua Bridge skywalk, where trains once carried goods and later tourists over the valley.

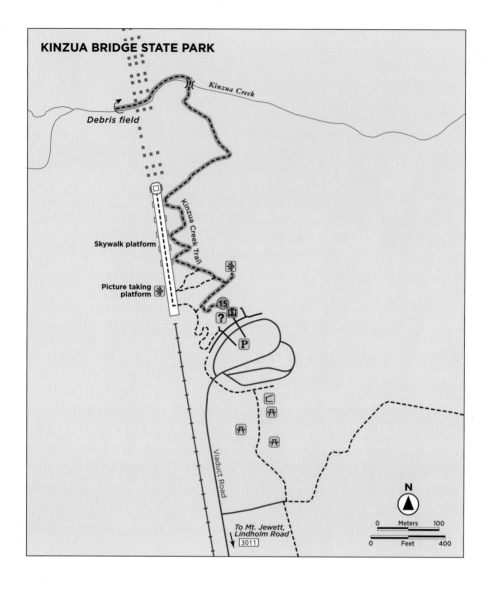

KINZUA BRIDGE STATE PARK

Kinzua Creek

Debris field

Skywalk platform

Picture taking platform

Kinzua Creek Trail

15

P

Viaduct Road

To Mt. Jewett, Lindholm Road
3011

N

Meters 100

Feet 400

The finished bridge stood 301 feet tall—24 feet taller than the Brooklyn Bridge—and stretched 2,053 feet long. It weighed a little more than 3.1 million pounds.

It was updated as early as 1900. With larger, heavier, more powerful locomotives capable of carrying bigger loads the new norm, the bridge was rebuilt. Starting at each end and working toward the center, crews demolished the Phoenix towers and replaced them with towers built using 6.7 million pounds of steel.

The new bridge—built using 895,000 rivets in 105 days—carried trains until 1959, when the demand for freight traffic ended.

That wasn't the end, though. The state bought the bridge and the land around it in 1963 to create Kinzua Bridge State Park. A little while later the bridge was recognized for being the groundbreaking marvel it was. It was added to the National Register of Historic Places in 1977 and the National Register of Historic Civil Engineering Landmarks in 1982.

Not long after that, the bridge was put back in service. Between 1987 and 2001 tourist trains ran over the bridge—stopping in the middle for the view—to give people the feel of riding "tracks across the sky."

Then disaster struck.

A routine inspection of the bridge in June 2002 found that its steel columns were rusting through. All train traffic was halted in August. "Engineers determined that high winds could create lateral pressure on the bridge. The wind hitting the bridge could shift the center of gravity, increasing the weight on one side. Such an event could send the whole bridge crashing to the bottom of Kinzua Creek Valley," reads information from the park.

In fact, that's just what happened. A repair crew started working to refurbish the bridge in February 2003. On July 21 of that year, crews were actually engaged in doing repairs when reports of an approaching storm caused them to quit. That storm turned out to be an F1 tornado, marked by winds of 73 to 112 miles per hour. In 30 seconds, they lifted eleven of the bridge's twenty towers from their moorings and sent them crashing to the valley floor.

The bridge had come to an end.

At least as far as trains are concerned. The state did rebuild part of the bridge—the "skywalk" portion leading to an observation platform—while leaving the remnants of the rest on the ground. The result is hikers today can walk out to the platform and see the devastation from above and walk to the debris field to get a view of it from below.

Kane, who lived just long enough to see the bridge completed, would probably approve.

Miles and Directions

0.0 Start at the back exit to the visitor center. Follow the gravel path to the right. The trail starts into the woods on the left, by an overlook. After a few hundred feet the trail Ys. Go left and continue downhill.

0.1 You'll get your first close-up views of the standing train trestles.

0.2 Arrive at a switchback with a bench on the right. Soon you come to another switchback with another bench. The trail then Ys; go left.

0.3 The trail bears to the right, then Ys again. Follow the signs to the left.

0.4 Cross a small bridge over Kinzua Creek. The trail then bends left.

0.5 The trail hits the edge of the debris field. Entry is prohibited, but you can get some good views of what's fallen and what remains standing. Take a look, then turn and retrace your steps to the top.

1.0 Arrive back at the visitor center.

16 Woodring Farm

Start: At the trailhead off Winslow Hill Road
Distance: 0.9 mile
Type: Lollipop loop
Hiking time: 1 hour
Difficulty: Easy
Best season: April to October
Traffic: Hikers only
Fees and permits: None

Maps: Available by calling 570-398-4744 or emailing pgc-ncregion@pa.gov, or online at everybodyadventures.com
Trail contact: Pennsylvania Game Commission, Northcentral Region Office, PO Box 5038, Jersey Shore 17740-5038; (570) 398-4744; www.pgc.pa.gov/InformationResources/ AboutUs/ContactInformation/Northcentral/ Pages/default.aspx

Finding the trailhead: From DuBois, follow Route 255 North to Route 555 East. Go 9 miles to Benezette, then turn left onto Winslow Hill Road. Go around an S curve, up a hill past the Elk Country Visitor Center. Pass the Winslow Hill elk viewing area and look for Woodring Farm on the left. GPS: N41 20.565' / W78 21.567'

The Hike

Be warned: You won't be alone.

It's a thrill to see a Pennsylvania elk at any time. But unquestionably the best time—and most popular time—to see them is in the fall. Starting in September, males, called bulls, go into the "rut." That's the breeding season. They become different animals then. They go on the hunt for females, or cows, and herd them into groups. It's not uncommon for a dominant bull to have a dozen or more ladies grouped together at a time. He'll guard them jealously against others who might try to sneak off with a few, too.

Even when you don't see a bull with cows, though, you can often hear them. The bulls "bugle," or call to one another in a high-pitched, almost flute-like way. To hear those throaty challenges at dawn, standing on a mist-covered mountain, the light just breaking through the clouds, is a thrill unlike any other.

It's one lots of people seek out.

The town of Benezette—site of the most famous elk viewing area, Winslow Hill—was home to 207 full-time residents in 2010, according to the US Census Bureau. But between September and November of each year, the peak of the elk viewing tourist season, it's estimated that 200,000 people visit. So expect traffic on two-lane roads not really built for it.

This trail draws crowds at times, too. For years, Game Commission officials fielded calls from would-be visitors. Where, they always asked, could they get out of their vehicle and hike to see elk? The trail at Woodring Farm is the answer.

Elk, native to Pennsylvania but gone by the late nineteenth century, are now back in a big way and a major tourist attraction. Here a bull wanders through the town of Benezette.

It doesn't get as busy as the elk viewing areas. Many tourists who come to see elk are content to watch for them from their vehicles. But Woodring Farm draws people, especially on those weekends when the Game Commission offers guided interpretive walks. They're interesting, but if you want to avoid competition, try hiking midweek. You won't be alone in peak seasons, but you'll have a bit more of a lonesome feel.

The trail isn't long, nor is it particularly difficult. It starts with a short climb up a gravel road, then levels out the rest of the way. Informational signs along the way—the artwork of which was done by local high school students—make for some good conservation reading.

Either way, plan to do this walk early or late in the day. Elk are grazers, like cattle, and leave the woods for open fields to feed. It's at dawn and dusk when they're most active.

This hike never really goes into the woods, instead circling a field along its edges, so if you time it right, there's the chance to either see elk there or catch them coming or going. The field itself is a wonder, too. It's a reclaimed strip mine, though it's so pretty you'd never think it.

A map of the hiking trail at Woodring Farm as seen at the trailhead, with trees from the surrounding landscape reflected in the cover.

If you don't see elk in the field here, try searching for them from the overlook located along the trail. It looks down on a valley where elk sometimes congregate if feeling too pressured elsewhere.

One last bit of advice? If you do see elk, don't try to get too close. These are wild animals, and the bulls—especially when they've got breeding on the mind—can be short-tempered. Keep your distance. There are often brochures with "elk viewing safety tips" at the trailhead, so pick one up for more information. Be safe, be smart, but do look for elk.

Not everyone's been able to see a Pennsylvania elk over the last century-plus. Don't miss your chance.

The History

They don't look like passenger pigeons, that's for sure.

They're flightless. They have tawny hair rather than feathers. The males carry crowns of bone atop their head for parts of the year. Oh, and when at their peak of health, the biggest specimens will weigh nearly half a ton. Yet elk almost went the way of the now-extinct birds, at least in Pennsylvania. That they didn't is a matter of conservation history.

Elk were widespread and numerous in the Keystone State when the first European settlers arrived. As late as the 1800s, market hunters—operating at a time when there were no closed seasons and no rules regarding how animals could be killed—were still killing elk and sending their meat to hungry cities. The animals couldn't stand the relentless pressure forever, though.

Some believe Pennsylvania's last elk was killed in Flag Swamp, near the Clarion River and St. Marys in Elk County, in 1865 by a Jim Jacobs. Other records say maybe it was as late as 1877 that a man named John Decker killed the last one in Centre County.

Either way, by the late 1870s, elk were gone.

That wouldn't change until 1913. Then the Pennsylvania Game Commission—the state's wildlife management agency—paid $30 each for fifty wild elk captured in Yellowstone National Park. They were shipped east in train cars and released in Clinton and Clearfield Counties. Ninety-five more followed in 1915. At the same time, twenty-two elk bought from a Pennsylvania preserve were also released in Monroe and Centre Counties.

It was primitive wildlife management. "To be honest," reads a commission account, "it's amazing the Yellowstone elk survived to serve as the nucleus of Pennsylvania's resurrected elk herd. Hauled across America by trains to locations principally selected through political deliberations, the elk were chased off the boxcars into the wild without any acclimation period. The terrain they bounded into was vastly different, the vegetation unfamiliar. Consequently, the 'hard release' approach used at that time by the Game Commission fell considerably short of providing the desired results."

The report continues, "Shortly after they were released, the elk began to wander in search of food and cover, to distance themselves from the trains that delivered them,

The Elk Country Visitor Center offers the chance to see live elk while also examining many exhibits and watching a movie to learn about the animals and conservation at large.

to seek out areas where human activity was limited. Within a week, some had traveled as far as 40 miles away from the release sites."

The herd was slow to grow. Farmers upset about crop damage, illegal poachers looking for a trophy, disease such as a brain worm outbreak, and other causes of mortality kept it in check for decades. As late as 1981 there were just 135 wild elk in the state.

That finally began to change in the mid-1980s, when Pennsylvania's first elk management strategies were really developed. Farmers were provided with special fencing to keep elk out of their fields, habitat was created on public lands, and elk living in areas that put them in conflict with people were trapped and transferred to more remote locations.

Helping to fund that work, interestingly, was hunters. The money they spend on licenses—the Game Commission's chief source of revenue, as it gets no general tax dollars—and raise at annual banquets hosted by the Rocky Mountain Elk Foundation and Keystone Elk Country Alliance, primarily went to buy land and improve habitat for elk, among other things.

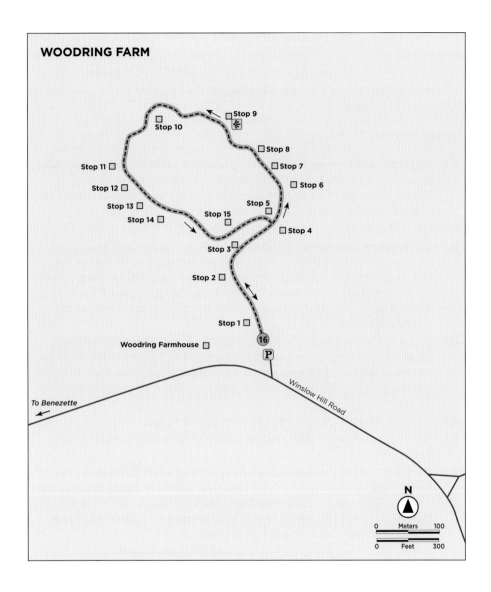

WOODRING FARM

Stop 9

Stop 10

Stop 8

Stop 11

Stop 7

Stop 12

Stop 6

Stop 13

Stop 5

Stop 15

Stop 14

Stop 4

Stop 3

Stop 2

Stop 1

Woodring Farmhouse

16

P

Winslow Hill Road

To Benezette

N

| 0 | Meters | 100 |
| 0 | Feet | 300 |

The result? Pennsylvania is now home to perhaps 1,000 elk. That's more than it's had in a century and a half, and more than any other state in the Northeast. Today the herd is an important economic driver for tourism in north-central Pennsylvania. It's large enough to support a limited elk hunting season, too.

If you'd like to see elk today, the Game Commission and state Department of Conservation and Natural History maintain elk viewing areas throughout the herd's range. Details can be found at www.pgc.pa.gov/Wildlife/WildlifeSpecies/Elk/Pages/ElkViewingDestinations.aspx. A video offering elk viewing tips, including how to see elk safely, can be seen at www.youtube.com/watch?v=xEtmEfhcrRE.

Be sure while in elk country, too, to visit the Elk Country Visitor Center. Located in Benezette, just moments away from Winslow Hill viewing area on Winslow Hill Road, it's not only a good place to see elk; it has a museum, store, and interactive exhibits focused on the elk herd too. Learn more about it at https:// elkcountryvisitorcenter.com.

Miles and Directions

0.0 Start at the trailhead, marked by a sign, at the parking lot just off Winslow Hill Road. Walk up the gravel road. Look for fifteen interpretive panels along the way. The first, stop 1, is a welcome sign on the left almost immediately after starting. After a few hundred feet come to stop 2, which describes what state game lands are.

0.1 Stop 3, which focuses on working for wildlife conservation.

0.2 Stop 4, which is about cool-season plants. The trail Ys here. Go right, past stop 5 on the left. It's an apple orchard behind a fence so the trees can get a start before elk eat them. Soon you come to stop 6, focusing on conifer trees. You can also see here how prescribed burns—intentionally set fires—are used to create wildlife habitat and why fire is such an important and increasingly common management tool. Next is stop 7, which is about planting clover for elk.

0.3 Here, at stop 8, learn about warm-season grasses. Soon after comes a highlight of this trail, stop 9. It's an observation deck that offers terrific views. Sometimes there are elk in the fields below. If not, the scenery alone is spectacular, especially in fall, when the leaves have changed colors. Follow the spur trail to the right to reach it, take it in, then return to the trail.

0.4 Stop 10 is about how elk change through the seasons of the year.

0.5 Stop 11 is a lovely field of wildflowers that often attracts elk and is colorful at certain times of year.

0.6 At this stop, number 12, look for birdhouses that are home to species like the kestrel, North America's smallest falcon. Stop 13 is a wetland, followed by stop 14, which is about a type of animal in trouble. Populations of some species of bats—so vital to controlling bugs like mosquitoes—have declined by 99 percent across the state in recent years because of a disease known as white-nose syndrome.

0.7 Here you find the final stop on the trail, number 15. It focuses on wildlife protection, or law enforcement efforts to protect elk and other species. Then the trail reaches the apple orchard again to close the loop. Turn right and retrace your steps to the parking lot.

0.9 Arrive back at the parking lot.

17 Pennsylvania Lumber Museum

Start: At the rear door of the Lumber Museum
Distance: 1.7 miles
Type: Loop
Hiking time: 2 to 3 hours
Difficulty: Easy to moderate
Best season: April to October
Traffic: Hikers only

Fees and permits: Admission is $8 adults, $7 seniors, $5 children 3–11, free to active-duty military and immediate family.
Maps: Available at http://lumbermuseum .org/map
Trail contact: Pennsylvania Lumber Museum, 5660 US Rte. 6, Ulysses 16948; (814) 435-2652; http://lumbermuseum.org

Finding the trailhead: From Galeton, follow Route 6 west for about 11 miles. The museum is on the right. GPS: N41 46.781' / W77 49.620'

The Hike

Things can always be worse, right?

There's a fair chance you'll encounter some mosquitoes when hiking the Sustainable Forestry Trail at the Pennsylvania Lumber Museum. Portions of it follow and even cross a small stream. Those low, wet spots draw bugs. It's nothing out of the ordinary, nothing that any regular use of insect repellent can't handle. So why mention it?

It's just a reminder of how well off we have things today, relatively speaking. During the lumber boom of the late 1800s and early 1900s—when men cutting trees for a nation still largely dependent on wood worked—conditions were often primitive. Very primitive.

As you'll learn at the museum, housing was especially nasty. Men—"woodhicks," they were called—would work 10- to 12-hour days, eat, then sleep in bunks or double beds in buildings with little in the way of heat aside from a central wood or coal stove. The bunkhouses often had poor ventilation, lots of dirt, no bathing facilities, and—lice.

So yeah, a few mosquitoes, that's OK. You may not even notice them really. And if you do, the hike is worth it.

Just be aware that this particular walk goes backwards, in one way. The Sustainable Forestry Trail has sixteen informational panels, numbered 1 through 16. Number 1 is located in the parking lot immediately where you pull off the highway and into the museum grounds. Sixteen is the last before you enter the historic area, with its many exhibits. That puts the museum at virtually the end of the journey.

We're not doing it that way. It's better to see the museum first—both to learn a bit and so be better able to understand what you're looking at, and to support the facility (the museum asks that people pay before walking the exhibits anyway). So check out the museum, then go out the side door and follow the plank sidewalks to the first

The Lumber Museum's Shay locomotive—nicknamed the "stem-winder"—dates to 1912. Last used in the mid-1950s and brought to the museum in 1964, it was capable of hauling twenty-two cars of logs.

set of buildings. Go down the hill to see the rest, then do the trail. The informational panels—which focus on everything from forest health and sawtimber value to the benefits of dead trees and forest openings—will make more sense then.

This is neither a particularly long walk nor a hard one, but there are benches in a couple of spots along the way in case you want to stop and just enjoy. You'll have it better than the woodhicks did, for sure.

The History

It was the time of the great purge, you might say.

When the first European settlers arrived in America, Pennsylvania was largely one vast unbroken virgin forest. Trees—white pines and hemlocks chief among them—towered hundreds of feet above the forest floor just about everywhere. Indeed, as late as colonial times, the forests were so expansive that the saying was a squirrel could travel from Pittsburgh to Philadelphia and back without ever touching the ground.

Things aren't too different today. The state is again heavily forested. According to the US Department of Agriculture, roughly 58 percent of Pennsylvania—about 16.7 million acres worth—is covered with trees. But in between those eras?

That was a time for cutting.

The steam-powered sawmill at the Lumber Museum is representative of the hundreds of mills that existed across the state at the dawn of the twentieth century.

In the span of a few decades from the late 1800s to the early 1900s, with American cities hungry for wood, tanneries demanding bark for treating leather, and the locomotive age making it possible to move and ship lumber like never before, Pennsylvania was turned into a giant clear-cut. Whole mountains were laid bare. Big trees were cut. Little trees were cut. Boards were produced. Shingles were made. Bark was collected. If little went to waste, little was left behind either.

An old photo from the state Bureau of Forestry tells the tale. It shows a perhaps 1930s-era car driving through a state forest—and there's nothing in the picture even half as tall as the vehicle. By the end of World War I, Pennsylvania's forest was as small as it was ever to get.

Armies of men made it so. Logging operations then required lots of workers, as the Lumber Museum explains. Each operation had saw filers, blacksmiths, carpenters, teamsters to take care of dozens of horses, men swinging axes and working hand saws, others running the sawmill, yet more operating boilers and railroads.

And men they were. Usually the only woman in camp—if there was any at all—might be the wife of the jobber, or foreman, as she could serve as camp cook. It was rugged, dangerous, dirty, noisy work, and paid little. Many men earned just $2 a day; even the foreman got only $3.50. But they fed a nation growing into an industrial power.

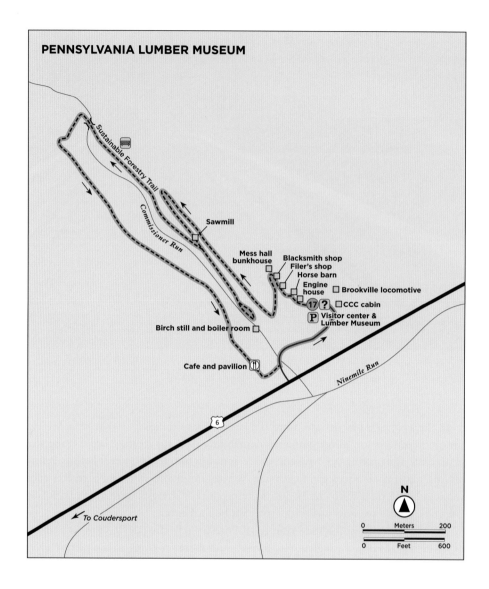

PENNSYLVANIA LUMBER MUSEUM

Sustainable Forestry Trail

Commissioner Run

Sawmill

Mess hall
bunkhouse

Blacksmith shop
Filer's shop
Horse barn
Engine
house   Brookville locomotive

17 ?   CCC cabin
P Visitor center &
   Lumber Museum

Birch still and boiler room

Cafe and pavilion

Ninemile Run

6

To Coudersport

N

0   Meters   200
0   Feet   600

The miracle is how the forests have come back. Indeed, that's one of the great ironies here.

The Lumber Museum is located in north-central Pennsylvania, that portion of the state known as "the big woods" for its giant chunks of state land. It's surrounded by many of the 4 million acres of land that make up the current state park and forest and state game lands systems. Those are all public properties open to hiking, camping, fishing, hunting, and the like. They're in state hands only because state leaders had the foresight to buy them up a century ago, after they'd been totally denuded by timbering, reduced to worthless "wastelands" in the eyes of some. What was once all but destroyed was saved for the benefit of future generations.

Timbering continues, of course, on those properties and on private lands. The business has changed—it's all done today in a much more sustainable manner—but has hardly faded away. Today Pennsylvania is still the largest producer of hardwoods in the country, accounting for about 10 percent of the nation's total output on its own. That's got economic benefits. Timbering, according to the Pennsylvania Forest Products Association, supports 90,000 jobs statewide. That's more than 10 percent of the state's total manufacturing workforce.

Cutting trees helps wildlife, too. It provides what biologists call "early successional habitat." That's young growth, the kind that some wildlife species, like ruffed grouse, absolutely need to survive.

The museum explains all that and more, while offering lots of cool information on the men, machines, and techniques that started it all more than a century ago. You'll learn about setters and doggers, jay-holes, marking hammers, bark slides and bark peelers, red row houses, and more.

You'll leave almost imagining you can smell the sawdust.

Miles and Directions

0.0   Tour the Lumber Museum, then go out the side door toward the engine house. Follow the plank sidewalk to the horse barn. In succession, check out the filer's shack, blacksmith shop, and mess hall.

0.1   Backtrack from the mess hall to go down the steps to the sawmill.

0.2   Arrive at the wooden plank walkway leading to the sawmill. Check it out, then walk out the far end of the building, turn left at the pond, and go down the hill.

0.4   Check out the boiler house, saw carriage house, and birch still, then retrace your steps back to the pond.

0.6   Arrive back at the pond. Follow it around the left side on the Sustainable Forestry Trail.

0.7   The trail enters the woods. Soon there's a bench on the right and a marker for stop 16.

0.8   Cross a bridge.

1.0   The trail Ys. Go left, passing stop 9.

1.3   Arrive at a small pavilion by a parking lot and the entrance to the museum. Turn left and walk the road back toward the parking lot.

1.5   Pass the visitor center by walking across the parking lot to a Civilian Conservation Corps cabin.

1.6   Past the CCC cabin, arrive at the Brookville locomotive and tannery exhibit. Then retrace your steps back to the beginning.

1.7   Arrive back at the start.

18 Leonard Harrison State Park

Start: At the Nessmuk sign just outside the entrance to the state park's main overlook area
Distance: 1 mile
Type: Loop
Hiking time: 2 hours
Difficulty: Easy to moderate
Best season: May to October
Traffic: Hikers only

Fees and permits: None
Maps: Available at www.dcnr.pa.gov/ StateParks/FindAPark/LeonardHarrison StatePark/Pages/Maps.aspx
Trail contact: Leonard Harrison State Park, 4797 Rte. 660, Wellsboro 16901-3061; (570) 724-3061

Finding the trailhead: From Wellsboro, follow Route 660 west for 2.6 miles. Turn left to stay on Route 660, go another 6.8 miles, then make a slight right to stay on Route 660. Go a little less than a mile, then go right again to stay on the same road to the state park. GPS: N41 41.781' / W77 27.278'

The Hike

Leonard Harrison State Park is deceptive. It's located on the east rim of what's known as Pennsylvania's Grand Canyon. Visitors who take in the view from its overlook are treated to unbroken green forests stretching to the horizon in each direction. Yet Leonard Harrison is just 585 acres. What's all the rest of those woods?

Colton Point State Park sits on the west rim. But at just 368 acres, it's smaller still and less developed. The majority of what you see is the Tioga and Tiadaghton State Forests. They encompass more than 300,000 acres. That's a lot of country, no matter how you label it.

What's not deceptive? The topography.

Look down from atop Leonard Harrison, and the canyon—through which flows Pine Creek—is every bit as narrow and deep as it appears. The canyon stretches 50 miles long and goes 1,000 feet deep in places. Here, the walls are nearly vertical. What that means is there's nowhere to hike that doesn't involve going sharply up and down.

There are two trails that originate from the park. One is Turkey Path Trail. It's a 2-mile round-trip, down-and-back walk via a series of switchbacks, steps, bridges, and decking. It's beautiful, with some very nice waterfalls to see along the way. If you're up to it and prepared—I've seen people try to hike it with baby strollers and in flip-flops, despite signs warning of its difficult nature—it's definitely worthwhile. But it is, quite frankly, beyond some people.

The more accessible trail—and the one outlined here—is Overlook Trail. It's also one that's perhaps perfect for campers. That's not to say it's easy. Granted, it's less than half as long as Turkey Trail, and never drops completely to the creek. But it still has some short, steep sections.

A view of Pennsylvania's Grand Canyon from the overlook at Leonard Harrison State Park

The first downhill portion—which leads past the ruins of a 1930s-era incinerator built by the Civilian Conservation Corps—leads to Otter Overlook, another view of Pine Creek looking downstream. It's been left in a more natural state than the main overlook—the only trappings here in the middle of the woods are some wooden fencing—but it's certainly scenic. Just be careful on the walk down. The trail runs right along the canyon rim; to the right are some steep drop-offs. They're wooded, but not the kind of slope you'd want to try and negotiate. From the overlook the trail climbs steeply back up.

If you're camping here—the campground is small, but all the better for it—there's a side trail that leads back to the campground. So you can walk this in a loop: from the campground, to the overlook, to this trail and back.

Otherwise, the trail ultimately takes you to a Civilian Conservation Corps display, complete with a statue of a 1930s-era worker. Seven parks around the state that had an especially big CCC presence have this same statue.

One other thing to try while you're here? The Pine Creek Trail is a hiking and biking path that runs along the canyon floor, following an old railroad grade. It's been rated as one of the top 10 such trails in the country. Take water with you if you go—there's about an 8-mile stretch here with no amenities, including no cell service—but it offers solitude, good fishing, and the chance to see wildlife, including numerous bald eagles.

The History

It's one of my favorite outdoor quotes of all time. George Washington Sears was a Pennsylvania outdoorsman and writer who went by the pen name Nessmuk. It means "wood drake" and was the name of the Narragansett Indian who taught him to appreciate and survive in nature. And do that he did. Sears loved to explore, often by lightweight canoe, and share his first-person stories in print.

Readers adored him, too. From the 1870s on he was one of the most popular writers for *Forest and Stream*, then the nation's premier outdoor magazine. His standing with the public only grew when in 1884 he wrote a book titled *Woodcraft and Camping*. Filled with tales of exploration and practical camping tips, some of which still remain relevant, it remains in print today and is considered a classic of outdoor literature.

At one point in the book, Sears talks about why people go outdoors. Some, he argued, view it as a man's attempt to challenge himself somehow, to prove his worth through hardship. Not so, Sears said. In his case, he went to the woods when "the straight jacket of civilization becomes too oppressive."

In short, immersing oneself in nature was less about struggle and more about restoration. "With a large majority of prospective tourists and outers, 'camping out' is a leading factor in the summer vacation. And during the long winter months they are prone to collect in little knots and talk much of camps, fishing, hunting and 'roughing it.' The last phrase is very popular and always cropping out in the talks on matters pertaining to a vacation in the woods. I dislike the phrase," Sears said.

He continued, "We do not go to the green woods and crystal waters to rough it, we go to smooth it. We get it rough enough at home; in towns and cities; in shops, offices, stores, banks anywhere that we may be placed—with the necessity always present of being on time and up to our work; of providing for the dependent ones; of keeping up, catching up, or getting left."

Amen to that, brother.

Sears is long gone—he died in 1890—but his legacy remains. An early and ardent conservationist, he championed protection of wild places and wild things. That advocacy is especially evident in this rural and rustic part of Pennsylvania, where state forests, state parks, and other public lands are set aside forever. That's fitting, as this is where he ultimately settled and took up writing.

Born in Massachusetts, he was a commercial fisherman in Cape Cod, sailed on a whaling ship from New Bedford, taught school in Ohio, mined silver in Colorado, edited a newspaper in Missouri, and was a cowboy in Texas and a hunter in Michigan.

The main overlook area at Leonard Harrison State Park is well developed and easy to access.

Yet when it came time to settle down, he chose Wellsboro, on the edge of what is now Tioga State Forest.

That was in 1848, when he was 27 years old. He spent the rest of his life here. Oh, there were periodic excursions. He joined the Pennsylvania Bucktails, a Civil War regiment of sharpshooters, though a medical condition kept him from ever serving. He explored Florida and the Amazon on assignment for magazines, as well. But he always returned to Wellsboro.

Fittingly, he's still remembered throughout the area. Leonard Harrison State Park has a historical marker bearing his name. You can see it adjacent to a log cabin near the entrance to the visitor center and overlooks of the Pine Creek Valley, known here as Pennsylvania's "Grand Canyon" for its high, steep walls and stream far below. There's also a lake and a mountain in this area that bear his name.

Assuredly, not all those who visit the area today know who Sears was or what he cared about. But if they love the outdoors, and this part of the world in particular, they share a passion with a man gone, but not forgotten.

Miles and Directions

0.0 Start at the Nessmuk sign, near a reconstructed log cabin. Cross the road and enter the main overlook area, passing the visitor center and gift shop along the way.

0.1 Come to the first area of overlooks. Follow them left.

0.2 Pass the entrance for Overlook Trail and follow the steps along the rim of the canyon. Check out the views, then turn around and retrace your steps to the Overlook Trail trailhead on the right. Turn and follow it.

0.3 Go right and then make another immediate right. Notice here a stone incinerator. It was built by Civilian Conservation Corps workers. Turn right and start downhill.

0.4 There's a bench on the left. The trail gets steeper and rocky here.

0.5 Arrive at Otter View. Check it out, then continue straight on the trail, winding back uphill.

0.6 Notice a small streambed on the right.

0.7 Find a bench on the right by a sign pointing right for the lower picnic area. Go left.

0.8 Find yourself back at the incinerator. Going to the right leads to the park office. Turn left and head back toward the main overlook.

0.9 At the top of the hill, turn right. Here find a memorial, with a statue and informational panels, paying tribute to the men of the Civilian Conservation Corps.

1.0 Arrive back at the Nessmuk sign.

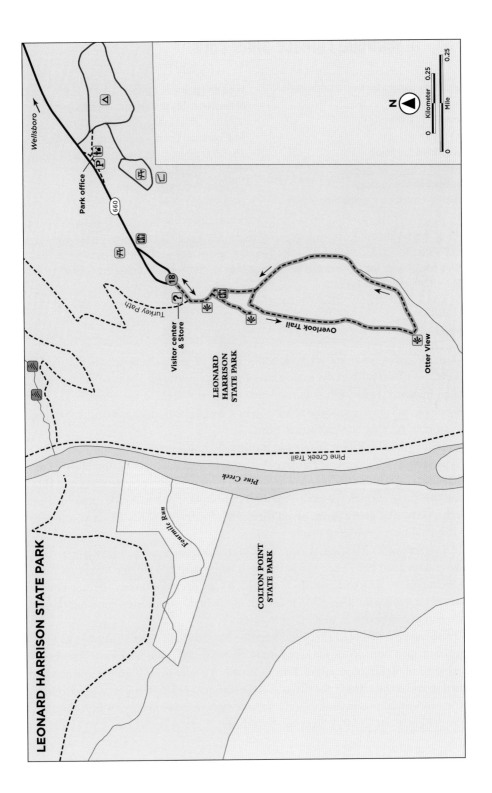

LEONARD HARRISON STATE PARK

Wellsboro

Park office

660

Turkey Path

Visitor center
& Store

18

LEONARD
HARRISON
STATE PARK

Overlook Trail

Otter View

Pine Creek Trail

Pine Creek

Fourmile Run

COLTON POINT
STATE PARK

N

0   Kilometer   0.25
0   Mile   0.25

19 Greenwood Furnace State Park

Start: At the parking lot for the Ironmaster's Mansion
Distance: 1.3 miles
Type: Loop
Hiking time: 1.5 hours
Difficulty: Easy to moderate
Best season: May to October
Traffic: Hikers usually; vehicles in spots

Fees and permits: None
Maps: Available at www.dcnr.state.pa.us/ stateparks/findapark/greenwoodfurnace
Trail contact: Greenwood Furnace State Park, 15795 Greenwood Rd., Huntingdon 16652-5831; (814) 667-1800; www.dcnr.state .pa.us/stateparks/findapark/ greenwoodfurnace

Finding the trailhead: From Huntingdon, follow Route 26 to a right turn onto Route 305 East/Greenwood Road. Go about 0.9 mile, then turn right to stay on Route 305 eastbound. Go 5 miles and look for the Ironmaster's Mansion parking lot on the left, just past the park office. GPS: N40 39.088' / W77 45.035'

The Hike

It's a miracle that anything survives, really. Think of the pace at which the world moves these days. Think of the mountains of garbage produced. Think of the demand for newer, bigger, better. Who's got time for saving the old? Far too often, in far too many places, what once was important at worst gets bulldozed, or at best is left to rot and crumble. It's why antiques stores exist.

At Greenwood Furnace State Park, fortunately, history remains visible.

The village of Greenwood Furnace that once existed here had 127 buildings at its peak. Only eight or so remain, and one of them is an off-limits private residence. But taking this walk through the park—on a mix of blacktopped sidewalks, gravel roads, wooden sidewalks, grassy paths, paved roads, and dirt forest trails—allows you to see the rest. And how interesting that is.

The Ironmaster's Mansion, where you'll start, was known as "the big house" to the workers who lived here, since it was so much larger than the average tenant's abode. It is an impressive structure, too. Built in 1833, it's got fourteen rooms on three floors. Chances are it was a bustling place. It housed not only the ironmaster, but often clerks, office staff, and servants, as well.

From there you'll get to check out Furnace No. 2. What's it like? Imagine a typical pyramid-shaped homemade backyard stone charcoal grill, then imagine it somehow growing to immense proportions. Sort as if your friendly neighborhood salamander turned into Godzilla. That's the furnace. Informational panels along its edges explain how it worked. It's interesting to walk up and explore it, knowing that in its heyday, it was pumping out 3,000 degrees worth of heat.

Furnace stacks like this one are the reason Greenwood Furnace existed as a village.

From there you'll pass the "charcoal demonstration area." It's basically your average fire circle most times of the year, though when the park hosts its annual heritage days, complete with charcoal demonstrations, it's interesting.

You'll next pass the blacksmith shop, the site of some fairly regular historical and environmental programming, and then the park's 6-acre lake. It's a pleasant place to swim, paddle, or fish. If you're just hiking, though, be sure to take note of its dam and spillway. The stonework there is absolutely incredible.

Next up, the hike leads to a cemetery, the final resting place of many Greenwood Furnace workers. Two Revolutionary War veterans are interred here, along with six Civil War veterans. There are twenty-seven marked graves and sixty unmarked. Notice the variation in even the marked graves, though. Some are fairly elaborate. Others are merely small rectangular stones with initials carved into them. One of those buried here lived to 79 years of age. Another was a baby of 6 months, 24 days.

The next spot of note on the hike is the Methodist Episcopal Church. It was built in 1867 at the request of village residents looking for an alternative to the sometimes wild ways of some workers. Today it holds "come as you are" services for campers and others on Sunday mornings from Memorial Day through Labor Day.

Greenwood's Methodist Episcopal Church, built in 1867, still holds services during the camping season for visitors to the park.

Crossing the road from the church leads to what was the company store. It's gone now, but in its day was where furnace workers—earning no more than $28 a month—shopped for necessities of all kinds. Leather boots went for $3.75 a pair, coffee for 30 to 35 cents a pound, hams for 10 cents a pound, flannel for 35 cents a yard. Money rarely changed hands. Clerks kept a record of what individuals spent and it was simply deducted from their pay before they ever got it.

The "meathouse" adjacent to the store remains, though. It was where hams, bacon, and other meats were kept before being moved into the store.

From here you'll walk back to the mansion to close the loop. Be sure before leaving, though, to visit the small visitor center inside the park office. There are some nice displays, along with a small store where you can buy gifts to support the park.

The History

If their uniforms weren't gray to start with, they probably turned that color in a hurry. Call it one price of prosperity.

The village of Greenwood Furnace had its own baseball team, the Energetics, in the early 1880s. Had its own brass band, too. There would have been plenty of potential players for each. Perhaps as many as 300 employees lived in the community then, when things were really booming economically. All, though, would have played in a world almost certain to be constantly smoky, sooty, ashy, and loud.

A wagon sits outside the blacksmith shop at Greenwood Furnace State Park. The shop is the site of periodic educational events.

Greenwood Furnace the town was built on Greenwood Furnace—or furnaces—Nos. 1, 2, 3, and 4. They were giant, pyramid-shaped structures of stone that burned charcoal to make high-quality pig iron ingots.

The first furnace went into operation in June 1834. The town sprang up around it and grew over time, from twenty or so tenant houses originally to ninety or so later. Also coming into existence were a blacksmith shop, company store, wagon shop, church, stables, gristmill, and more.

By the 1880s Greenwood was at its peak. It turned out 3,000 tons of iron annually, enough to rate it as one of the largest charcoal furnace operations in Pennsylvania. Most of that metal went to supply the burgeoning railroad industry, serving as the raw material for wheels, axles, and other parts.

That supported families, no doubt. But the look of the town?

It certainly wouldn't have been as quiet and idyllic as Greenwood Furnace State Park is today. Not by a long shot. The furnaces gobbled up hundreds of acres of forests each year, given their need for charcoal. That would have meant lumbermen cutting, horses dragging jangling chains, creaking wagons. Then, when lit, the furnaces burned at 3,000 degrees Fahrenheit, creating a constant roar. There would have been a constant hiss of steam, too.

The furnaces provided lots of light—it was said residents could walk around the village at night without a lantern, the skies were so lit up—but lots of dirt, too. They would routinely belch clouds of smoke and cinders into the air. Ash constantly rained down on people, homes, the ground, animals, everything. It must at times have been like walking through a perpetual, if light and warm, snowstorm. No wonder the town was described as being "built on top of an inferno."

It didn't last forever. Greenwood Furnace as an industrial enterprise closed up for good in 1904, a victim of its own ravenous appetite for wood—it was harder and harder to find it nearby—and changing technologies.

As it turns out, though, that was just another beginning. Ironically, the residue of the very thing its furnaces gobbled up—namely trees—gave it a second life. Foresters determined that the soil around Greenwood Furnace, having been enriched for years by charcoal and fly ash, was perfectly suited for growing trees. The state bought the land and, from 1906 through 1993, operated the Greenwood Furnace Tree Nursery here. Its seedlings were used to reforest the immediate area initially. Later, those seedlings went out all over the state, to restock forests elsewhere that had been largely cut over.

Along the way, in 1936, Furnace Stack No. 2 was refurbished as a monument to what had been. The site's been recognized for its historical value twice since. The National Park Service established the Greenwood Furnace Historic District in 1989. And in 1995, the area was designated a Historic Landmark by ASM International, formerly the American Society for Metals. It was at the time the 95th site in the world to be so honored.

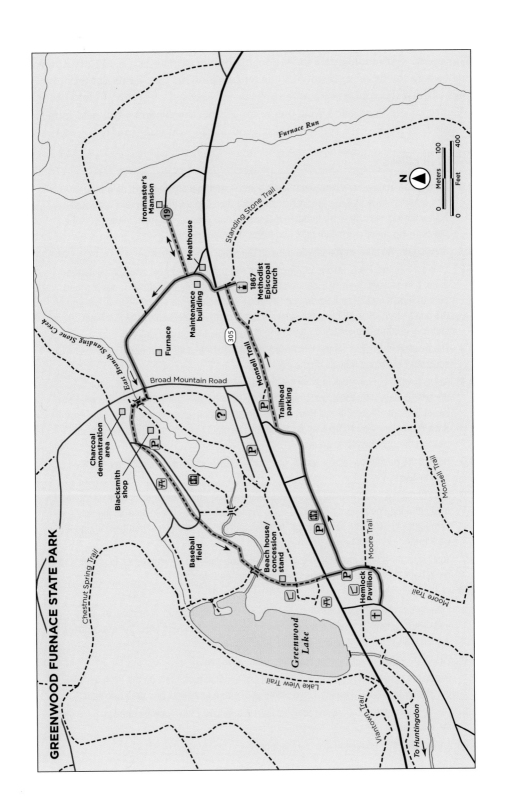

GREENWOOD FURNACE STATE PARK

Furnace Run

Ironmaster's Mansion

19

Meathouse

Standing Stone Trail

1867 Methodist Episcopal Church

Maintenance building

Furnace

305

Monsell Trail

East Branch Standing Stone Creek

Broad Mountain Road

Trailhead parking

P

P

Charcoal demonstration area

Blacksmith shop

P

?

P

Baseball field

P

Beach house/ concession stand

Moore Trail

Monsell Trail

Hemlock Pavilion

Chestnut Spring Trail

Greenwood Lake

Lake View Trail

Vanown Trail

To Huntingdon

N

Meters   100

0

Feet   400

0

Maps of what is now Greenwood Furnace State Park—which seems bigger than it is, given the surrounding state forest—highlight where many of the old structures dating back to the furnace era stood. Some remain; most are long gone. But they give a sense of the scale of what was.

And as for the Energetics? Well, they're long gone. But there is a ball field in the park, very near the furnace and blacksmith shop, in case you want to play.

Miles and Directions

0.0 Start at the Ironmaster's Mansion (there's some limited parking here, but on a busy weekend, you may have to leave your car at the park office and visitor center and walk over). Follow the sidewalk. In a few hundred feet the sidewalk meets the road. To the left is the old company meathouse. Turn right and follow the road downhill.

0.1 Stay left on the road as you pass a barn on the right.

0.2 Look for Furnace No. 2 on the left. There are a few picnic tables here and some informational panels worth reading. Soon the path meets Broad Mountain Road. Cross the road, then turn right and cross East Branch Standing Stone Creek via a footbridge. At the end of the bridge, turn left and follow the sidewalk. Notice immediately on the right, though, the charcoal burning demonstration area.

0.3 The blacksmith shop is on the left. Pass a maintenance building, restrooms, volleyball court, and unnamed trail, all on the left.

0.4 Arrive at what is essentially the left field corner of the baseball field. Turn left onto the unnamed, really unmarked, trail here, and follow the edge of the outfield, toward what would be center field. The trail Ys at a small bridge. Go left, crossing the bridge over East Branch Standing Stone Creek again. Soon the swimming beach is to the right. Stay left, passing through the picnic area.

0.5 Behind the beach concession stand, the trail Ys. Going left leads to a gate; go right instead.

0.6 Pass through a small parking lot and cross Greenwood Road/Route 305. Walk up the road leading to the campground. The road Ys. To the left is Hemlock picnic area, to the right the campground. Go right just far enough to check out the old cemetery. Then turn around and walk toward Hemlock picnic area on the gravel road.

0.7 You'll walk for a brief moment through a parking lot, then the gravel road Ys. To go left is to cross back over Route 305 to the beach area. Instead, go right.

0.8 Spruce Pavilion is on the right.

0.9 Enter another small gravel parking area, directly across Route 305 from the park office and visitor center. Go straight, passing a sign for Monsell Trail, and enter the woods following the orange blazes of Monsell toward Standing Stone Trail.

1.0 Pass a mileage marker sign for Standing Stone Trail.

1.1 Reach the driveway for Methodist Episcopal Church. Turn right, walk up the hill to check it out, then return back downhill. Cross Route 305 at the crosswalk and then turn right.

1.2 On the right is the company meathouse. Pass it and follow the sidewalk back to the mansion.

1.3 Arrive back at the mansion to close the loop.

20 Little Buffalo State Park

Start: At the parking lot by the classroom annex

Distance: 6 miles

Type: Loop

Hiking time: 4 hours

Difficulty: Easy to moderate on the south side of Holman Lake, difficult on the north side of the lake

Best season: April to October

Traffic: Hikers only, though it does cross some roads

Fees and permits: None

Maps: Available at www.dcnr.pa.gov/StateParks/FindAPark/LittleBuffaloStatePark/Pages/Maps.aspx

Trail contact: Little Buffalo State Park, 1579 State Park Rd., Newport 17074-9255; (717) 567-9255; www.dcnr.pa.gov/StateParks/FindAPark/LittleBuffaloStatePark/Pages/default.aspx

Finding the trailhead: From Newport, follow Route 34 South/Route 849 East for 0.6 mile. Turn right to stay on Route 34 South and go 0.4 mile. Turn right onto Route 4010 and follow it to the park. GPS: N40 27.341' / W77 10.257'

The Hike

Do you have any idea what volksmarching is? If not, here's your chance to learn.

According to the American Volkssport Association, volksmarching is "a non-competitive 3.1 mile (5 km) or 6.2 mile (10 km) walk. It's not a pledge walk, it's not a race, it is a fun activity you do with a club, with your family, with your pet, or all by yourself."

Why's that important here? Because, at Little Buffalo State Park, this hike follows—partially, though not completely—a volksmarching trail. We leave the volksmarching trail in spots.

For example, the volksmarching trail follows Little Buffalo Creek Trail for a while. And it is a pleasant walk, to be sure, following the edge of the stream. That offers the chance to see some wildlife. For this hike, though, we leave the trail and trade the possibility of seeing critters for a chance to walk a more historic route. The hike here follows an old railroad grade that's connected to the Little Buffalo's economic past. The Newport and Sherman's Valley Railroad carried goods to and from the early industrial center that existed here. Walking the old railroad grade allows you to explore—and take in a nice view—that would have been visible from the train.

Near the other end of the trail, meanwhile, we skip a portion of the Exercise Trail—a piece of the volksmarching path—to spend a little more time at the historic Blue Ball Tavern.

Besides, you'll get plenty of exercise on this trip. That's especially true when it comes to the northern leg of this hike, which follows Middle Ridge Trail. The

The waterwheel at Shoaff's Mill is one of the tallest east of the Mississippi River, at 32 feet.

park lists this 2.5-mile path as offering "most difficult hiking." And it is challenging, for sure.

You'll cross Little Buffalo Road at a bridge over Little Buffalo Creek. Middle Ridge Trail then immediately heads steeply uphill and, through a series of switchbacks, goes downhill and up, downhill and up, again and again. The park map promises some views of Holman Lake from the trail, and you will get some glimpses of the water. You'll certainly hear people paddling, too.

Don't expect overlooks, though, at least in summer. The vegetation of the trees largely blocks out any views. Hiking this in winter would offer better sight lines.

Regardless of the time of year you walk this, Middle Ridge eventually dumps you out at Exercise Trail on the far end of the park. The walking there, and on most of this hike, is comparatively easy. It's mostly wooded, though there is a short section that goes through the park's main picnic area. That involves walking on the road.

And if you really want to try volksmarching sometime, here or elsewhere, contact the American Volkssport Association for information. Details are at www.ava.org.

The History

Success and failure. The historic district at Little Buffalo State Park, which is on the National Register of Historic Places, is a testament to both.

The success is visible in the form of Shoaff's Mill. It's an 1840s-era facility designed to grind corn and, later, flour. It was built initially not as an afterthought, but certainly only to play a supporting role. Then, it outlasted the star.

The Juniata Iron Works—built just south of the present-day state park in 1808— is what prompted the settling of a community in this area. There had been Native Americans before that, and European pioneers and farmers afterward. But the opening of the furnace concentrated the settlement. That, in turn, made it feasible to operate a centralized mill where those farmers could turn their crops into something that would last throughout the year. Shoaff's Mill was born.

Ultimately, it outlasted the furnace. The latter ceased operations in 1848; the mill continued through 1940. Along the way it was improved several times—since 1900 it's featured one of the largest waterwheels east of the Mississippi River, a 32-footer— to make it more versatile.

And it still works today. Park officials use it to grind meal and make apple cider and more. That's all centered around public education programs, so be sure the check the park's schedule of events to see when you might explore things closer.

As for the failure here? That would be the railroad.

There were at one time two railroads— of two different kinds—that operated in the Little Buffalo area. The Perry County Railroad operated on "standard" gauge tracks, those 56.5 inches wide. It ran from Duncannon through New Bloomfield to Lloydsville.

Competing for business was the Newport and Sherman's Valley Railroad, owned by David Gring. He brought his railroad here from Huntingdon County to haul freight—largely logs from timbering operations—and later passengers. It was successful for a while, too. But there was one problem. The Newport and Sherman's Valley was a "narrow" gauge railroad. Its tracks were just 36 inches wide.

In time, locomotives grew larger and more powerful, to be able to haul more freight at one time. The bigger engines required the wider tracks, though. That spelled doom for Gring's operation. By 1937, forty-four years after he got his start at Little Buffalo, his operation went bankrupt.

Visitors to the park today can see one of his old rail cars, though. Way Car No. 12—oddly enough, decorated inside with a mix of authentic railroad memorabilia and Christmas decorations—sits off Blue Ball Trail, near the Holman Lake dam breast.

Aside from the mill and railroad car, there are two other historic structures here to see. They've had their moments, and continue to do so.

One is the Blue Ball Tavern. Starting in 1811, it offered food and lodging for travelers. Passersby knew whether they should stop or not by the presence or absence of a large blue ball outside the building. If it was visible, there were no overnight rooms left. The tavern was a hotbed of politics, too. Messenger riders stopped here during the War of 1812, for example. Today the Perry County Historical Society operates the tavern as a library and museum.

The other is Clay's Covered Bridge. Built in 1890, it's 82 feet long. It spanned Little Buffalo Creek about 1 mile west of where it sits now. The creation of Holman Lake necessitated its move. It's of Burr Truss architecture, meaning one large arch extends from one side of the bridge to the other. The roof and floor are attached to it as well, as are the many "king" posts. That type of construction allowed for building longer spans. The covered bridge is one of fourteen still existing in Perry County.

So there's plenty to see here, especially if you time it to be on hand when things are operational.

Miles and Directions

0.0 Starting at the parking lot by the classroom annex, go around the gate and follow the trail as it parallels the road. There's a volksmarch trailhead sign here.

0.1 Arrive at Clay's Bridge.

0.2 After crossing the bridge you come to Shoaff's Mill on the left. It's sometimes open for tours. Check it out, then go up the hill, keeping the mill on your left, on Mill Race Trail.

0.4 After passing under some power lines, you come to the remnants of the dam that existed when the mill was fully operational. Cross over the dam breast; the trail loops back around to the right.

0.5 Cross a small bridge. Soon Buffalo Ridge Trail is to the left. Go straight/right. When the trail meets a gravel road, turn left.

0.6 To the left are a few steps for Fishermans Trail. You'll turn here and follow this path. First, though, go straight long enough to check out Way Car No. 12, an old railroad car. Then backtrack to Fishermans Trail.

0.7 Steps on the right lead to the Holman Lake dam breast. Stay straight.

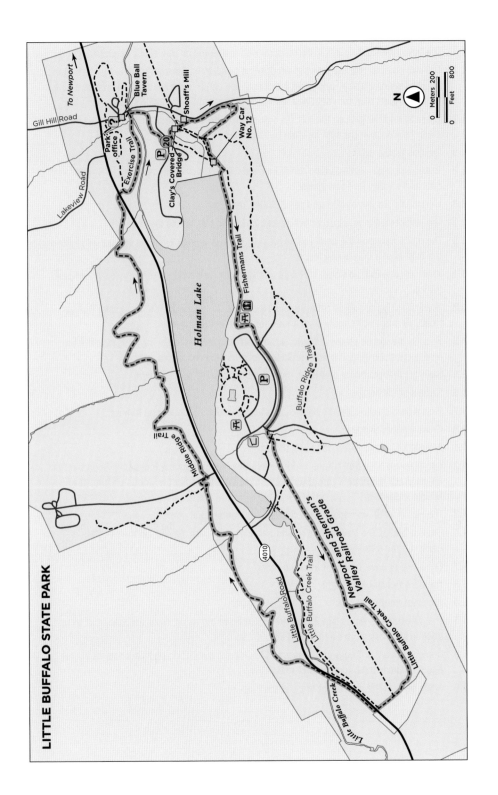

LITTLE BUFFALO STATE PARK

To Newport

Gill Hill Road

Lakeview Road

Blue Ball Tavern

Shoaff's Mill

Park office

P 2

Exercise Trail

P 20

Clay's Covered Bridge

Way Car No. 12

Fishermans Trail

Holman Lake

Buffalo Ridge Trail

P

Middle Ridge Trail

4010

Little Buffalo Road

Little Buffalo Creek Trail

Newport and Sherman's Valley Railroad Grade

Little Buffalo Creek Trail

Little Buffalo Creek

N

0   Meters   200
0   Feet   800

0.9 The trail Ys. Go left, following the white volksmarching arrow.

1.1 The trail comes to a four-way intersection with restrooms on the left. Continue straight.

1.2 The trail empties into the park's main day-use parking lot. Go straight, then turn left when the road winds that way and head uphill until you come to the road and, across it, a gate. Cross the gate, then turn right and follow the grassy path that parallels the parking lot.

1.7 Come to another gate on the left. Go around the gate, by another set of restrooms, and enter the woods at the sign for Little Buffalo Creek Trail.

1.9 The trail Ys. Go right.

2.0 The trail Ys again. Little Buffalo Creek Trail goes right. Go straight onto the old Newport and Sherman's Valley Railroad grade.

2.3 The trail Ys. Go left, back onto Little Buffalo Creek Trail.

2.7 The trail comes to a field, then winds just inside the tree line to the left.

2.9 The trail emerges in the field. Follow the field edge, keeping the woods on your left. Take the path past a private residence.

3.1 Arrive at Little Buffalo Road. Turn right and walk the mowed grass path, past a gravel parking lot.

3.2 The trail Ys. To the right is Little Buffalo Creek Trail. Go left, up the steps, to Little Buffalo Road, then turn right and walk the road for less than 100 yards.

3.3 Reenter the woods on the left side of the road onto Middle Ridge Trail. This is where the hike gets challenging. The trail Ys. Go left, following the red blazes.

3.5 Start the first of several descents. There are benches left and right here.

3.6 Cross a small bridge.

3.7 Pass a field on the right. It's a good spot to see wildlife like deer and turkeys.

3.8 Cross another bridge.

4.1 At another bench, go left, following the arrows.

4.2 Campground Spur trail comes in on the left. Stay right on Middle Ridge Trail. Soon the trail meets Black Hill Road. Cross the road, turn right, then reenter the woods on the left on Middle Ridge Trail.

4.3 The trail Ys at an unmarked path. Go right and switchback down the hill.

4.4 Cross a bridge. The trail then Ys at another unmarked path. Go left, up the hill. Pass a bench on the left.

4.7 Cross two bridges, one right after the other.

5.3 There's a bench on the right.

5.4 Cross yet another bridge.

5.5 The trail emerges onto Little Buffalo Road. Go down the steps, cross the road, and go up another set of steps to Exercise Trail. At the Y, go right.

5.8 Come to Blue Ball Tavern and Museum. Check it out if it's open (the park lists its hours) and then cross the bridge onto Blue Ball Trail.

6.0 Arrive back at the parking lot to close the loop.

21 Kings Gap Environmental Education Center

Start: At the Scenic Vista trailhead
Distance: 2.4 miles
Type: Lollipop loop
Hiking time: 2 hours
Difficulty: Moderate to difficult
Best season: May to October
Traffic: Hikers only
Fees and permits: None

Maps: Available at www.dcnr.state.pa.us/ cs/groups/public/documents/document/ dcnr_004117.pdf
Trail contact: Kings Gap Environmental Education Center, 500 Kings Gap Rd., Carlisle 17015-9306; (717) 486-5031; www.dcnr .state.pa.us/stateparks/findapark/kingsgap

Finding the trailhead: From Carlisle, head south on Route 465/Walnut Bottom Road for 6.8 miles. Turn right onto Montsera Road and go 5.3 miles. Turn right onto Pine Creek Road, go 200 feet, then turn left onto Kings Gap Road. Go about 4 miles to the park office. GPS: N40 05.593' / W77 15.840'

The Hike

Kings Gap is really two parks in one. Topography is the reason why.

It straddles South Mountain, which rises 700 to 1,400 feet above sea level. The forests at its upper and lower reaches are distinct. The woods in the lower elevations are full of spring seeps, vernal pools, and small natural ponds. Those wet spots sustain everything from wood frogs to spotted salamanders. It's here, among red and white oaks and tulips, that you might see Baltimore orioles, scarlet tanagers, and vireos.

The woods atop the ridges—which is where the historic mansion buildings and education center are located, and where this hikes winds—are drier and marked by thicker undergrowth. That's more beautiful than you might think, especially in late spring. In late May and early June the area's mountain laurel is in full bloom. Standing 6 feet tall, and sometimes more, it sprouts delicate pink and white flowers in big bouquets. To look into the woods when it's in its glory is to see random splashes of color against a dark green backdrop. It's amazing.

This hike, which uses several trails to form a loop, offers plenty of opportunities to take it all in. There are benches at a couple of spots along the way—including at the scenic overlook—so you can stop, relax, and just enjoy. To sit at the vista, in the quiet, not talking, is to know peace.

Getting there is a little challenging. This trail is wide, flat, and relatively easy in the beginning and at the end. But the final climb to the vista gains about 200 feet in elevation in a short time, so that's a little rougher.

More challenging is the walk back down. Leaving the vista, you'll descend a bit, jump onto Buck Ridge Trail, climb a short ways, then start downhill. The going is fairly steep. What's tricky is that the trail has a lot of loose rock. It's not terrible. But

This is the front of the James McCormick Cameron mansion. Despite having thirty-two rooms, it was used only as a summer home.

pay attention to where you're putting your feet to avoid slipping and sliding. A hiking stick is helpful here, too.

Make the trek, though. The scenery is worth the effort.

The History

Well, he didn't have to worry about crowding, that's for sure.

James McCormick Cameron, the son and grandson of US senators—his grand-dad, Simon Cameron, was Abraham Lincoln's secretary of war for a while—was born into wealth. Harvard educated, he owned, all at the same time, three homes. One was in Harrisburg, Pennsylvania's capital. Another was in nearby Lancaster. The third was his mountain retreat at Kings Gap.

This was no simple weekend cabin, though. His country home—which visitors to the park can tour today—is a 200-foot-long, thirty-two-room mansion sitting on 2,700 acres. Built to resemble an Italian villa, with a flat roof, huge windows, and a flagstone terrace, it's made of native Antietam quartzite quarried locally. Its internal construction features steel-reinforced concrete; it is one of the first buildings in this area to use that technique. The house is, simply, stunning. The commanding view from the back porch, looking over the surrounding countryside, is equally incredible.

The Cameron mansion and all of its outbuildings were serviced by this giant water tower.

For most of his life, Cameron had it to himself. Afflicted with a hearing issue that left him shy and soft-spoken, he didn't marry until he was 62 years old. Even then, he had no children. So space was never an issue.

Not that he spent all of his time there anyway. Despite the home's massive size, grand detailing, and support system—it has an ice house, its own water tower, a carriage house and stable, a stone-walled garden, a caretaker's house, and, later, an electrical generator house—Cameron only stayed in it from May through October. The threat of fire was the reason.

Most of Pennsylvania's forests were cut down in the late nineteenth and early twentieth centuries. Whole mountainsides were laid bare. The woody debris left behind, and the brush that sprang up from it, was perfect tinder. That was troublesome, given the transportation of the day. Those same denuded mountainsides were typically crisscrossed with railroad tracks over which traveled smoky, coal-burning, spark-throwing locomotives. Like rolling lighters, they often ignited blazes.

Cameron, not wanting to get caught in the middle of a wildfire, is thought to have avoided the home when the threat was highest. That means the mansion, time-consuming to erect, incredibly costly, huge enough to later serve as a corporate guest house for the Masland and Son Carpet Co., and just plain gorgeous, sat empty for months at a time.

It gets used now, though. Since passing into the state's hands in 1977, it's served as the focal point of Kings Gap Environmental Education Center. A part of the state park system, Kings Gap—as its name suggests—offers all kinds of outdoors programming to the public, from owl prowl hikes to youth discovery camps to beginner archery events.

Some of those are run by park staff. Check out the Department of Conservation and Natural Resources calendar for details on those at http://events.dcnr.pa .gov/kings_gap_environmental_education_center#.WTd8iJDyvIW. The Friends of Kings Gap group operates other events, from hikes to events like the "Music on the Mountain" festival. Details are available at www.friendsofkingsgap.org.

Many of those gatherings utilize the mansion, which has received $1.6 million in renovations, including construction of an enclosed fire escape and wheelchair-accessible restrooms. New carpeting, painting, tile, and furniture were added, too. That's all on view.

From Memorial Day through November, visitors to the park can take self-guided tours of the first floor of the mansion on Sundays from 1 p.m. to 5 p.m. The second floor can be seen on the first two Sundays in December, when the park hosts "Holiday Open Houses." Each year in mid-June the parks hosts a "Heritage Day," too, with early twentieth-century period music and games, doll making, tours of the mansion and carriage house, carriage rides, and more. And if you really want to use the mansion for something special? It can be rented for weddings and other events.

Be sure to check out the mansion garden, too. Cameron had it built along with his home, using wagonloads of soil brought up the mountain, to supplement his pantry.

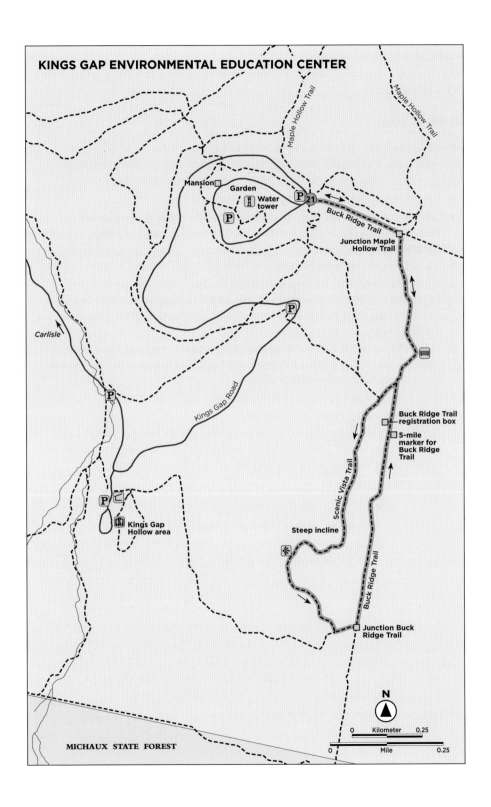

KINGS GAP ENVIRONMENTAL EDUCATION CENTER

Maple Hollow Trail

Maple Hollow Trail

Mansion

Garden

Water tower

P 21

Buck Ridge Trail

Junction Maple Hollow Trail

Carlisle

P

Kings Gap Road

P

Buck Ridge Trail registration box

5-mile marker for Buck Ridge Trail

Scenic Vista Trail

P

Kings Gap Hollow area

Steep incline

Buck Ridge Trail

Junction Buck Ridge Trail

N

| 0 | Kilometer | 0.25 |

| 0 | Mile | 0.25 |

MICHAUX STATE FOREST

Since 1992 it's been maintained by the Cumberland County Master Gardeners to showcase sustainable gardening.

All in all, it's definitely worth spending time here, even if—like Cameron—it's only for a little while.

Miles and Directions

0.0 Start at the Scenic Vista Trail trailhead, off Kings Gap Road. Follow the signs for Scenic Vista Trail on what is a level, wide pathway. Look for lots of mountain laurel right away.

0.2 Scenic Vista Trail meets Maple Hollow Trail. Go right at the Y to stay on Scenic Vista.

0.5 The trail Ts. Turn right, again following the signs for Scenic Vista.

0.6 Notice a bench on the left for sitting and resting. Then the trail Ys at a junction with Buck Ridge Trail. Go to the right. Soon there's an unmarked four-way intersection. Continue straight.

0.9 The trail narrows and begins its climb up to the vista.

1.1 Arrive at the scenic vista. The trees here obscure the view a bit—it's not like coming to the edge of a cliff—but it's possible to see quite a ways. The benches here are a wonderful spot for stopping, with more laurel to be admired. When ready to go on, continue on Scenic Vista Trail.

1.3 The trail Ts, with Scenic Vista Trail going to the right. Instead, turn left onto an unnamed connector path. After a bit the trail T's again as it meets Buck Ridge Trail. Turn left. The trail here is narrow, rocky, and surprisingly sunny.

1.4 Begin a steep, rocky descent. Watch for loose rock.

1.7 Pass a 5-mile marker for the Buck Ridge Trail.

1.8 On the left is a trail registration box for hikers who want to leave record of their passing. Ignore the trail you soon come to on the left. Continue straight and almost immediately Buck Ridge Trail runs into Scenic Vista Trail. Follow it back the way you came.

2.4 Arrive back at the trailhead.

22 Pine Grove Furnace State Park

Start: At the iron furnace
Distance: 1.3 miles
Type: Loop
Hiking time: 2 hours
Difficulty: Easy
Best season: April to October
Traffic: Hikers and bicyclists; trail also follows some roads with automobile traffic
Fees and permits: None

Maps: Available at www.dcnr.pa.gov/StateParks/FindAPark/PineGroveFurnaceStatePark/Pages/Maps.aspx
Trail contact: Pine Grove Furnace State Park, 1100 Pine Grove Rd., Gardners 17324; (717) 486-7174; www.dcnr.pa.gov/StateParks/FindAPark/PineGroveFurnaceStatePark/Pages/default.aspx

Finding the trailhead: From Shippensburg, follow I-81 north for 8.2 miles. Get onto Route 233 South and go 8 miles. Turn left onto Pine Grove Road. Make an almost immediate left into the park near the park office and follow it to parking along Quarry Road, near the furnace. GPS: N40 01.912' / W77 18.389'

The Hike

OK, so it's not the most scenic or challenging section of the Appalachian Trail by any means. But take this walk through Pine Grove Furnace State Park and you can say you trod the mighty Appalachian Trail. You'll accomplish something else along the way. That is, you'll see almost all of the historic structures in the park.

Begin by parking in the gravel lot in front of the furnace stack. First built in 1794 and last used in 1895, the stack has been renovated several times over the years. Most recently it got a new concrete top in 2014. It's possible to walk around the base of it and even stoop down to wander inside a bit, to get an up-close look.

This hike then takes you to the Ironmaster's Mansion. Definitely try to get a tour. A guide will talk about the home's past, while—if you're like me—you gawk at the tremendous fireplace in the kitchen. Park officials say this home was considered finer than most other mansions of the time, and it looks the part.

That done, come back down the stairs to Quarry Road to visit the paymaster's office, stable/general store, mill-turned-Appalachian Trail Museum, and stone walls of the charcoal house. The tables and chairs outside the stable make for a pleasant place to take a break, and the museum is worth exploring. Keep an eye out for through-hikers here. Backpacks on the benches outside the museum are a giveaway if you don't see them in person.

The hike next takes you past the site of what was the blacksmith and carpenter's shop. They're gone but for a marker. Across the parking lot, past the restrooms, you'll hit a paved multi-use trail that runs through the park's main picnic area. That, tame though it seems, is the Appalachian Trail here. Follow it past the concession stand by

The Ironmaster's Mansion at Pine Grove Furnace State Park, which was opulent by the standards of its day, is open for regular tours. It also serves as a hostel for Appalachian Trail hikers.

the beach to reach an old cabin and then Fuller Lake. Before it was a lake, this was a pit reaching 90 feet deep, where iron workers for a century mined their raw materials. When they left, it filled with groundwater and eventually became the lake you see now.

Next, loop back past the brickworks (a foundation remains if you go a few steps out of your way) and school (gone completely) to the water race, or channel, and then your starting point.

If you really want to do this hike when you can get a feel for history, stop by in mid-October. The park hosts a Fall Furnace Festival then. It's part craft show and food festival, but tours of the mansion are offered, too, and there are usually demonstrations in charcoal making, woodworking, axe and saw use, muzzleloaders, and more. It's crowded, as all these things usually are, but a nice event.

The History

At Pine Grove Furnace State Park, history sometimes meets history in the form of a worn-looking, rangy, and obviously hungry backpacker trying to down a half gallon of ice cream in one sitting.

Yeah, really.

What was once the grain mill for the community of Pine Grove now serves as the Appalachian Trail Museum.

The park sits along the Appalachian Trail, the 2,190-mile Georgia-to-Maine foot-path. The midpoint of the trail, in fact, is just a few miles south of the park in Michaux State Forest.

The Appalachian Trail, or AT as it's known, is the nation's oldest official long-distance trail. Efforts to build it began in 1921. Despite lots of hard work and advo-cacy, though, it wasn't completed until 1937. The first through-hiker—defined as someone who walks the trail end to end in one season—was a recovering veteran of the Pacific Theater in World War II named Earl Shaffer. He actually grew up not far away, in York, Pennsylvania.

No one at the time, not even trail organizers, believed such a feat was possible. Shaffer proved otherwise and changed how hikers looked at the trail. These days, about 2,000 people a year set out to replicate his experience. About one in four suc-ceed. By tradition, those who get to Pine Grove stop in its general store and attempt the "half gallon challenge." Hikers can write about the experience in a register in the store. It makes for colorful reading.

It's there that hikers meet another kind of history. The general store was, at one time, a stable for mules, back when this area was home to an iron furnace (the bars on some of the store's windows are visible reminders of that time). It later hosted dances when men of the Civilian Conservation Corps from Camp S-51 were here in the 1930s.

It's just one of several historic structures still standing in the park, though. All are tied to the area's industrial past.

The Pine Grove area was settled as early as 1764, when three partners built an iron furnace and named it Pine Grove Iron Works. They kept it just a short while; the furnace subsequently passed through many owners over the years.

Several were famous in their own ways. When the iron works went bankrupt dur-ing the financial panic of 1837, for example, it was bought at sheriff's sale by two men, Frederick Watts and his law partner, Charles Bingham Penrose. Watts would found Penn State University in 1855 and serve as chairman of agriculture under President Ulysses S. Grant in 1871; Penrose would become a state senator and solicitor of the treasury for President Benjamin Harrison.

Later, in 1864, Jay Cooke and Company bought the iron works. Cooke is often called the "Financier of the Civil War" because he sold bonds to raise nearly $1.2 bil-lion for the war effort. He collected a percentage of each sale and for a while was the wealthiest man in America. He ultimately went bankrupt, though.

The furnace changed hands again before hitting its peak of production in 1883, when it turned out 6,000 net tons of cast iron. That was under the guidance of John Birkinbine, who went on to found the Pennsylvania Forestry Association.

Ultimately, it was changing technologies and not poor ownership that put the furnace out of business. It went cold by 1895.

The old mill still stands, though. Today it houses the Appalachian Trail Museum. Home to displays about the trail's past, it also features a hall of fame for people

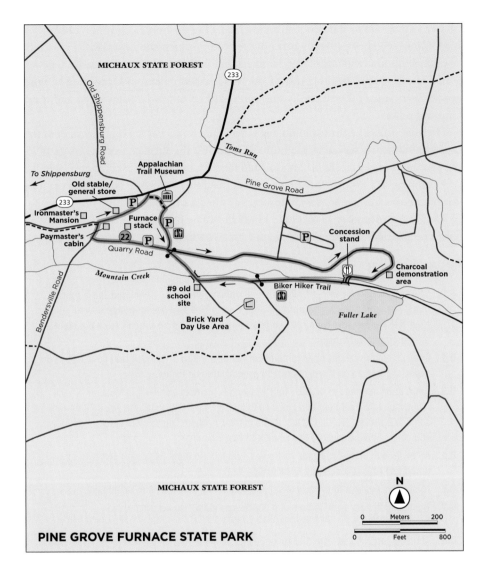

PINE GROVE FURNACE STATE PARK

0	Meters	200
0	Feet	800

important in the trail's development, a museum store, and more. There's even a children's section in the basement. Visitors are asked to sign in. For fun, check out the register. Through-hikers typically go by trail names while hiking. All have a story behind them, and some are interesting, if you can catch a hiker willing to share.

Another historic building in the park is the redbrick, English Tudor Ironmaster's Mansion. It was built in 1829 by then furnace owner Peter Ege for his wife, Jane Arthur. A magnificent structure, it hosts weddings and youth group retreats. It's open to public tours on Sunday afternoons from Memorial Day through Labor Day, too.

Most notably, perhaps, it serves as a hostel for backpackers. As many as twenty-eight at a time can stay in dormitory-style rooms, men on one floor, women on another, with access to showers, bathrooms, and all of the home's common rooms. For an additional fee, they can get a pizza dinner and breakfast the next day.

Outside, on the wide front porch, hikers will find a "trail magic" box. Such boxes, located at various points along the AT, are places where hikers and "trail angels" who support them drop off gear, treats, and more. Hikers take what they need and leave things for others.

There are still other historic buildings here. The furnace stack remains, as does the paymaster's office. It served as the business office for the furnace from 1764 to 1895. It's been modernized inside and is available for rent, in case you ever want to spend a week camping in a historic building. Contact the park for details. One of two original boardinghouses still stands as well. It serves as the park office.

That's a lot of history of a couple kinds all in one place, right? Stop by, take it all in, and keep an eye out for an ice cream eating machine.

Miles and Directions

0.0 Start at the iron furnace (there's a small parking lot there). Check out the furnace, then, with your back to it, turn right onto Quarry Road. At the stop sign several hundred feet farther, turn right on Bendersville Road and go up the hill. Take the steps to the Ironmaster's Mansion.

0.1 Reach the mansion. It's open for tours on Sunday. Return to the road and go left. Pass the paymaster's cabin on the right and the general store on the left.

0.3 Arrive at an information board. Straight ahead is the Appalachian Trail Museum. Check it out, then turn right here and go down the hill on the trail through the grass. Soon you come to a parking lot. On the left, at the marker, is where Pine Grove's blacksmith and carpenter shops used to be. Go straight through the lot.

0.4 At the far end of the lot, by the restrooms, turn left. Go around the gate and follow the paved trail (this is part of the Appalachian Trail).

0.6 The trail comes to a four-way intersection, with a bridge to the right. Go straight.

0.7 The trail four-ways again in front of a concession stand. Go left around the concession stand.

0.8 At an old log building—site of charcoal demonstrations—you'll notice the trail goes straight toward a bridge. Instead, turn right and walk through the grass toward the beach.

0.9 Just past the concession stand, there's a bridge to the left. Cross it, then make an immediate right on the trail.

1.0 Notice a playground on the left. Soon, just past a bridge on the right, the path comes to the Brick Yard Day Use Area. Go around the gate and straight on the path.

1.2 On the left, at the marker, is where Pine Grove's school used to stand. After a short bit you will find yourself back at the parking lot. On the left, by the marker, is the water race that was used to help operate the furnace. Turn left toward the furnace.

1.3 Arrive back at the start to close the loop.

23 Caledonia State Park

Start: At the Dock Memorial
Distance: 1.5 miles
Type: Loop
Hiking time: 1.5 hours
Difficulty: Easy
Best season: May to October
Traffic: Hikers only on the Thaddeus Stevens and Midland Trails; bicycles and horses possible on the Chambersburg Water Line; vehicles possible when crossing roads
Fees and permits: None
Maps: Available at www.dcnr.state.pa.us/stateparks/findapark/caledonia
Trail contact: Caledonia State Park, 101 Pine Grove Rd., Fayetteville 17222-8224; (717) 352-2161; www.dcnr.state.pa.us/stateparks/findapark/caledonia

Finding the trailhead: From Gettysburg, follow Route 30 west for 15 miles to the state park. GPS: N39 54.385' / W77 28.672'

The Hike

Thaddeus Stevens was not, by any measure, an ambiguous man. A lawyer and politician, he was passionate and principled, with a fierce and oftentimes biting wit. Editorial writers at the *New York Times* in his day called him "the evil genius of the Republican party."

It's ironic then that the historical trail that bears his name in Caledonia State Park is so subtly misleading.

The Thaddeus Stevens Historic Trail allows visitors to check out remnants, some original, some reconstructed, of the iron furnace he operated at the site for years. All is not as it seems, though.

Stop No. 4 on the trail—there are ten—is a beautiful little series of waterfalls. The stream bubbles and gurgles over rocks. A wonder of nature, right? Not necessarily. The stream not only flows between two gorgeous stone walls, but is man-made itself. Iron workers dug the "race," as such watery pathways were called in the 1830s, to turn the 30-foot waterwheel that in turn powered the furnace. And where does the water for the stream come from? That's the No. 9 feature on the trail, lovely Furnace Dam. Popular with anglers these days, and a neat spot for resting and observing wildlife, it's man-made, too.

Even the trailhead is deceiving.

The hike starts at the "Dock Memorial." It looks like a miniature log cabin. With its Appalachian Trail sign on the outside—the trail does pass through the park—it also appears like a place where weary hikers might spend a night. Its beginnings were more humble, though. According to the book *At Work in Penn's Woods*, it was originally a latrine built by the men of the Civilian Conservation Corps in the 1930s.

The colors of fall are reflected in the lake of Furnace Dam.

No matter, though. This trail makes for a very pleasant walk. Hikers will follow the mostly level Thaddeus Stevens Trail for just under a mile, switch to the Chambersburg Water Line—wide, flat, and sunny—for a bit, then jump onto the Midland Trail near the park office before walking some sidewalks and across a picnic area to return to the start.

Parking is available along Route 30. One parking lot is near the Dock Memorial; another, the more popular, near the iron furnace.

No matter where you start, it's a wonderful walk that can begin or end with a picnic or dip in the park pool. And if you visit during summer weekends, stop by the blacksmith shop. The Thaddeus Stevens Society opens it on Saturday and Sunday, with a working blacksmith on-site occasionally.

The History

Talk about a bargain. Visitors to Caledonia State Park get a three-fer for their history dollar.

First there's Thaddeus Stevens and his iron furnace. Remnants of the furnace and its operation still stand today. What's amazing is the story behind them.

Stevens, born in Vermont, rose from poverty to become a successful lawyer— and the largest landowner—in Gettysburg and later Lancaster. Known as "the Great

Horseshoes hang in a row in the Thaddeus Stevens Blacksmith Shop, which dates to 1830.

Commoner" for things like his impassioned efforts to maintain free public education, he also operated the Caledonia Iron Works. It never made him rich. Indeed, it was for a long time a draining source of debt. But he operated it for decades, employing hundreds. Those families lived in houses that stood near the current park pool and ball field.

Stevens was also twice elected to Congress, the second time in 1859. There, as an early anti-slavery advocate, he made many ardent enemies.

If that wasn't abundantly clear before June 1863, it was after. That month, Gen. Jubal Early led a force of Confederate soldiers into south-central Pennsylvania. Early, like all Confederate commanders, was under orders from Gen. Robert E. Lee not to disturb the civilian population. He largely obeyed.

With one exception.

Early's forces burned the Caledonia furnace works and village to the ground on June 23 on their way to Gettysburg. The issue was Stevens's abolitionist views. He was one of several lawmakers backing a proposal to break up the holdings of wealthy Confederates and divide that land among soon-to-be-freed slaves. He was also a key backer—some say the father—of the 14th Amendment, which guarantees equality under the law regardless of color.

That infuriated the likes of Early. When he came to the iron works, he said "I (am) determined to destroy them." That he did. His soldiers also looted the village.

Stevens was not cowed. "If finally, the government shall be reestablished over our whole territory and not a vestige of slavery left, I shall deem it a cheap purchase," he said.

He lived to see the nation reunited, passing away in 1868. True to his beliefs, he was buried in a segregated cemetery, below a tombstone with an epitaph he wrote himself. "I repose in this quiet and secluded spot, not from any natural preference for solitude; but finding other cemeteries limited as to race, by charter rules, I have chosen this that I might illustrate in my death the principles which I advocated through a long life, equality of man before the Creator."

Second, Caledonia—the second-oldest state park in Pennsylvania and originally known as Caledonia Forest Reserve Park—exists in part because of the historic road that fronts it. Caledonia was once a popular trolley stop, complete with an amusement park. It's no wonder then that when it came time to build a massive highway, Caledonia would be along it.

Route 30, known as the Lincoln Highway, was America's first coast-to-coast highway. It was the brainchild of Carl Fisher, founder of the Indianapolis Motor Speedway. Together with Henry Joy, president of Packard Motor Co., he proposed a route running from New York City to San Francisco. That was pretty radical thinking at a time when most of the nation's roads were still unpaved. The highway came to be, though. It was ultimately completed in 1925.

Before then, when the paved section near Caledonia was completed, a massive celebration ensued. In October 1921 an estimated 30,000 people and 6,000 vehicles

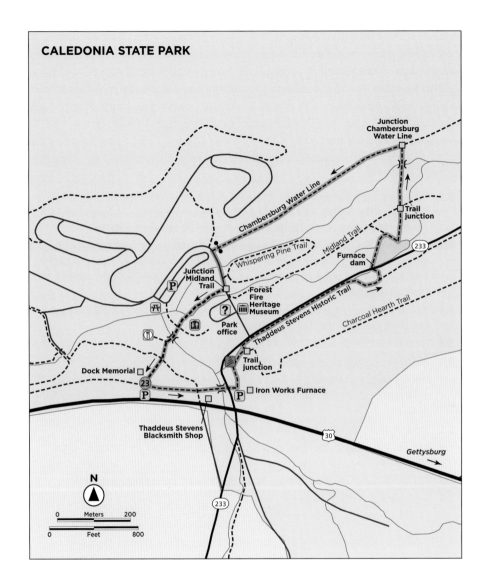

CALEDONIA STATE PARK

turned out for what was billed as the "Good Roads Jubilee Pageant," the world's longest parade. Two colleges even cancelled classes so students could see it. You can learn about that and more history of the road courtesy of the Lincoln Highway Heritage Corridor at www.lhhc.org.

Third and finally, Caledonia State Park is home to Pennsylvania's Forest Fire Heritage Museum. Inside its doors are artifacts from firefighting's earliest days. They are primitive. Fighting wildfires is hazardous duty today, no doubt. But at least today's crews have some evolved gear to work with. In the early days, firefighting was as much about determination as anything, as the assortment of rakes, shovels, tin water containers, and other hand tools attest. There's even a Smokey Bear collection. As much as the museum is about the past, though, it's also got information on how fire—prescribed fire, it's called—is now being used to grow the forests of tomorrow.

The museum is located directly across the road from the Caledonia State Park office. It's open from 1 to 5 p.m. on Friday, Saturday, and Sunday. For more information, check out the Pennsylvania Forest Heritage Association's website at www.paforestheritage.org.

Miles and Directions

0.0 Start at the Dock Memorial. Access it by walking down the wooden steps leading from the gravel parking lot that sits along Route 30 westbound (or from the parking lot at the furnace). After 500 feet arrive at the blacksmith shop, originally built in 1830.

0.2 Arrive at the iron furnace. After checking out the information kiosks, head up the hill via the paved walkway. Soon you come to the site of the former waterwheel. Enjoy the small falls, then cross the bridge on the left to stay on the Thaddeus Stevens Trail. (Avoid the Charcoal Hearth Trail.)

0.4 Turn right, crossing a footbridge, to go up the hill. This is the one slightly challenging section of the hike, given the climb and rocky, rooted terrain.

0.5 Cross Route 233. Go around the gate by the Furnace Dam.

0.6 The trail Ys. Go right to keep following the edge of the lake.

0.7 The trail intersects Midland Trail. Go straight, keeping the stream on your right. Soon you arrive at another old dam. Go to the left, cross a bridge, then turn left onto Chambersburg Water Line.

1.1 Arrive at a gate. Go left, on the park road.

1.2 Turn into the woods on the right, just across the bridge and before the park office, onto Midland Trail.

1.3 The trail Ts. Go left, across the bridge. Follow the sidewalk and cut through the grass.

1.5 Arrive back at the Dock Memorial.

24 Gettysburg National Military Park

Start: At the visitor center
Distance: 2.9 miles
Type: Out and back with some loop sections
Hiking time: 3.5 hours
Difficulty: Easy
Best season: April to October
Traffic: Hikers only, though it crosses roads used by vehicles
Fees and permits: None to hike; fees associated with the visitor center, with prices determined by whether you want to visit the museum only or add the movie and cyclorama (group rates available)
Maps: Available at www.nps.gov/gett/plan yourvisit/brochures.htm
Trail contact: Gettysburg National Military Park, 1195 Baltimore Pike, Gettysburg 17325; (717) 334-1124; www.nps.gov/gett/index.htm

Finding the trailhead: From Chambersburg, follow Route 30 east for about 25 miles. At the traffic circle, go right onto Baltimore Street/Lincoln Square, then straight on Baltimore Street and then Baltimore Pike. Turn right into the park. GPS: N39 48.682' / W77 13.607'

The Hike

The battle of Gettysburg lasted three days, spanned more than 17 square miles, and involved about 160,000 men. To say it's a sprawling place would be an understatement. To walk to the site of every skirmish, every pitched battle, every troop movement, would take days on end. It's why bus tours, self-guided automobile tours, and even horseback tours are so popular. This hike, though, hits several of the most important spots to be explored, all in one afternoon.

Start at the visitor center, being sure to leave yourself lots of time for it alone. There's a spectacular movie to see, along with plenty of exhibits on everything from weapons to uniforms to how the 2,400-person town of Gettysburg dealt with the battle and its horrific aftermath.

Afterward, exit the building out the back, near the cafeteria, to the tents where park rangers begin most of their programs. Follow the signs on the paved trail toward Meade's headquarters. The walking is pleasant enough here, but it's when you cross Taneytown Road that the history starts. On the left is the Lydia Leister farmhouse. It served as Union Gen. George Meade's headquarters during the battle and as a field hospital immediately after.

It's also a testament to the suffering of the people who lived here and got caught up in the battle. A widow, Leister lived in the home with two of her daughters. The same thing that made this location perfect for Meade's headquarters—it was on the opposite side of Cemetery Ridge—also put it in line of shelling. It suffered as a result.

Leister reported returning to her home after the battle to find her house pockmarked with shell holes, her cow and horse gone, apple and peach trees destroyed,

Visitors walk through Soldier's National Cemetery in Gettysburg, very near where President Abraham Lincoln delivered the Gettysburg Address.

her spring spoiled by some of the seventeen dead horses left lying about, two tons of hay gone from the barn, her wheat trampled, and all her fence rails burned. She was never paid for the damages. All she was able to recoup was the money she got—50 cents per 100 pounds—by selling the bones of the dead animals.

This hike goes on, passing several monuments, to reach what's known as the "high water mark" of the Confederacy. It's here, at what's famously known as "The Angle," that Gen. Lewis Armistead and his Virginians temporarily broke through the Union lines on Cemetery Ridge. A marker approximates where Armistead, hat on his sword, reportedly reached out and touched a Union cannon before being mortally wounded. His men couldn't hold their gains and were repelled. This is as far into Northern territory as the Southern armies ever got.

After exploring The Angle you'll backtrack a bit, turning left on Taneytown Road to walk to the Soldier's National Cemetery. More than 6,000 veterans are buried here, 3,200 of them Union soldiers who died at Gettysburg. There are monuments here, too, along with some absolutely magnificent trees representing states all over the country.

Most famously, though, this is where—or near where—President Abraham Lincoln delivered the Gettysburg Address.

This spot marks "The Angle," the farthest that Confederate troops pierced into Union territory.

Unbelievably, at least in hindsight, he wasn't the main speaker. Pennsylvania officials purchased the site of the cemetery in October 1863. To dedicate it a little less than a month later, on November 19, they asked Massachusetts orator Edward Everett to deliver the primary speech. Lincoln was asked to show up and just deliver "a few appropriate remarks."

Everett spoke for more than 2 hours; Lincoln offered 272 words. Yet today it ranks as one of the greatest speeches in American history.

Don't be confused here as to the location where Lincoln delivered his speech. Enter the cemetery from Taneytown Road and immediately on the right you'll see a monument with a bust of Lincoln. That was erected in 1912. Lincoln actually gave his speech about 300 yards away. The cemetery lists the site as being where the large soldiers' memorial is; others say the platform where he spoke was actually in the adjoining civilian Greenwood Cemetery.

Regardless of the exact spot, the cemetery is worth visiting before turning and retracing your steps to the start.

The History

The carnage must have been staggering to witness.

There were Civil War battles involving more men than Gettysburg. There were battles that produced more casualties in a 24-hour period. There were battles, like Chancellorsville with Stonewall Jackson, that ultimately claimed the lives of more prominent individuals. But none led to more misery overall than Gettysburg, where about 51,000 either died, were wounded, captured, or went missing. It is the deadliest battle ever fought on American soil.

It was every bit as gruesome as might be imagined.

Soldiers afterward told of lying wounded in fields, surrounded by the moaning of comrades and the sound of hogs feasting on the flesh of dead and dying combatants. At temporary field hospitals, meanwhile, amputated limbs were stacked in giant piles until they resembled stacks of cordwood. Dead horses were dragged into piles and set afire. The stench of death in a hot Pennsylvania summer had to be overwhelming.

Evidence of that suffering would linger a long while. Farmers here for years after the battle would uncover detritus of all kinds, from belt buckles and canteens to human bones, when plowing their fields.

Perhaps no less should be expected, though, of a battle that was a major turning point in the war that pitted Americans against Americans.

In the summer of 1863, fresh off having scored a big victory at Chancellorsville, Confederate Gen. Robert E. Lee was looking to capitalize on his momentum. He decided to take the fighting to the North. His hopes were two. On one hand, he dreamed that a victory on Union soil might spur the "Copperheads"—Northerners opposed to the war—to press for peace. On the other, he believed such a victory might finally convince France and Great Britain to recognize the Confederacy as an independent nation.

One of Gettysburg's many monuments, seen through the spokes of a cannon wheel.

Lee headed for Pennsylvania. When he heard that Gen. George Meade and the Army of the Potomac were marching to meet him, Gettysburg—which had ten roads leading into and out of it, and was thus a convenient place for troops to assemble—became the focal point.

Fighting began on July 1. Lee, looking to take the initiative before Union reinforcements could arrive, attacked, or at least ordered subordinates like Richard Ewell to do so. The Union forces dug in. Day two brought more of the same, with entrenched Union lines battling Confederate attackers to a bloody standstill.

On day three, July 3, Lee went all in. Believing he was close to victory, and desperate for a win that would turn the tide of the war, he ordered a frontal assault against the Union center at Cemetery Ridge. A 150-cannon artillery bombardment began, designed to soften up the Union lines. It proved ineffectual. When the famous Pickett's Charge—an attack by fewer than 15,000 men who had to walk across nearly a mile of open field under withering fire—began, the Union army was waiting, largely intact and ready.

It was a bloodbath. Pickett's division took fire from the front and both sides. Still, in fighting so close and desperate that Union forces were shooting double and triple loads of grapeshot from their cannons, his men would reach the corner of a stone fence forever after known simply as "The Angle." They engaged in fierce

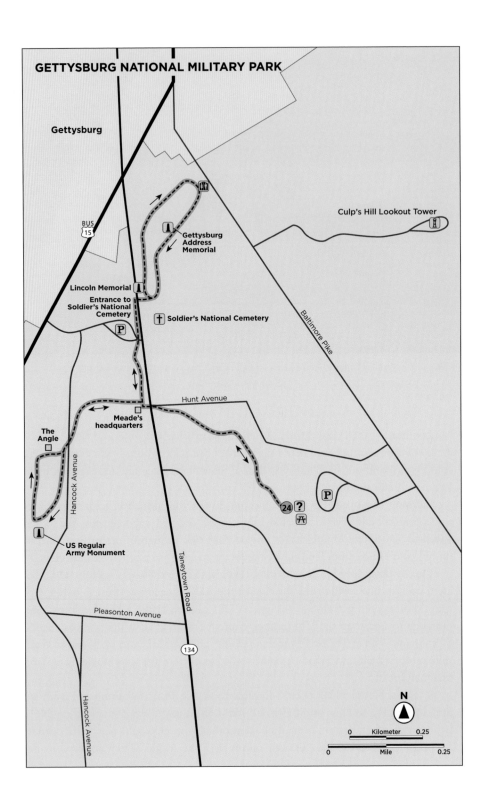

GETTYSBURG NATIONAL MILITARY PARK

Gettysburg

BUS
15

Culp's Hill Lookout Tower

Gettysburg
Address
Memorial

Lincoln Memorial
Entrance to
Soldier's National
Cemetery

Soldier's National Cemetery

Baltimore Pike

P

Hunt Avenue

Meade's
headquarters

The
Angle

Hancock Avenue

24 ?

P

US Regular
Army Monument

Taneytown Road

Pleasonton Avenue

134

Hancock Avenue

N

0   Kilometer   0.25
0   Mile   0.25

hand-to-hand combat with the enemy. But they couldn't sustain the attack. Pickett's division lost two-thirds of its men. Ultimately repulsed, the survivors returned to the Confederate lines, devastated and defeated.

What happened after was controversial.

Lee braced for a counterattack, but it never came. That allowed him to slip away on July 4, taking his battered army and leaving Gettysburg behind as he retreated south. Meade—believing his own army was too beaten down to take the offensive—had decided not to pursue, something that caused him to be the object of great criticism later. Some, including President Abraham Lincoln, thought he missed a chance to rout Lee and end the war.

A distraught Lee—he offered his resignation, something Confederate president Jefferson Davis rejected—looked around him and saw an army in tatters. He lost 28,000 men, more than a third of his force, at Gettysburg. The South lost more than that, as hopes for international recognition and a course-altering victory disappeared.

Still, the war would go on for nearly two more years and cost many more lives. But in some ways it ended on those Pennsylvania farm fields. The "high water mark" of the Confederacy was also its undoing.

Miles and Directions

0.0 Start at the back of the visitor center, outside the cafe, at the tents where park rangers present programs. Follow the paved sidewalk toward Soldier's National Cemetery and Meade's headquarters.

0.3 The trail Ys. Stay right.

0.4 The trail crosses over Taneytown Road to reach the Lydia Leister home on the left. It served as the headquarters of Gen. George Meade, known as "Ol Snapping' Turtle" because of his stern disposition. Stay straight on the trail as it goes uphill.

0.6 Go left when the trail Ys.

0.7 At a marker for the Army of the Potomac's 2nd Corps, cross Hancock Avenue, then go left past several monuments to a stone wall.

0.8 At the wall, turn right and follow the edge of the field to The Angle. Stop there, then turn and walk back to Meade's Headquarters.

1.2 At Taneytown Road, before crossing, turn left and go toward Soldier's National Cemetery.

1.4 Turn right and cross Taneytown Road into Soldier's National Cemetery. Follow the paved path to the left, noting the magnificent old trees, from hemlock and red oak to sweet buckeye and bald cypress.

1.8 Pass restrooms on the left.

1.9 Come to a marker for the Gettysburg Address, near the main monument. Lincoln reportedly gave his speech just behind this spot, in Greenwood Cemetery.

2.0 On the left is a memorial to Lincoln. Check this out, then exit the cemetery and go left back toward Meade's headquarters. Retrace your steps to the start.

2.9 Arrive back at the visitor center.

25 U.S. Army Heritage and Education Center

Start: At the visitor center
Distance: 2.1 miles
Type: Loop
Hiking time: 1.5 hours
Difficulty: Easy
Best season: March to October
Traffic: Hikers only

Fees and permits: None
Maps: Available at https://ahec.armywar college.edu/trail/aht.cfm
Trail contact: U.S. Army Heritage and Education Center, 950 Soldiers Dr., Carlisle 17013-5021; (717) 245-3972; https://ahec .armywarcollege.edu

Finding the trailhead: From the Carlisle exchange of the PA Turnpike, follow Route 81 South for 2.9 miles to exit 49. Turn left and follow Route 641 for approximately a quarter mile, then turn left onto Army Heritage Drive. Go 1.3 miles to the entrance. GPS: N40 12.451' / W77 09.593'

The Hike

More than 250 years of military history in about 2 miles. That's the best way to describe the Army Heritage Trail hike around the grounds of the U.S. Army Heritage and Education Center.

It starts at the facility's visitor center and museum. That's not to be missed. The key is to get here early, though. Show up too late in the afternoon and you can find yourself spending all your time inside, with too little daylight left before you ever start walking.

Once you hit the trail, you'll follow it around the grounds, starting with the big outer loop. One thing you'll notice right away is the different ways soldiers have protected themselves—or tried to—over time.

In Afghanistan, soldiers used HESCO, or Hercules Engineering Solutions Consortium barriers, for defense. They're welded steel-mesh containers lined with "nonwoven polypropylene geotextile"—it looks like heavy-duty cardboard, though it obviously isn't—and filled with local dirt and rock. They take the place of sandbags.

Go a little farther and you'll wander through a replica of a World War I trench. About as wide as a typical hallway, the trenches could be deep and lined with simple wood planks. As the notes of some soldiers make clear, though, they weren't all that big or nice. Some were "burrows" more suitable for animals than people. It's easy to see how even the best would be crowded and dirty and loud.

Still farther down the trail are examples of a World War II–era concrete bunker and a Revolutionary War–era fort. At around the halfway mark, meanwhile, is a Memorial Garden for those who served. It's a beautiful spot for reflection.

Before and after the garden, you'll see quite a few tanks. It's easy to forget sometimes just how young the people driving these in combat really are, at least until you

The U.S. Army Heritage and Education Center has as one of its goals to showcase "land-power." Tanks play a big part in that.

see the little touches they sometimes add. A Hellcat symbol here, a fancy paint job there, and you're reminded of someone who might have a muscle car back home.

Throughout the hike there are informational panels. Some tell the story behind certain weapons, like the M101A1 Howitzer. Introduced in 1940, and used in World War II and Korea, it proved too cumbersome when fighting a guerilla war in Vietnam and had to be replaced.

Other panels tell the story of soldiers who fought. Some lived, some came home wounded, others died.

There's a panel where Bill Beck of Steelton talks about what it was like being pinned down by the enemy at LZ-X-ray in Vietnam. He stepped out of a helicopter and saw six comrades killed immediately before he ever saw the enemy. He ended up at a machine gun, wounded, with another Pennsylvanian who had likewise been hit. That soldier was alive, and would ultimately survive, but was out of the fight.

Beck engaged in a firefight with the enemy at just 25 yards. He battled on, alone, for the next two hours. "It was lonely as hell up there . . . I don't know what the hell's happening. I'm out there by myself. I'm only a 20-year-old kid. I don't know what's going on. . . . Fear, real fear hit me. Fear like I had never known before. . . . Once you recognize and accept it, it passes just as fast as it comes. . . . You just do what you have to do, but you learn the real meaning of fear and life and death," he said.

Such tales of sacrifice will surely make you pause.

The hike leads around almost back to the start, but then—if you want to see everything—you have to follow a second, smaller inner loop and then head back to the start a second time.

The History

There's no missing the U.S. Army Heritage and Education Center. Glance out the window of your vehicle when traveling near Carlisle on I-81, and the helicopters and missiles and cannons catch the eye unlike most roadside attractions. That's by design.

The center has a goal of making available "contemporary and historical materials" related to the "global application of landpower." Mission accomplished there. Nothing says landpower like a tank, right?

The U.S. Army Heritage Center is about more than just massive tools of destruction, though. It showcases the challenges and triumphs faced by soldiers throughout American history.

Sometimes they varied from era to era, based on conditions. Soldiers in the Continental Army often wrote home of needing firewood to stay warm. Their descendants fighting in the jungles of Vietnam almost 200 years later wrote about praying for snow.

There are currents of shared daring and bravery and heroism and sacrifice among soldiers of all time frames, too, though.

Consider the twenty men of the 4th Connecticut Infantry who captured Redoubt No. 10—a temporary fortification—at the Battle of Yorktown, thereby playing a large role in the surrender of Lord Cornwallis on October 19, 1781. Or Captain Joseph Dawson of the 1st Infantry Division, who went ashore on Omaha Beach on June 6, 1944, with one thought in mind, "to get to the enemy." How about Corporal Eugene Rivera of the 8th Ranger Company, who climbed a desolate hill and braved fierce enemy fire on April 25, 1951, to radio in coordinates so that the wounded men of his unit could be evacuated by helicopter? Or Specialist Fourth Class Robert Law, who on February 22, 1969, threw himself on a grenade to save five other Rangers.

They were all born years apart. They served in different parts of the world. They fought different enemies wearing different uniforms and using different weapons. But are they not all related? The heritage center shows how that's so.

It's not all blood and guts here, though. The center focuses on the life in camp experienced by soldiers throughout time. There are details on how the men—and later women, too—lived.

Some of the most interesting information here, though, comes from ordinary soldiers themselves. They talk, in letters and oral histories, about their experiences at war and what they encountered, good and bad, upon returning home.

Some of the exhibits are permanent. Others change over time. They range from the earliest conflicts on American soil, around the Revolutionary War, to the modern War on Terror. Still others are interactive. For example, a Vietnam War exhibit allows

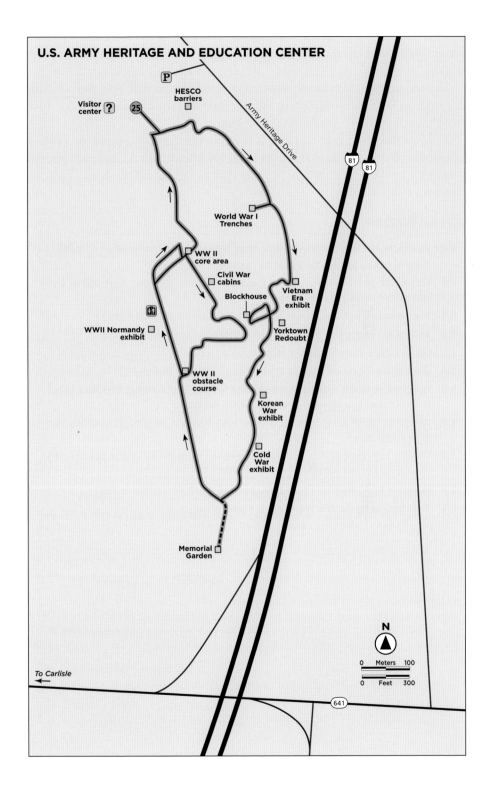

U.S. ARMY HERITAGE AND EDUCATION CENTER

P

Visitor
center ?

25

HESCO
barriers

Army Heritage Drive

81
81

World War I
Trenches

WW II
core area

Civil War
cabins

Blockhouse

Vietnam
Era
exhibit

WWII Normandy
exhibit

Yorktown
Redoubt

WW II
obstacle
course

Korean
War
exhibit

Cold
War
exhibit

Memorial
Garden

To Carlisle

N

0   Meters   100
0   Feet   300

641

visitors to experience a "spider hole" and "booby trap" to see what soldiers fighting in that conflict were up against. There are stories, too, on the experiences of prisoners of war.

Visitors can enjoy regular lectures and programs here, as well. There are scholarly programs on leadership—exploring, say, the contradictory natures of George Armstrong Custer—and living-history reenactments.

None of those will get you inside one of the tanks on the grounds or a ride in a helicopter. But if you have an appreciation for military history, and the men and women for whom sacrifice was and is more than just words and deeds on a page, this center is a must-see place.

Miles and Directions

0.0 Pick up the trail near the Soldiers Walk Plaza. Follow it toward the interstate. After 300 feet come to HESCO barriers, the first of the displays.

0.2 On the right are World War I trenches. Take time to explore them, and the Hellcat tank they lead to, then return to the main trail.

0.7 The trail Ys by a Vietnam-era helicopter. Go left, toward the Yorktown Redoubt.

1.0 Arrive at the Korean War exhibit, followed immediately by one for the Cold War.

1.1 On the left is a lovely Memorial Garden.

1.4 Come to a replica of an obstacle training course. Continue straight.

1.5 This is the World War II core area, with a mess hall and other buildings to explore. Check these out, then turn right and go to the Civil War cabins.

1.7 The trail Ys. Go left to the French and Indian War waystation. Make a right when you come to an intersection.

1.8 Pass the forge and blockhouse, continuing until you reach the obstacle course again, this time on the left. Turn right toward the parking lot.

2.0 Reach the World War II core area again; this time go left around the buildings.

2.1 Arrive back at the Soldiers Walk Plaza to close the loop.

East

26 Lacawac Sanctuary

Start: At the visitor center
Distance: 1.6 miles
Type: Loop
Hiking time: 2 hours
Difficulty: Easy
Best season: April to October
Traffic: Hikers only

Fees and permits: None
Maps: Available at www.lacawac.org/
uploads/4/6/4/4/46449361/lacawac_
board_3-21.pdf
Trail contact: Lacawac Sanctuary, 94 Sanctuary Rd., Lake Ariel 18436; (570) 689-9494;
www.lacawac.org

Finding the trailhead: From Scranton, follow I-84 East for about 24 miles to exit 20. Turn left onto Route 507, go 0.7 mile, then make another left on Ledgedale Road. Go 2.8 miles, take the first right onto St. Marys Church Road, and go 0.25 mile. Take the first right onto Lacawac Road. After 0.6 mile, turn right onto Sanctuary Road. Go 0.5 mile to the visitor center and parking. GPS: N41 22.599' / W75 17.983'

The Hike

Odds are you'll never experience anything like this ever again. I mean, c'mon. How many hikes through the woods lead to a 10,000-pound, 14-foot-tall, sixteen-tone set of chimes?

You won't see them right away. Initially it's Lacawac's natural beauty that will catch your eye. You'll experience it by walking parts of several trails to make this loop.

Upon leaving the visitor center, for example, you'll swing around Heron Pond on Big Lake Trail. Pay special attention as you do. At one location, you'll notice an upright pole—it looks like a telephone pole—on the edge of the lake. There's a flat platform on the top. In most years there's a large nest there, home to a pair of breeding ospreys.

Sometimes called "fish hawks" because that's their preferred prey, ospreys are relatively big raptors, with wingspans approaching 6 feet. They're brown on top and white underneath, with dark stripes around their eyes. They thrive in situations like this, where there's water surrounded by trees. The nesting platform is critical, too. About 80 percent of the ospreys in Pennsylvania these days use them rather than natural tree nests.

From there the trail winds past mountain laurel. That's something to see around mid-June, the peak of the bloom, and again after, when the ground is littered with white flower petals.

Of course, in time you'll come to Lake Lacawac itself. The view from the dock by the boathouse is incredible. With no development anywhere around the lake, it looks like something out of a wilderness setting.

The Deagan chimes stand in Lacawac Sanctuary, held up by what looks like a giant tree house.

But about those chimes. They're located in between the ospreys and Lake Lacawac, near what was once the carriage house. The horses and wagons that hauled people 7 miles from the community of Lake Ariel were housed here. Its lower floor still showcases the horse stalls.

The chimes came here only after following their own curious path.

Col. Louis Watres—who bought the Lacawac property in order to flood just a portion of it for a power plant—had the chimes made by the Deagan Chime Factory for his Scranton estate. The company made just 438 sets; only 6 went to private interests like Watres. Only 96 remain working across the world today. Watres had them installed along with an organ run by a clock. They rang out over the countryside every 15 minutes, though a keyboard allowed for special music to be played on occasions like Christmas and the Fourth of July, too.

Ultimately, though, tragedy struck. Fire destroyed Watres's mansion in 1937. He died three months later. His wife, Isabel, and son Arthur, unwilling to part with the chimes, kept them, took them to Lacawac Sanctuary when they moved there in 1948, and stored them for nearly half a century.

It wasn't until 1998—the one hundredth anniversary of Isabel's birth—that they sounded again. Volunteers discovered the chimes to be sound and developed a home-made computer system to play them. That system is gone now, but the chimes remain.

They're positioned upright, attached to what looks like a tree house. Hikers strolling by can tap them with a rubber mallet that hangs on a post to hear their music again.

How's that for something different?

The History

Conservationists will appreciate Lacawac Sanctuary for what it is today—specifically, a field research station where scientists and students learning to be scientists study things like water quality, climate change, forest ecology, and more. Lake Lacawac, one of the 510-acre property's most prominent features, plays a big part in that. It's recognized as the southernmost unpolluted glacial lake in the United States.

Arthur Watres and his mother, Isabel, who lived here for years, championed the site as being special for its beauty and ecological importance. They longed to preserve the site in its natural state after they were gone. Together, they gave birth to the sanctuary. The importance of their vision can't be understated.

History lovers, though, will appreciate Lacawac for what it was—namely, a retreat, a private zoo of sorts, and a hunting lodge. Visitors can explore much of that past in the form of five buildings collectively on the National Register of Historic Places.

They were the dream of a man named William Connell. He was an industrious sort, who went from driving a coal wagon as a youth to owning that same coal company in his middle years. That, combined with the financial success of owning a huge button making factory, among other enterprises, allowed him to buy the 400-acre Lacawac estate in 1902 and 1903. He renamed it Connell Park.

It became his summer home. But this was not the site of some mere cabin in the woods. Connell was a wealthy man and he lived like one. His main residence, now known as the Watres Lodge, was built in the style of the day and was comparable to the homes of wealthy industrialists in the Adirondacks. It featured gas lighting, hot and cold running water, indoor plumbing, central heating, and even a walk-in cooler stocked with ice year-round. No other home in the region at that time could boast of such things.

The lodge—one of eight buildings on the property in Connell's day—remains standing and is used by visiting scientists as an on-site residence.

Four other buildings also survive. One is the coachman's house. It was the bunkhouse where the men who drove the Connells to and from the estate lived. It was much more primitive, as the outhouse out back makes clear. The building also had a second purpose. It housed a generator, which made the acetylene gas that powered the lanterns inside the main lodge (a few of those vintage gas lamps remain).

The ice house—used to store ice cut from Lake Lacawac until electric service came to the property around the time of World War II—still stands, as does the pump house, or spring house, used to supply water to the lodge.

Then there's the carriage house. This was the social center of the property in some ways. It housed horses and wagons on a daily basis. But on special occasions, it hosted barn dances. The Connells would hire an orchestra, decorate the building, and spread

A large, open sitting porch facing Lake Lacawac is one of the hallmarks of Watres Lodge.

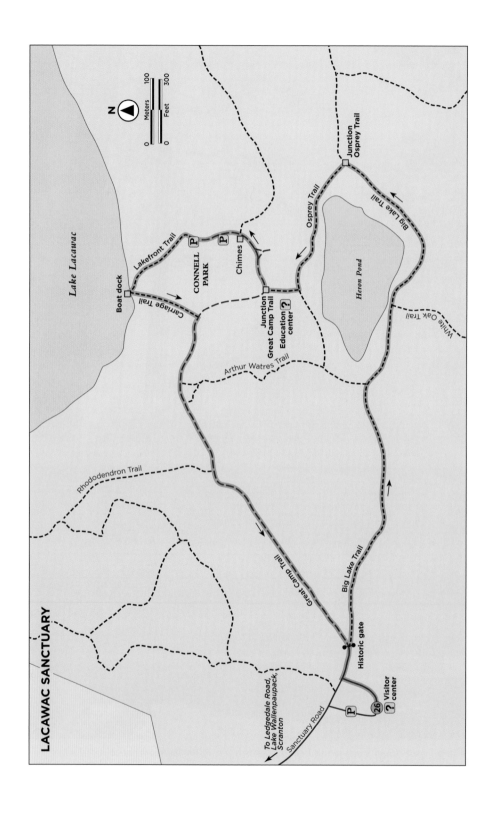

LACAWAC SANCTUARY

Lake Lacawac

Boat dock

Lakefront Trail

Carriage Trail

CONNELL PARK

Chimes

Rhododendron Trail

Arthur Watres Trail

Great Camp Trail

Junction
Great Camp Trail
Education
center

Osprey Trail

Junction
Osprey Trail

Heron Pond

Big Lake Trail

White Oak Trail

Big Lake Trail

Historic gate

To Ledgedale Road,
Lake Wallenpaupack,
Scranton

Sanctuary Road

26

Visitor
center

N

Meters   0   100

Feet   0   300

the word of an impending party. People from all over would travel to the estate for what became community celebrations. It's still used in that same way, at least to a degree. The building plays host to all sorts of public educational programs. There's a gift shop on the first floor, too.

As for the buildings now gone, the most interesting and noteworthy was the "deer house." A marker near the carriage house tells its tale. At the dawn of the twentieth century, when Connell built this estate, white-tailed deer—today Pennsylvania's official state mammal—were largely gone. Unregulated market hunting and habitat destruction all but wiped them out. They were so rare, in fact, that Connell and other wealthy types imported deer—in this case, from Virginia—to keep as exotic pets and to hunt. He built a 4-mile-long fence around a portion of the property to keep the deer in and poachers out. The deer house stored feed to make sure his animals survived. It was torn down in 1947 because of termite damage, but deer are once again plentiful—perhaps too much so, in places—in part because of herds kept by Connell and others.

His descendants later sold the estate to the Watres, setting the sanctuary on its current path.

Today visitors can take in the area's beauty while exploring its history in some detail. Hikers can wander among the buildings and check them out from the outside anytime. On special occasions, though, indoor tours are offered. Contact the sanctuary for specifics.

Miles and Directions

0.0 Starting with the visitor center to your rear, go right on the gravel road. After a couple hundred feet the road Ys. To the left is Lake Lacawac Trail. Turn right. Almost immediately the trail Ys again. Great Camp Trail goes left. Turn right onto Big Lake Trail.

0.3 The trail Ys. Arthur Watres Trail is to the left. Go right to stay on Big Lake Trail. Heron Pond is on your left here. Look for the osprey platform and nest.

0.4 White Oak Trail branches off to the right. Stay straight on Big Lake Trail.

0.5 The trail Ys. Big Lake Trail goes right. This time, turn left onto Osprey Trail. Make a right when you reach a small home, then go right again on Great Camp Trail.

0.6 The sanctuary's education center is on the left.

0.7 Notice the chimes on the left as you enter what was Connell Park. Follow the road past the ice house and lodge.

1.0 The trail Ys. Go left toward the boat dock and soon arrive at the lakefront. Check it out, then take Carriage Trail (a left as you were coming down the hill, a right if you're walking back from the lake). This was the road wagons took to enter the property years ago.

1.1 Carriage Trail meets Great Camp Trail. Go right on Great Camp.

1.3 Rhododendron Trail branches off to the right. Stay left on Great Camp.

1.5 Great Camp Trail meets Big Lake Trail. Turn right and retrace your steps back to the start.

1.6 Arrive back at the visitor center to close the loop.

27 Promised Land State Park

Start: At the gated entrance to Conservation Island

Distance: 1.2 miles

Type: Loop

Hiking time: 1 hour

Difficulty: Easy

Best season: April to October

Traffic: Hikers only

Fees and permits: None

Maps: Available at www.dcnr.pa.gov/StateParks/FindAPark/PromisedLand StatePark/Pages/Maps.aspx

Trail contact: Promised Land State Park, 100 Lower Lake Rd., Greentown 18426-9735; (570) 676-3428; www.dcnr.pa.gov/StateParks/FindAPark/PromisedLand StatePark/Pages/default.aspx

Finding the trailhead: From Milford, follow I-84 west for about 20 miles. Take exit 26 onto Route 390 South and go a little less than 5 miles. Turn left onto Park Avenue and follow that to the trailhead. GPS: N41 18.393' / W75 12.285'

The Hike

It's hard to appreciate the sarcasm today.

In the late eighteenth century, devotees of the Shaker religion moved into the area of what is now Promised Land State Park with the goal of building a village centered around farming. That proved difficult in the extreme, given the rocky nature of the terrain. Later, they switched to lumbering and built sawmills to process the abundant timber. Plenty of cutting went on—by the dawn of the twentieth century, few trees remained—but that venture wasn't entirely successful either.

So, in time, after enduring all that hardship, the Shakers faded away, but not before tabbing this area—with what legend says was a real lack of sincerity—"the promised land."

They surely had their troubles. But visit Promised Land State Park today and take this hike around Conservation Island, and it feels more heavenly than not.

The island sits just west of Pickerel Point and Deerfield Campgrounds, both of which were built by Civilian Conservation Corps crews during their stay here in Camp D-139-PA between 1933 and 1941.

The loop trail around the island is not overly long. But it's a beautiful path to take in early summer—mid-June is prime time—because of the abundant and colorful mountain laurel in bloom then. This is also a great hike for seeing wildlife. White-tailed deer are common here, as are glimpses of bald eagles, ospreys, and water birds like great blue herons. There are any number of little spurs off the trail that lead to views of Promised Land Lake, as well (some of which offer pretty good fishing, if you're inclined to occasionally cast a line while hiking).

A monument to the men of the Civilian Conservation Corps stands outside the Masker Museum in Promised Land State Park.

Expect lots of roots. They stick up along the trail like hardened varicose veins pretty much everywhere. But the hike is mostly flat, so they're not bothersome.

As for how to get here, there's a small parking lot by the bridge leading to the island, so you can drive and then walk. That's the hike described here. It's possible, though, to park at the Masker Museum, check out its exhibits, then walk to the island. That adds about a mile each way. It's on park roads, too, so there will be traffic, both from vehicles and campers on bicycles. But it's not a bad walk by any means.

However you get to the island, enjoy your time, more than the Shakers did apparently. Promised Land—the fourth-oldest in the state park system—is a place to be enjoyed rather than just endured.

The History

Poverty. Numbing, grinding, soul-crunching, relentless poverty. That's what gave birth to Promised Land State Park. It's hard to imagine. Tour the park these days and you'll see people fishing from boats and from shore, camping in tents and recreational vehicles, riding bicycles, swimming, picnicking, and watching wildlife. And smiling, always smiling.

The change was brought about in part by the young men memorialized here, the CCC boys.

In early 1933 America was engulfed in the Great Depression, a period of economic hardship unlike anything seen before or since. Forty percent of the country was unemployed, and more than that were barely hanging on.

President Franklin D. Roosevelt prompted Congress to authorize the Emergency Conservation Work Act. It aimed to take young men ages 18 to 25 and put them to work restoring America's public lands, which had been used, abused, and largely abandoned for decades. "I propose to create a Civilian Conservation Corps to be used in simple work, not interfering with normal employment, and confining itself to forestry, the prevention of soil erosion, flood control, and similar projects," Roosevelt said. The Civilian Conservation Corps was born.

The men went to camps—more than 2,500 nationwide—where they lived in military-style encampments. Up at 6 a.m., with breakfast by 7:15, they would then put in 8-hour days—when not battling wildfires—before returning to camp.

Roosevelt had said the "moral and spiritual value of such work" would prove lasting, and it likely did. But there's no underestimating the economic value of the program, too. The pay was $30 a month, $25 of which by rule had to be sent home to their families. That kept many a family afloat. The other $5 the men could spend on themselves, whether to have someone launder and repair clothes or to buy a meal in a local restaurant. Combined, all those expenditures brought people, if not to prosperity, at least to a level where life was better than it had been.

CCC boys were able to attend classes at night, too. Alternately called the "College in the Woods" and the "College of Calluses," the Corps led to an estimated 40,000 learning to read and write.

Many of the young men who enrolled had never been out of their hometowns, let alone their states. Yet they were shipped all across the country to work planting trees (more than 3 billion), building state facilities like cabins and campgrounds, erecting dams to create lakes and beaches, restoring historic structures, and even completing the final leg of the Appalachian Trail in Maine.

That impact can still be seen today in places like Promised Land State Park. Here they planted the forest that now stands, and built Pickerel Point Campground, the Bear Wallow cabins, North Shore Road, and Egypt Meadow Dam, for instance.

A number of state parks around Pennsylvania have similar ties to the CCC. That's not surprising, considering that the state benefited more than almost any other from CCC workers.

Gifford Pinchot, then governor of the state, had already enacted a state-level program very similar to the CCC, so when the federal version came along, Pennsylvania already had a structure in place. And it made good use of it. The state eventually had

Civilian Conservation Corps workers commonly fought forest fires using hand tools like these.

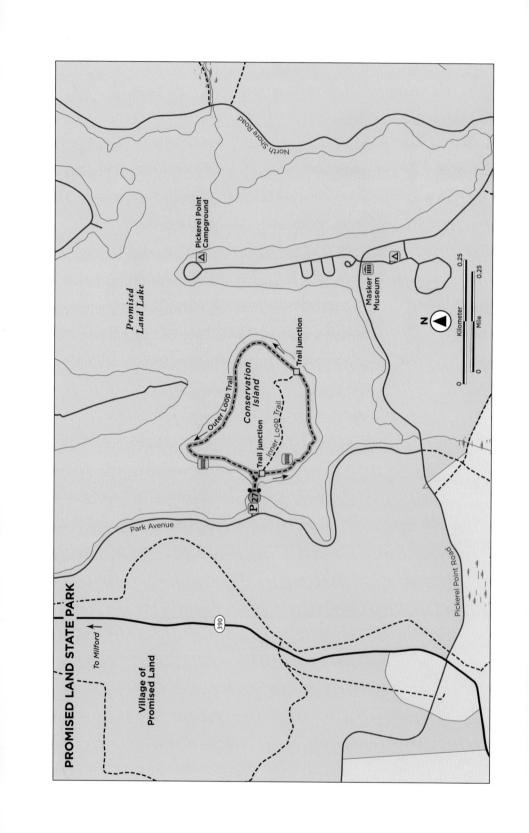

more than 150 CCC camps—second only to California nationally—and provided work for nearly 975,000 men.

The Masker Museum at Promised Land tells the tale of those men working around the Keystone State. It is home to artifacts from the era, along with plenty of background information on the CCC itself. Most interesting, though, is the abundance of information about what life was like in the camps. Letters and oral histories provided by men, since grown old, who once worked for the CCC, shed a lot of light on the songs, games, dances, practical jokes, and camaraderie spawned by the giant social experiment. If there was ever any doubt of the value of the program, their stories, in their words, erase them.

The museum holds a festival each August to celebrate the CCC and the men who staffed it. That's a great time to visit the park and hike here. Veterans of the Corps have grown few—it ended in 1942, with the outbreak of World War II—but their legacy lives on.

Miles and Directions

0.0 Start at the gated entrance to Conservation Island. There's a portable toilet here but no other restrooms. Cross the bridge to enter the island. After 200 feet the trail Ys. Go right. There are lots of mountain laurel here. Expect to see white-tailed deer on occasion, too. After another 300 feet the trail Ys again. Go right.

0.1 Find a bench with views of Promised Land Lake to the right.

0.3 A spur trail on the right leads to another bench with views of the lake. Check it out, then continue on the trail.

0.5 Come to a trail intersection. Go straight, keeping the lake on your right.

0.6 Another spur on the right leads to a lake view with a bench. Check it out, then continue straight on the main trail.

0.9 The trail Ys. Go right to follow the blue blazes.

1.1 There's a bench on the right. Soon the trail Ys. Go right. Then the trail Ys again. Go right again, then retrace your steps to the start.

1.2 Arrive back at the start to close the loop.

28 Grey Towers National Historic Site

Start: At the parking lot behind the mansion
Distance: 0.6 mile
Type: Loop
Hiking time: 1 hour
Difficulty: Easy
Best season: Memorial Day to October
Traffic: Hikers only
Fees and permits: None to hike; fees to tour the Grey Towers mansion

Maps: Available at www.greytowers.org/resources/publications/ and at www.fs.usda.gov/Internet/FSE_DOCUMENTS/stelprd3826318.pdf
Trail contact: Grey Towers National Historic Site, PO Box 188, Milford 18337; (570) 296-9630; www.fs.usda.gov/greytowers

Finding the trailhead: From Lords Valley, Follow I-84 east for 13 miles, to exit 46. Get onto Route 6 East toward Milford. At the base of the hill, just past the Apple Valley shops, make a hard right onto Old Owego Turnpike. The entrance to Grey Towers is on the left. GPS: N41 19.721' / W79 49.170'

The Hike

This is another hike that's somewhat deceiving.

Officially, it's about 0.6 mile long. But when you figure in the walk from the parking lot to Gifford Pinchot's home, the walk through the home, and, if you care to take it, the walk around the grounds to explore the various trees—including Cornelia Pinchot's famous apple trees—you'll easily double that. Not to worry, though. Aside from the tour of the home, which is by guide only, you can do this at your own pace.

As for the hike outlined here, there are three main things to see.

You'll notice the first one early on in the walk. Not long after entering the woods behind the home on Forestry Trail, your way will be blocked by a gate. That's not to keep visitors out. But deer? Yes.

Undeniably beautiful creatures, white-tailed deer can, if their numbers are allowed to get too high, literally change the composition of a forest. They prefer to browse on certain species, like oak, and if not held in check by hunting or other means, will dictate what the forests of tomorrow look like.

This part of the property is surrounded by a deer exclosure, or fence meant to keep them out. Walking through the gate allows you to go where the deer can't.

Next up you'll come to a re-creation of the tent campsites students pursuing a forestry career would have lived in between 1901 and 1926. James and Mary Pinchot endowed the Yale School of Forestry with a gift of $150,000 in 1901. That was later increased to $300,000. The school was the first of its kind in the United States.

Students here had access to a mess hall, lecture hall, club house, and athletic field—they were students at Yale, after all—but their "dorms" were wall tents outfitted only

The Grey Towers mansion has fourteen bedrooms among its many, many rooms.

with washbasins, cots, a pitcher, and a bucket. They're not quite as primitive as they might have been otherwise—the tents have wooden floors—but were accessible only by dirt paths nicknamed "Broadway" and "Fifth Avenue." Take time to listen to the recorded message played here. There's a reading of a letter home written by Aldo Leopold, a student who went on to become the father of wildlife management.

Lastly, right before you leave the woods for the maintenance road, look on the right for a crumbling water tower. If you take the house tour, you'll learn that the Pinchot home originally had no running water—at least not in the way we think of it—and no indoor plumbing. Rather, water was stored in this giant tower, which looks like a supersize wooden bucket. It was then routed downhill so that it ran through the home powered only by gravity.

It's startling, in some ways, to see this giant castle of an abode and realize that, when constructed, it was still primitive in so many ways. That doesn't lessen it in any way, though. If anything, it magnifies the home's grandeur.

It's fitting for a giant of conservation.

The History

It's not every man who can twice get elected as state governor and still have that rate as, at best, the second most impressive thing he ever accomplished. But that's Gifford Pinchot's tale.

Born in 1865 to wealthy merchants, Gifford Pinchot could easily have gotten into the family business—a grandfather suggested that, more than once—and coasted through a life of luxurious privilege. Instead, he chose to get dirty. Literally.

At the urging of his father, Pinchot decided to pursue a career in forestry. He admitted later in life that he didn't know exactly what he was agreeing to. "I had no more conception of what it meant to be a forester than the man in the moon. . . . But at least a forester worked in the woods and with the woods—and I loved the woods and everything about them," he said.

There was one problem. No school in America taught forestry. It didn't exist as a profession. So what did Pinchot do? He just became the father of American forestry, that's all.

It didn't happen overnight, of course. After graduating from Yale, he went to France to study forestry from the world's leading experts. Impatient with the slow pace of studies, though, he dropped out after a year, returned home, and set about working in the woods. That eventually led him to Theodore Roosevelt, who as president made Pinchot the country's first ever chief of the US Forest Service. Together, they elevated conservation to the level of national policy.

Pinchot championed the notion that it was possible to both make use of the forest and still sustain it for future generations. Such "wise use," he argued, should be done always "for the greatest good for the greatest number for the longest time." It was a mantra he lived by forever.

The outdoor dining room at Grey Towers has a 6-foot-deep "dining table" where visitors floated food to one another in bamboo bowls—Cornelia Pinchot's method of stimulating conversation.

His career path was not always smooth. He was fired—a move he sparked intentionally to bring to light reverses he thought were untenable—as chief forester by Roosevelt's successor, William Howard Taft. But throughout his life he fought for conserving natural resources.

He looked out for the citizens of Pennsylvania as governor, too. During the Great Depression, for example, he used public money to put people to work building roads. The program, something he said was meant to "get the farmers out of the mud," was the forerunner of the Civilian Conservation Corps enacted on a national scale by President Franklin Delano Roosevelt.

And as for his home, Grey Towers? Pinchot didn't build it. His parents did that, as an homage to their French heritage—hence the bust of the Marquis de Lafayette outside a second-floor window—but he inherited it.

It's a stunning building, or rather an estate full of stunning buildings. Some of the highlights?

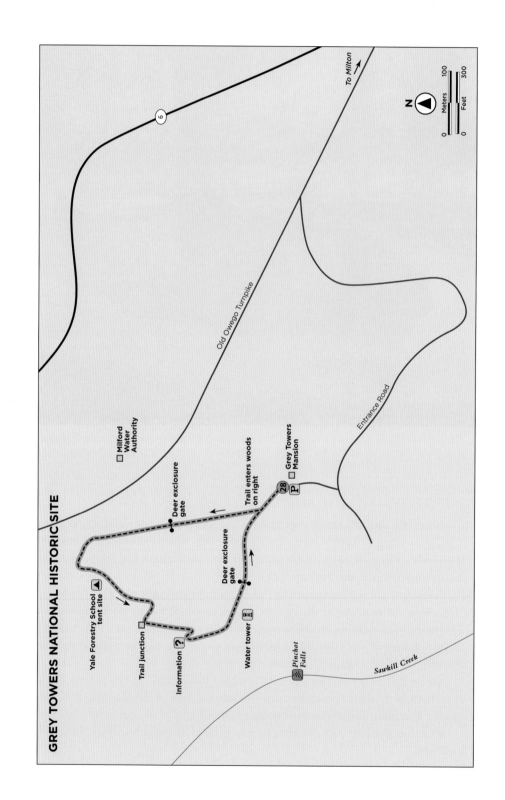

GREY TOWERS NATIONAL HISTORIC SITE

If you love to fish or read—Pinchot was fanatic about both, and was in fact buried with his favorite fly rod—his library is fabulous. When you do the tour, be sure to ask the guide to reveal the hidden compartments where he kept a few rods, always close at hand, in case he felt the need to slip off to Sawkill Creek to chase native brook trout.

Check out the outdoor dining room favored by his wife, Cornelia, too. A political activist who fought for women's right to vote, Cornelia loved to entertain, bringing in titans of industry, art, journalism, and other fields. She wanted her guests to engage in lively discussion, though. So rather than seat them around a table that might limit conversation to those immediately left and right, she had built a relatively small, though 6-foot-deep, "table" of stone. The Finger Bowl, as it was called, was filled with water. Diners would push food from one to another in floating bamboo bowls so that everyone interacted.

There are other buildings here worth exploring—the Letter Box, which was Pinchot's office; the Bait Box, which was his son's playhouse; and others—as well as a moat, garden, swimming pool terrace, and more.

It's all unbelievably interesting.

There's a hint of tragedy, too, in one way. The site was recognized as a National Historic Landmark in 1963. Ceremonies marked the occasion, as it was set aside as the Pinchot Institute for Conservation Studies, "for greater knowledge of the land and its uses." Speaking at the dedication was none other than President John F. Kennedy. His speech—parts of which can be seen in a film shown in the Letter Box—came almost exactly two months to the day before he was assassinated.

Miles and Directions

0.0 Start at the parking lot behind Grey Towers mansion. A sign marks the trailhead. It follows a paved service road initially. After 200 feet, turn right into the woods at the trail sign. Follow the yellow blazes on the mulched path.

0.1 Enter the deer exclosure through the gate.

0.2 Reach a tent site that re-creates how Yale forestry students lived while studying here.

0.3 The trail Ys. Go left on the road toward an informational panel.

0.4 The panel talks about forest plants and pests, and shows how a 139-year-old red oak was a witness to history.

0.5 Look on the right for the leaning water tower that once supplied Grey Towers with drinking, cooking, and bath water. Soon you leave the deer exclosure through a gate.

0.6 Arrive back at the parking lot to close the loop.

29 Ricketts Glen State Park

Start: At the Beach Lot #2 parking area
Distance: 4.5 miles
Type: Loop
Hiking time: 5 hours
Difficulty: Moderate to difficult
Best season: May to October
Traffic: Hikers only
Fees and permits: None

Maps: Available at www.dcnr.pa.gov/
StateParks/FindAPark/RickettsGlenStatePark/
Pages/Maps.aspx
Trail contact: Ricketts Glen State Park, 695
State Rte. 487, Benton 17814; (570) 477-
5675; www.dcnr.pa.gov/StateParks/
FindAPark/RickettsGlenStatePark/Pages/
default.aspx

Finding the trailhead: From Wilkes-Barre, take Route 309 North for 9.2 miles to a left on Route 118. Take Route 118 West for about 18 miles, then turn onto Route 487 North. Go 3 miles and turn right into the park. GPS: N41 20.280' / W76 16.771'

The Hike

You don't find many waterfalls on the prairies. Not big, spectacular ones anyway. It's a matter of topography.

Water causes erosion wherever it flows, carrying small stones and gritty sand along and scouring out a course through soft earth. Only the hardest rock withstands the pressure. Solid ledges are the result. Waterfalls occur when the water pouring over those iron-like spots has to fall a ways before plunging into a pool. That takes elevation, or rather, changes in elevation.

Ricketts Glen State Park has that.

To understand what the area known as the Glens is like, imagine the letter Y laid on a table. Then picture each section of that Y—the two arms and the main trunk—as being surrounded by steep walls. Not vertical walls, like in a canyon, but harshly angled ones. That's the Glens.

This hike starts at the park's main picnic area—Beach Lot #2—and is fairly level at first. Eventually, though, when you get to about what's known as Glen Leigh, it gets steep and challenging.

And once you're in, you're in. The park has signs at both ends of the Y's arms warning people they're at basically a point of no return. Once you descend into the Glens area, there are no loop trails that will get you back out. Hikers are advised to wear sturdy boots, pack in water and snacks, and use caution.

And the going, while well blazed and obvious, is challenging. This hike is constantly downhill on the first leg, largely on steps of stone. They're uneven and typically wet, so they can be slippery. The way back up and out is just as steep, again largely on wet, cut stone steps. This way is closed to use in winter unless you're a "properly equipped" ice climber, so that tells you what it can be like.

Hikers explore and take pictures at one of Ricketts Glen State Park's twenty-two named waterfalls.

So, given all that, is the hike really worth it? Absolutely.

There are twenty-two waterfalls significant enough to have names here. This hike allows you to see eighteen of them. They range in height from 11 feet—that's Cayuga Falls—to 94 feet—that's Ganoga. It's neither easy nor wise to get off the trail to get real close to many of the falls, but Ganoga is the exception. A spur trail leads down to it. From there, you can take in the view, soak your feet in Kitchen Creek, or—if you're willing to hopscotch your way across rocks when flows aren't too high—even get your picture taken in front of the falls.

The Waters Meet spot—where the two branches of Kitchen Creek come together, at about the halfway point of this hike—is, meanwhile, a great place to stop and take a break and maybe have a snack. There's a marker here noting the Glens' place in history. You won't get in much quiet reflection here; these trails, despite their challenging nature, get a lot of use, and this is a common rendezvous point. But it's a good-natured crowd.

Something else interesting you'll see along the way is what's known as the "Midway Crevasse." Located on Highland Trail, it's a spot full of giant, bus-size boulders. The trail winds among them, so in spots it's like you're walking a hallway between stony walls. It's another nice spot for taking a break.

The hike into and out of Ricketts Glen State Park's waterfalls area is challenging, with lots of rocky steps that can be slippery.

Be sure when doing this hike to leave yourself plenty of daylight. The rocky conditions and steep terrain will slow you down. Figure on covering ground about half as fast as you might elsewhere. You'll want time to stop and check out the waterfalls anyway. After all, it took eons to create this natural wonder. Spend some time enjoying it.

The History

A kind of historic guy himself, by modern standards, with a sense of history of his own, lies behind Ricketts Glen State Park.

Robert Bruce Ricketts was a Civil War veteran. He enlisted as a private in 1861 and—unlike so many—lived to see the war's end, despite fighting in at least one of its most pivotal battles. He led the Grand Army of the Potomac's Battery F, an artillery force, during the fighting at Gettysburg. They successfully held off the Confederates in fighting at Cemetery Hill. He'd moved up through the ranks by then, of course. In fact, by the time the fighting concluded, he'd become a colonel.

After the war, and together with his father and an uncle, Ricketts went into the timber business. He began buying property in this area of Pennsylvania—he amassed 66,000 acres in less than a decade—built a sawmill, and worked at producing lumber for a nation hungry for it. Despite a few downturns in the lumber market, Ricketts prospered, with his holdings totaling roughly 80,000 acres at one point.

One section of all that land proved especially memorable. Fishermen exploring the lower reaches of Kitchen Creek "discovered" the many waterfalls that make this area so famous today. Ricketts, thankfully, appreciated them. A lumberman who made his fortune cutting trees, he could have viewed this area from a purely monetary standpoint.

In this area, southern and northern hardwood types meet, meaning that there's a greater variety of trees here than in most places to the immediate north or south. Ricketts, though, didn't mow them all down. Instead, he left the trees standing to protect the waterfalls and the nature of the area.

Then he went further and took steps to share it all. Astonished by the beauty of the forest here—it's still home to giant pines, hemlock, and oaks, some of them 100 feet tall, 4 feet across, and 300 years old—and the waterfalls, he built trails into the area known today as the Glens Natural Area. The rocky stairs you descend along one branch of Kitchen Creek and climb along the other, with the area of Waters Meet in the middle? Such paths were Ricketts's idea.

He gets credit, too, for the names given to the waterfalls here. Ricketts was a member of the Wyoming Historical and Geological Society, the local county group. He had a passion for the past. So it's not surprising that he named many of the waterfalls for American Indian tribes. Others bear the names of family members and friends.

Fortunately, those who came after took care to conserve this area, too. Ricketts died in 1918. His heirs sold about half the land to the Pennsylvania Game Commission between 1920 and 1924. Another 12,000 acres—including the Glens area—was slated to be sold to the state for a park in the 1930s, but World War II changed that.

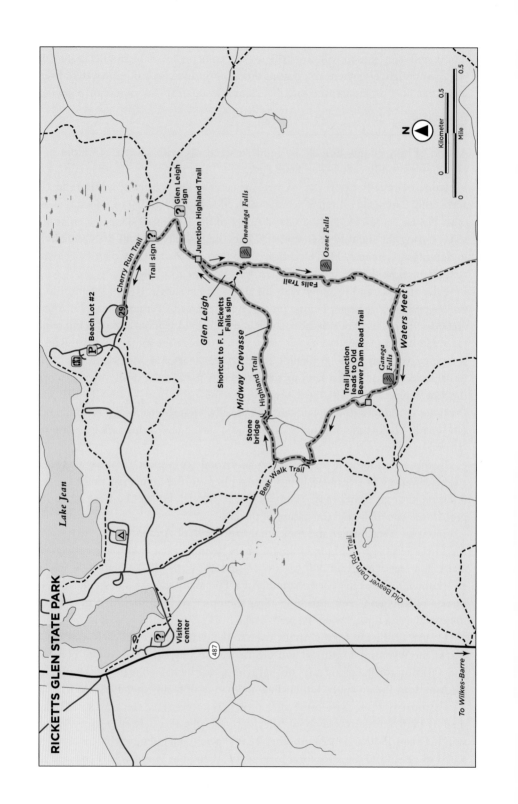

The state purchased just 1,261 acres in 1942. Additional land bought from the family in succeeding years brought the park to nearly 10,000 acres by 1949. The state park was developed along the way.

All the while, the Glens stayed safe. It became a National Natural Landmark in 1963, and a state park "natural area" in 1993, meaning it will be forever protected from development.

Surely that's something Ricketts would have wanted.

Miles and Directions

0.0 Start at Beach Lot #2. Follow the signs to the trailhead.

0.2 At a kiosk, turn right onto the wide, flat trail.

0.5 At a trail map sign, go right for Falls Trail. Start downhill.

0.6 Follow the sign for Glen Leigh, which goes to the right.

0.9 The trail Ys. To the right is Highland Trail. You'll return via that route, but for now go left toward Onondaga, the first named waterfall.

1.1 Cross a bridge at Onondaga Falls. Then go straight, avoiding the shortcut to Highland Trail. The trail gets rocky and wet here. Soon cross another bridge.

1.2 At Huron Falls, the steps get steeper.

1.4 Cross a bridge by Ozone Falls.

1.5 Cross another bridge.

1.6 A bridge below B. Reynolds Falls.

1.7 Come to the bridge at Waters Meet. This is where the two branches of Kitchen Creek come together, and is a prime resting place.

1.9 Cross another bridge.

2.0 Arrive at Ganoga Falls, the tallest in Ricketts Glen at 94 feet. Soon Old Beaver Dam Road Trail is to the left. Stay straight on Falls Trail.

2.2 Just after Mohawk Falls, the trail Ts. Go right, across a bridge toward Highland Trail.

2.4 The trail Ts again. Go right on Highland Trail.

2.6 Cross a stone bridge.

2.7 Enter the Midway Crevasse, an area of giant boulders among the trees.

3.2 The trail Ts. The shortcut is on the right; go straight on Highland Trail.

3.4 Close the loop at the Y trail intersection from the start of the hike. Right is to Glen Leigh. Go left, retracing your steps back to the start.

4.5 Arrive back at the start.

30 Delaware Water Gap National Recreation Area

Start: At the Lake Lenape trailhead
Distance: 4.1 miles
Type: Loop
Hiking time: 4 hours
Difficulty: Moderate to difficult
Best season: May to October
Traffic: Hikers only

Fees and permits: None
Maps: Available at www.nps.gov/dewa/planyourvisit/upload/sb2Hikes-2.pdf
Trail contact: Delaware Water Gap National Recreation Area, 1978 River Rd., Bushkill 18324; (570) 426-2452; www.nps.gov/dewa/index.htm

Finding the trailhead: From Stroudsburg, follow I-80 East for 3.3 miles to Broad Street. Go about 0.4 mile on Broad Street to a left onto Main Street. Go about .4 mile, then take a right onto Mountain Road and go less than half a mile. GPS: N40 58.782' / W75 08.503'

The Hike

Now this is what the Appalachian Trail is supposed to feel like.

This hike begins at the Lake Lenape trailhead, just out of the town of Delaware Water Gap. The drive to the parking area takes you past long-distance backpackers, kayakers, rafters, and others in a town that looks and feels outdoorsy. You'll likely encounter a number of backpackers on the trail, too.

That's all pretty cool, and pretty obvious. The history here—in terms of visible remnants of what once was—is more hidden. No matter how much of it you see, though, this is an enjoyable, though challenging hike. You'll climb about 1,000 feet in 2 miles, then come right back down.

The hike starts out on a gravel road. Just past Lake Lenape, you'll bear left to follow the white-blazed Appalachian Trail into the woods. It's here you'll want to keep your eyes open if you want to see any old foundations.

As the trail climbs uphill—and it does, consistently—look for small spur trails off to the left, toward the river. Some lead to "just" nice views. You'll see kayakers and rafters on the river far below. Others will reveal stone walls and the like. They can be hard to spot. Nature is expressing its dominance over the man-made features of the landscape, slowly reclaiming everything.

The trail is generally narrow and rocky, so expect to make slow time. There are several small creek crossings, too. Only one—Eureka Creek—is large enough to require any rock-hopping, and even it can be handled without much trouble. Wet feet shouldn't be an issue.

Keep your eyes open for the white blazes, too. There are a few spots where they are found not on trees, but on rocks. It's about here, at roughly 1.3 miles or so, that you're high enough to notice vultures and other birds soaring not above you, but below you. They're riding air currents above the river, but below eye level.

Things like the views from near Mount Minsi are what made the Delaware Water Gap so popular with late nineteenth- and early twentieth-century visitors.

Go beyond where the trail meets Minsi Fire Road and there's a section where—because of the overgrowing mountain laurel and rhododendron—it feels like you're walking through a tunnel.

Finally, the trail brings you to the Mount Minsi overlook where you can see, across in New Jersey, Mount Tammany. This is also the area known officially as "the gap." It's not uncommon to find an Appalachian Trail staffer here, too, offering advice and helping hikers as needed.

When you're ready, turn around and backtrack to Minsi Fire Road. Follow it downhill rather than taking the Appalachian Trail. The Fire Road is wider, but still steep and rocky, though not like you experienced coming up. There are some old stone foundations along it, too, so keep an eye out for those. You'll follow it back to the lake and then the parking lot.

Be aware that the Lake Lenape parking lot is a busy one. Appalachian Trail hikers park here to launch trips, and others park here to pick up hikers. Day-trippers use the lot as well. There are times when finding a space is difficult. Weekends are, of course, busiest.

The Appalachian Trail, the granddaddy of all long-distance hiking trails in America, follows trails made for wealthy tourists in the Delaware Water Gap area.

The History

There was a time when the Delaware Water Gap was the most popular tourist destination in America.

It's a deep, narrow cut in the Kittatinny Mountains, with the Delaware River following a lazy, if scenic, path through. Pennsylvania lies on one side of the river, New Jersey on the other. Everywhere there are majestic forests and views. That majesty gained popularity early on.

The Kittatinny Hotel, which could handle twenty-five guests in 1832, was the first in the area. Others followed, especially after the close of the Civil War. Railroads began offering cheap fares, and a nation of people who had grown accustomed to seeing new places under the worst of conditions went on the move in search of fun.

The Gap benefited from that as much as anywhere. From the mid-nineteenth through early twentieth centuries, it was a playground for people from all over. According to one account, the town of Water Gap had about 400 full-time, year-round residents. In summer, though, there would be 2,500 or more, what with all the tourists.

They came in part for the natural beauty and atmosphere. "The Water Gap is about the nearest accessible mountain wilderness to the large cities," reads an October 17, 1872, article in the *Stroudsburg Jeffersonian*. "And its fame as a healthful and pleasant resort is constantly extending."

Some of those who visited each year were the wealthy socialites of the country. They traveled from Philadelphia, New York, and elsewhere to stay for weeks at a time, if not entire summers.

The Kittatinny and Water Gap House catered to that clientele. The Kittatinny grew so that at its peak in 1892 it could house about 300 guests at a time. So, too, could the Water Gap House, which sprang up in 1872, just a little higher up on the mountain than its competitor. Such was their fame that by the 1890s the *New York Times* kept a correspondent in town to report weekly on guest arrivals and their activities.

Those people came to fish, hike, row, and do more outdoors. They didn't want to leave their city life behind entirely, though. The resorts responded by hosting ballroom dances, building billiard halls and other common areas where guests could mingle, and more. Some of the most famous people in the country stopped by. One was Theodore Roosevelt, who visited in 1910, shortly after the end of his presidency.

It was not to last, however.

The automobile boom spelled the beginning of the end for these resorts and others like them, which had been largely dependent on railroads delivering guests. When Americans could suddenly go wherever the road took them, they began exploring other places. By the time the Water Gap House burned down in 1915 and the Kittatinny in 1931, demand for their services was gone. Neither was rebuilt. The golden era of the Water Gap resorts was officially over.

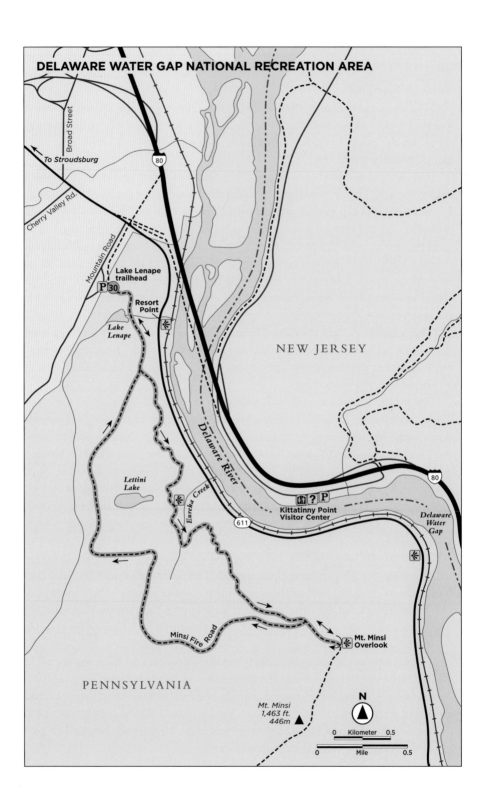

DELAWARE WATER GAP NATIONAL RECREATION AREA

Broad Street

To Stroudsburg

Cherry Valley Rd

Mountain Road

80

Lake Lenape
trailhead

P 30

Resort
Point

Lake
Lenape

Lettini
Lake

Eureka Creek

NEW JERSEY

Delaware River

611

Kittatinny Point
Visitor Center

80

Delaware
Water
Gap

Minsi Fire Road

Mt. Minsi
Overlook

PENNSYLVANIA

Mt. Minsi
1,463 ft.
446m

N

0 Kilometer 0.5

0 Mile 0.5

The crossing at Eureka Creek is one of the landmarks of this hike.

Remnants of those structures still stand in spots in the form of scattered foundations. The most lasting contribution of the resorts, though, may be their trails, which were laid out in the mid-nineteenth century for the benefit of their well-to-do guests.

Today the Appalachian Trail in part follows some of the old trails designed a century and more ago. To walk it here is to literally walk through history.

Miles and Directions

0.0 Start at the Lake Lenape trailhead. Follow the white blazes. After a few hundred feet you will see a "pack it in, pack it out" sign, with Lake Lenape and a bench on the right. Go straight.

0.3 The trail Ys. Go left on the Appalachian Trail, following the white blazes.

1.0 The trail crosses Eureka Creek.

1.2 The trail Ys. Go right, up some rocky steps, and switchback up the hill. Soon the trail climbs a small rock face.

1.3 Look for views of the river on the left.

1.6 The trail Ts when it meets Minsi Fire Road. Go left, following the white blazes. At the almost immediate Y that follows, go right, following the white blazes through a tunnel of rhododendron and mountain laurel.

1.7 Reach the Mount Minsi overlook. Turn and retrace your steps back to Minsi Fire Road.

1.8 Turn left on Minsi Fire Road.

3.1 A small unmarked trail goes left. Stay straight on Minsi Fire Road.

3.4 Another trail goes left. Stay straight on Minsi Fire Road. Notice some rocky cliffs on the left.

3.8 Minsi Fire Road meets the Appalachian Trail again to close the loop. Go left, back toward the start.

4.1 Arrive back at the trailhead.

31 Hugh Moore Park

Start: At the National Canal Museum entrance
Distance: 1.3 miles
Type: Loop
Hiking time: 1.5 hours
Difficulty: Easy
Best season: April to October
Traffic: Hikers only
Fees and permits: None to hike. Museum admission, which includes a canal boat ride, is $12 adults, $11 seniors, $9 children ages 3-15 (group packages available).
Maps: Available at https://canals.org/visit/use-the-dl-trail
Trail contact: National Canal Museum, 2750 Hugh Moore Park Rd., Easton 18042; (610) 923-3548; https://canals.org

Finding the trailhead: From Allentown, follow Route 22 East. Take the 25th Street exit and turn south at the end of the ramp. Go about 1.5 miles, then turn right onto Lehigh Drive, then right again at the stop sign onto the green metal bridge. Turn right at the end of the bridge to go into the park. GPS: N40 39.727' / W75 14.355'

The Hike

Like all walks along a canal, this one is flat, so the travel is easy. It's also interesting, for a couple of reasons.

It starts at the National Canal Museum. A 14,000-square-foot, two-story building, it houses exhibits on the first floor. It's worth your time to start here—check https://canals.org for hours, admission, and seasons—so that you have a feel for what you're looking at and how and why it was so vitally important to this region and the country as a whole.

When you're done, turn right outside the museum doors and follow the canal along the Delaware & Lehigh Canal Trail. You'll pass some historic remnants along the way. The mechanics of the canal system are striking. The size of the gears—with impressive steel teeth, like something appropriate for a shark—speak to how serious was this business.

The trail continues to a lock and, next to it, the locktender's house. The last one built on this canal, it's open Friday, Saturday, and Sunday in-season. It's surrounded by a white picket fence, has a beautiful flower garden, and offers lovely views of the river. It all seems so serene.

But as you'll learn—especially if you stop here when there's a volunteer interpreter—the life of the locktender really was a difficult one. They had Sundays off. But the rest of the week? "The boatsman had a hard life. But the locktenders did, too, because they couldn't go nowhere. They had to be on the job all the time," reads a quote from locktender Harvey Brant.

The locktender's house at Hugh Moore Park stands adjacent to the lock.

Indeed, locktenders had to be available to open and close gates 18 hours a day, from early spring through late fall, all by turning gears in a building called the "dog house." It wasn't just the locktender, though. Family members pitched in to operate the locks. Locktenders got to live in their house—provided by the canal company— year-round. But they only got paid during the months the lock operated. To make ends meet, entire families worked the locks, each member taking his or her turn, so that the father could also hold down a job somewhere else. Mothers, meanwhile, often took in laundry and traded vegetables and baked goods with canal boaters for coal to heat their home.

Be sure to explore all that, then continue beyond the locktender's house to a few more informational panels explaining some local history. There's the story of the amusement park that existed on the island in the river here, for example. That island—known as Uhler's Island or Smith's Island at various times—is totally wooded these days. But starting in 1894 it housed an amusement park. Easton Transit Company built it, then shuttled passengers out there to enjoy its rides, games, dancing, entertainment, boating, and swimming. It lasted until 1919, when heavy ice flows destroyed the trolley trestle and eliminated access.

Operating the lock at High Moore Park involves some serious gears and other machinery.

Turn around, then head back to the museum. Follow a little spur to get a good look at Chain Dam on the Lehigh River before continuing on. You'll eventually return to the museum to close the loop.

One more thing, though. Before you leave, trade your hiking boots for a unique seat.

Hugh Moore Park has an operating canal boat, the *Josiah White II*. One of just two like it in the state, it's 50 feet long, with two levels and seating for 110. It makes daily runs though the canal, pulled by the museum's resident mules, Hank and George. The out-and-back trip, from the museum to the locktender's house, takes 45 minutes.

If you want to try something even more unique, the *Josiah White II* also plays host to dinner cruises. Each begins with a history lesson and ends with themed music and dinner. Details are available at the museum.

The History

You'd never know it today, given all the trees and grass and picnic areas and play-grounds and people walking, biking, and playing. But Hugh Moore Park—site of the National Canal Museum and the Lehigh Navigation Canal—was home to one of America's first industrial parks.

As with all real estate, location was the key.

In the early nineteenth century, the anthracite coal mined in northeastern Pennsylvania was seen as the perfect fuel. It was not only abundant, but burned clean and hot, too. Urbanites seeking heat wanted it.

Then, when David Thomas, a Welsh ironmaster, came to America and realized that anthracite coal could be made to ignite via a blast of air, the blast furnace was born. Suddenly, iron could be produced easier than ever before. That, too, sent demand for coal skyrocketing.

There was one problem. Getting coal to markets as far away as New York and Philadelphia was time consuming and cost prohibitive. Enter the town of Easton, Hugh Moore Park, and its canal.

The Lehigh Navigation Canal was built between 1827 and 1829. It was an engineering marvel in its day. It had to be. The Lehigh River upstream offered challenges aplenty. "A few miles above Easton, the Lehigh was pocked with white water at almost every turning. To navigate it seemed impossible," said Josiah White, one of the founders of the Lehigh Coal and Navigation Co. Engineers, though, used dams, hand-dug channels, and calm river straits to weave a path downstream, handling a 1,000-foot drop in elevation in the process. So well did they do their job that Lehigh Navigation became known as the canal capable of handling more freight, by capacity, than any other.

The fact that it met here with the Delaware Canal, which went on to Philadelphia, and the Morris Canal, which went to New York, made Easton a hub of goods coming and going, just like a highway interchange today. Industry sprang up accordingly.

At certain times, visitors to the National Canal Museum can take a ride on the Josiah White II *as it's pulled by mules.*

So important and so centrally located was the area that, even with the coming of the railroads, the canals here were able to make money long after others faded from the scene. The Lehigh Navigation Canal—which stretches 47 miles from Mauch Chunk to Easton—remained in full operation until 1932 and in partial operation until 1942. As such, it was America's longest-operating towpath canal. Today it remains the only fully restored section of towpath in Pennsylvania or New Jersey.

What's amazing is the manpower a successful canal required. Typically, boats were pulled by a team of mules. Those mules—the offspring of a male donkey and a female horse—were preferred because they were more surefooted than horses, ate less, and could go farther with fewer health problems. Indeed, it was common for mules to haul a boat 25 miles a day.

Canallers—the men who worked the mule teams—typically acted as independent contractors, owning their own animals. They worked just as hard as their teams. Canallers stopped only when the locks closed, which was from 10 p.m. to 4 a.m. They had to take care of their animals at the end of the day, though, and be up and

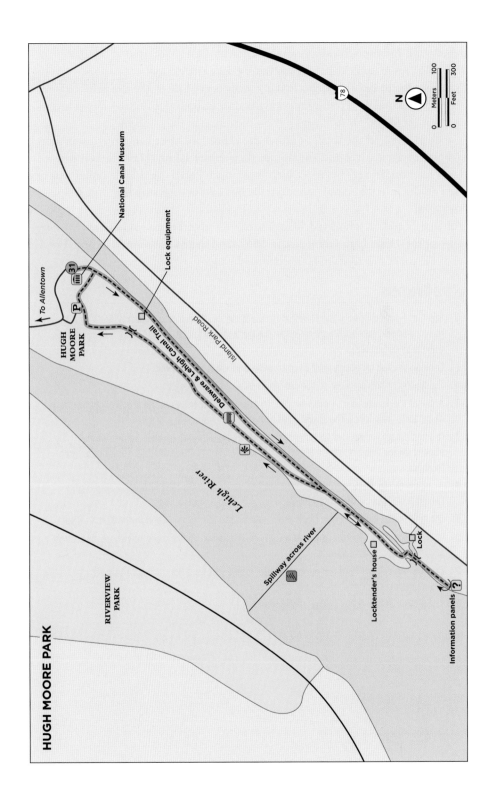

ready to go when the gates opened in the morning. "One thing, you were never bothered with insomnia," said one canaller, Joseph Lum. "You rose about 3:30 a.m. and wouldn't retire until 11 p.m." That was six days a week, too.

Such was the price of making a living. Canallers got paid by the ton delivered, not hours or days worked, so resting too long wasn't an option. Even the mules had to learn to eat on the go via feed bags put on their faces as they walked.

Canallers lived on the road, or rather the canal, too. Most had a tiny cabin atop their boat for themselves and sometimes their entire family. Hauling 100 tons of coal at a time on "hinge" boats—which were much like those double trailer trucks you see on the interstate now—they'd trade bits of it at each stop for food, supplies, and services.

All that history is preserved here. Thanks for that begins with Hugh Moore, founder of the Dixie Cup Company. In 1962 he donated the money to purchase 6 miles of the canal and adjacent land from the Lehigh Coal and Navigation Co.

Miles and Directions

0.0 Start at the front door of the National Canal Museum. Walk to the *Josiah White II* and the mule paddock, then turn right to follow the Delaware & Lehigh Canal Trail (the same one walked by the mules).

0.1 Look on the left for equipment used to raise and lower water levels.

0.4 The trail Ys by the spillway on the Lehigh River. Continue straight.

0.6 Arrive at the locktender's house on the right and the old canal on the left. Walk out on top of the lock, then follow the gravel path upriver.

0.7 Cross a bridge where river water enters the lock and continue to a few informational panels. Check them out, then return to the locktender's house, which is sometimes open for tours.

0.9 Just past the locktender's house, turn left and go down a few steps to get a view of the Lehigh River. Then return to the trail.

1.0 The trail Ys. Go left this time. Soon after, look on the left for an island in the Lehigh River.

1.1 Look on the right for a bench, near a sign—unlike any you'll likely see anywhere else—that says "Caution, mules at work."

1.2 Cross a bridge. This is where water from the lock escapes. Soon turn right toward the museum.

1.3 Arrive back at the start to close the loop.

32 Boulton Historic Site and Jacobsburg Environmental Education Center

Start: At the Boulton Historic Site parking lot off Henry Road
Distance: 2.3 miles
Type: Loop
Hiking time: 2 hours
Difficulty: Easy to moderate
Best season: April to December (Note: The Longrifle Museum and Henry House is only open select weekends.)
Traffic: Hikers only in places, horseback riders and cyclists in others
Fees and permits: Free to hike; $5 admission for those older than 12 to the Longrifle Museum and Henry House

Maps: Available at www.dcnr.pa.gov/State Parks/FindAPark/JacobsburgEnvironmental EducationCenter/Pages/Maps.aspx
Trail contacts: Jacobsburg Environmental Education Center, 400 Belfast Rd., Nazareth 18064; (610) 746-2801; www.dcnr.pa .gov/StateParks/FindAPark/Jacobsburg EnvironmentalEducationCenter/Pages/ default.aspx. Jacobsburg Historical Society, 402 Henry Road, Nazareth 18064; (610) 759-9029; www.jacobsburghistory.com.

Finding the trailhead: From Bethlehem, go north on Route 33 for about 15 miles. Take the exit toward Belfast. Go a little less than half a mile on Henry Road and look for the parking lot on the right. GPS: N40 46.594' / W75 75 17.162'

The Hike

Pennsylvania longrifles. Converted Civil War firearms, some of European origin. Nineteenth-century wedding dresses. Horse-drawn sleighs. Dam ruins. Old, if not exactly ancient, forest. You'll see all these things and more on this hike.

It begins at a small parking lot off Henry Road. There's a collection of informational panels offering details on the Henry family and its rifle-making legacy. Starting with William I, the family produced firearms from 1750 to 1895, all but seven of those years here in the Lehigh Valley.

Beware, though. Those signs reference the blue-blazed Homestead Trail. They also talk about following the 0.5-mile Boulton Heritage Walk, which is said to be marked with a yellow flintlock symbol. Both trails exist. The blazes and symbols, though? Those markings can be hard to find or can be almost unreadable. Don't let that deter you, though. This is a fascinating walk that is, for the most part, easy except for one challenging section.

Just be sure to time your visit to those days when the Pennsylvania Longrifle Museum and John James Henry House are open. That's not necessarily often. Both are run by volunteers from the Jacobsburg Historical Society, so the schedule is understandable. But it pays to heed it. The Longrifle Museum is open only

Pennsylvania longrifles on display at the Longrifle Museum

certain weekends from May through December. The Henry House is open even less frequently—one Sunday a month from July through September and during special events other months.

It is possible to schedule appointments to both sites, though. To do that, or just to check schedules and hours, visit www.jacobsburghistory.com or call (610) 759-9029.

Meanwhile, when you do start this walk, take time to pay attention to the subtle history as well as the overt. Early on, for example, you'll cross a metal bridge over picturesque Bushkill Creek. Imagine what it would look like if it was dammed. That's how it was back when the Henry family lived here.

There were practical reasons. The Henrys used water to power their rifle factory, for example, so pooling the water guaranteed a source of energy. The family made good use of the "mill pond" for recreation, too, though. The Henrys alone had twenty-seven picnics in a two-month period in 1891.

Others in the community also played here. Perhaps too hard, sometimes? Granville Henry once posted a sign reminding visitors that permission to visit the woods and dam was granted only to "well-behaved persons." Swimming and fishing on

A reenactor in period clothes fires a muzzleloader outside the Pennsylvania Longrifle Museum.

Sunday was strictly prohibited, for example. And bathing suits? They were an absolute requirement, the sign noted, saying that "persons who appear in the water during the week, without swimming breeches, will be prosecuted."

The dam's mostly gone. Only a few foundation walls and other remnants remain, visible if you're willing to bushwhack along the water's edge. The stream remains popular, however, as you'll see.

A portion of the hike follows the Henrys Woods Trail through what is billed as the "oldest forest in the Lehigh Valley." The walk upstream can be rough in spots. Indeed, a sign you'll pass as soon as you start on it warns of hazards like irregular roots, rocky surfaces, and steep terrain. Coming downstream is much gentler.

While traveling both directions, though, you'll likely see people wading, swimming, playing, and fishing in Bushkill Creek, just like way back when. That hasn't changed, even with the passage of time.

The History

A cabin? Really? A cabin? Are you kidding me? No way. That kind of reaction is pretty much what led to construction of what is now known as the John Joseph Henry House at Boulton Historic Site. Apparently, being essentially the chief executive officer and president of a rifle-building empire doesn't make you immune to the wishes of your better half.

To understand the story behind the Henry House requires starting a bit further back, though, to the start of a family whose life took many interesting turns.

It begins with William Henry I. He was born in Pennsylvania's Chester County in 1729. In 1744, at age 15, he became an apprentice gunsmith in Lancaster County. By 1750 he had his own shop and was producing his own rifles. He led a life of adventure and intrigue thereafter.

Henry served as an armorer with the British military in America, meeting George Washington and helping to capture Fort Pitt from the French. He later experimented with building steam-powered paddleboats. Next up was revolution. He joined the American Philosophical Society—his membership application was signed by Ben Franklin—and became involved in the American Revolution, serving as a member of the Continental Congress.

His son William II followed him into the family business, producing fine Pennsylvania longrifles from his shop in Nazareth starting in 1780. A dozen years later—after creating Nazareth's first fire company and serving as its first chief—he moved his operation to Jacobsburg. There, sons John Joseph and William III got involved.

That's when things really took off. The family had fulfilled various military contracts off and on for years. But during the War of 1812, they became the largest civilian contractor supplying rifles to the United States. On the heels of that, in 1826, under John Joseph's guidance, the Henrys became chief rifle supplier for John Jacob Astor's American Fur Co. In no time, Henry rifles were among the most prominent on the western frontier. Hunters, explorers, trappers, and others loved their accuracy, relatively low cost, and durability. The business was booming.

Enter Mary Rebecca Smith. John Joseph married her in 1808. Four years later he left Philadelphia to oversee construction of the family's new riflemaking facility, the Boulton Gun Works. With demand for his rifles skyrocketing, he tried to move Mary to Boulton. Forget it. She took one look at what was to be their home—a rustic, rough-hewn place more typical of the frontier than the civilization she knew—and quickly prepared to go back to the city unless he came up with something better.

The Henry House—an impressive Philadelphia-style townhouse—is the result. Unfortunately for John Joseph, he didn't live there long. The home was finished in 1834; he died in 1836. It would, though, serve as home to five generations of Henrys. The last descendant lived there until 1989.

It was then donated to the Jacobsburg Historical Society, which operates it today. Visitors can tour the home—and its adjacent carriage house—and see how the Henrys lived. The furnishings, right down to a couple of wedding dresses, a piano, furniture, and more, are original pieces.

The family association with rifle building didn't end with construction of the house, of course. The Henrys stayed busy in the years leading up to and during the Civil War and—unlike many competitors—stayed afloat afterward, too. They did that by taking surplus army rifle barrels and turning them into inexpensive shotguns, among other things. Later still, they switched to making breech-loading rifles and shotguns.

Eventually, though, the company was surpassed by competitors like Winchester and Remington. It ceased making gun parts in 1895, nearly 150 years after William I got his start, and assembled its last one from leftover pieces in 1907.

The Pennsylvania Longrifle Museum, located across the street from the Henry House, tells those tales and more as a repository of all things Henry rifles. It has many firearms on display and outlines the family's story, with some odd tidbits thrown in.

Take the case of James Henry. He was, perhaps, the one family member who might have pursued interests other than gunmaking, given the chance. Born in 1809, the only son of John Henry and Rebecca, he attended a theological seminary initially. He would return to lead the family business—with four sons following—only upon his father's death. But he didn't stay forever. When his own son Granville joined the business in 1859, he turned to writing, drafting an unpublished study of forests around the world that same year. He later encouraged Pennsylvania universities to teach forestry. Finally, before he died in 1895, he played a key role in establishing Arbor Day in Pennsylvania.

The Henrys left quite the legacy, didn't they? From steamboats to trees, with rifles at the heart of it all.

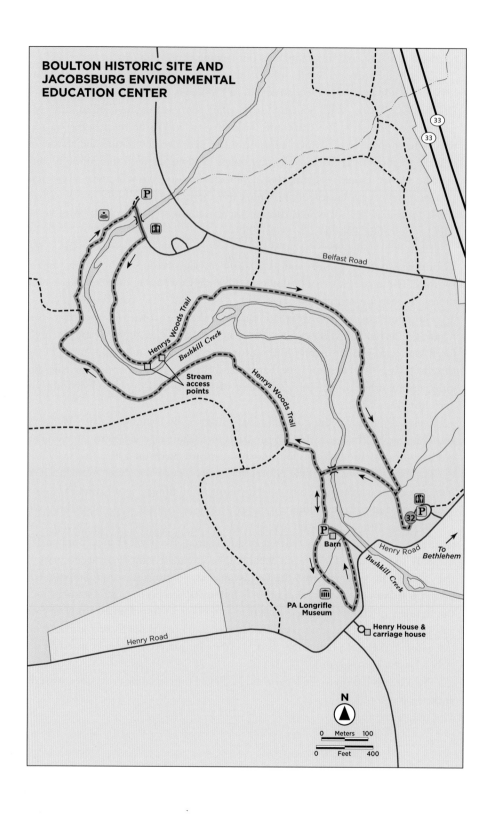

BOULTON HISTORIC SITE AND JACOBSBURG ENVIRONMENTAL EDUCATION CENTER

Belfast Road

Henrys Woods Trail

Bushkill Creek

Stream access points

Henrys Woods Trail

33

33

32

P

Henry Road

To Bethlehem

Barn

P

PA Longrifle Museum

Henry House & carriage house

Bushkill Creek

Henry Road

N

| 0 | Meters | 100 |
| 0 | Feet | 400 |

Miles and Directions

0.0 Start at the Boulton Historic Site trailhead. Pass the informational signs, go through the wooden gate and bear right. After a few hundred feet the trail Ys. Straight ahead is Woods Trail. You'll come back that way later. For now, turn left just before crossing the bridge.

0.1 Cross the bridge over Bushkill Creek. Soon the trail Ys. Go left for now.

0.2 The trail enters a parking lot. Go straight through it, up the hill.

0.3 The Pennsylvania Longrifle Museum is on the right. Explore it, then return to this spot and continue straight up the hill.

0.4 The trail meets Henry Road. Cross over to explore the Henry House and associated buildings. When done, return to the road, cross back over, and turn right to follow the blue-blazed trail.

0.6 The trail brings you to a barn on the left. This is the parking lot you entered before. Turn right and go back to the bridge over Bushkill Creek.

0.7 Back at the bridge. Stay left to go up the hill.

0.8 The trail Ys. Go right onto orange-blazed Henrys Woods Trail. This is the most challenging part of the hike.

0.9 Stairs on the right lead down to Bushkill Creek. Avoid those and continue up the hill.

1.0 The trail Ys. Go right.

1.1 Cross a small bridge, then go right at the Y.

1.2 Take the stairs down to stream level.

1.3 Notice a small amphitheater on the left. Pass this and walk to the edge of the parking lot. Soon turn right and cross the bridge over Bushkill Creek. Restrooms are located on the left. This is also Henrys Woods Trail, leading back to the start. It's largely wide and flat, and easy walking.

1.5 At a kiosk about Maurice K. Goddard, note one of the first official access points to Bushkill Creek on the right. Stairs on the right lead to the creek.

1.7 The trail Ys. Go right, following the orange blazes.

2.1 Overlook on the right.

2.2 The red-blazed trail goes left. Stay straight to follow the orange blazes. Soon cross the wooden bridge, then stay left to return to the parking lot.

2.3 Arrive back at the trailhead.

33 Hawk Mountain Sanctuary

Start: At the visitor center
Distance: 2.3 miles
Type: Loop
Hiking time: 2 hours
Difficulty: Easy to moderate
Best season: May to November
Traffic: Hikers only
Fees and permits: Admission is $10 adults, $7 seniors, $5 children ages 6-12;

memberships that include visitation privileges also available
Maps: Available at www.hawkmountain.org/ visit/hiking/hiking-hawk-mountain/page .aspx?id=239
Trail contact: Hawk Mountain Sanctuary, 1700 Hawk Mountain Rd., Kempton 19529; (610) 756-6961; www.hawkmountain.org

Finding the trailhead: From Pottsville, follow Route 61 South for 11.5 miles. Turn onto Rolling Mill Road and go about 0.1 mile, then continue on Route 895 East for 2.5 miles. Turn right onto Hawk Mountain Road and go 1.5 miles. The visitor center and parking are on the right. GPS: N40 38.026' / W75 59.234'

The Hike

If you go to Penn State University's Beaver Stadium in, say, oh, March, and somehow sneak in, you can pick the seat you want without any competition. Of course, there isn't much to see either. The action comes on Saturdays in the fall, when the Nittany Lions are actually playing football. Then you'll have to share the stadium with about 100,000 other folks.

So it is when hiking at Hawk Mountain.

Visiting here in summer is nice. Very nice, in fact. The hike through the forest is lovely, offering the chance to see woodland birds and mammals from gray squirrels to white-tailed deer. Benches along Lookout Trail offer tranquil spots for reflection. And the views from the various overlooks are simply breathtaking.

But it's the raptors that make you want to come here. And their numbers peak in fall. Not surprisingly, that's when human crowds are at their heaviest, too. On weekends especially, the trails can seem busy enough to need traffic lights. And at the overlooks, seemingly every rock big enough to offer a seat will have a person perched on it.

That's not a reason not to visit in autumn. Far from it. The opportunity to see and count so many raptors of so many kinds is unique enough to make a lack of elbow room tolerable. But know what you're getting into. That advice applies to the hike in, as well.

This particular hike leaves the Hawk Mountain visitor center and follows Lookout Trail to North Lookout, the main raptor viewing area. Early on, the walking is easy. There's a slight grade, but the trail is wide and groomed. In fact, the path is wheelchair accessible as far as South Lookout. If there's someone in your group with

The North Lookout is the largest and most popular viewing site at Hawk Mountain Sanctuary. On peak weekends in fall, it can be crowded with people.

limited mobility, getting even this far has benefits, as there are informational displays here, a count of birds seen, and, in fall, staff on hand to answer questions. This spot offers a view of the "river of rocks," too. That's the mile-long boulder field to the front. It's called that because a stream runs below the boulders.

If you're hiking, continue on Overlook Trail, passing a number of other overlooks, all worth stopping to see. The trail remains easy going all the way to Bald Lookout, which is about halfway. Then, things change. From here on out, the trail is increasingly rocky. Sturdy hiking boots help even when it's dry. When things are wet, the rocks can get slippery, so use caution.

Pass the Escarpment, River of Rocks, and Express trail junctions to stay on Overlook Trail and eventually you'll come to a junction for Sunset Overlook and The Slide. The Katter trail is one that goes straight up a rock face; it's fun to explore, so long as you realize it requires using handholds to get up.

For the sake of this walk, we'll bypass that and continue on to North Overlook. You have to climb a set of steep, narrow, irregularly spaced stone steps. The way is not overly wide, so in fall, expect the occasional bottleneck as people are coming and going.

It's worth the effort to get here, though. The North Lookout offers a 200-degree field of view. It's possible to see 70 miles in some directions. That's beautiful enough at any time of year, but especially so in fall, when the woods seem on fire with splashes of red, yellow, and orange leaves. And over it all are majestic soaring raptors. Bring

Hikers on Lookout Trail can check out running totals of raptors seen.

binoculars to get the best look at them. Sanctuary staff members man this ridge, so they'll help identify what you're seeing, but the closer look you can get, the better.

Raptor migrations begin in earnest in August and continue through December. The days following a cold front on strong north–northwest winds in October and November are the absolute best, though.

That's when the crowds come. But what's a little traffic so long as you get to see the action, right?

The History

It's an event today billed as "nature's greatest airshow." But way back when? It was seen as more of an opportunity for retribution.

In the early part of the twentieth century, eagles, hawks, falcons, owls, and vultures were rarely viewed as regal objects of wonder, capable of soaring through the sky seemingly without effort. They were competitors. Farmers, hunters, and others saw them as pests that preyed on the same livestock and game species the people themselves were after. And as with all competitors, the object of the game was to put them out of business.

In 1929 the Pennsylvania Game Commission—the agency responsible for managing the birds in Pennsylvania—offered bounties for every one killed. Goshawks alone were worth $5, a princely sum at a time when the average person's monthly wage might be $30. People took advantage as best they could. That was especially true right here.

Raptors pass over Hawk Mountain Sanctuary today because of the lay of the land. Birds migrating south—the timing of their movement sparked by seasonal changes in the availability of prey—soar over the Kittatinny Ridge because of its deflected winds and thermals. Deflected currents occur when northwesterly winds strike the ridge and are forced up and over the top. Thermals are bubbles of heated air that spiral up from the valley floor. Both naturally give birds a boost, allowing them to soar—covering miles and miles—without expending much energy. That's critical considering that some will go as far as South America before stopping.

Those same environmental factors led them to migrate here a century ago, too. People knew that and turned out en masse to kill them on their way by.

Things started to change, here anyway, thanks to a curious birder. Richard Pough was a recent college graduate and amateur ornithologist living in Philadelphia. He heard of the shoots occurring at "Hawk Mountain" and decided to visit.

The carnage was probably worse than he had even imagined possible. He saw rows of gunners socializing and, when the opportunity presented itself, killing birds. He stayed after they left and collected the carcasses. He took pictures, too. Those images caught the attention of Rosalie Edge, a wealthy New Yorker and, like Pough, a conservationist.

She visited Hawk Mountain herself in 1934 and immediately leased 1,400 acres on the ridge. She next hired a New England birder, Maurice Braun, and installed him

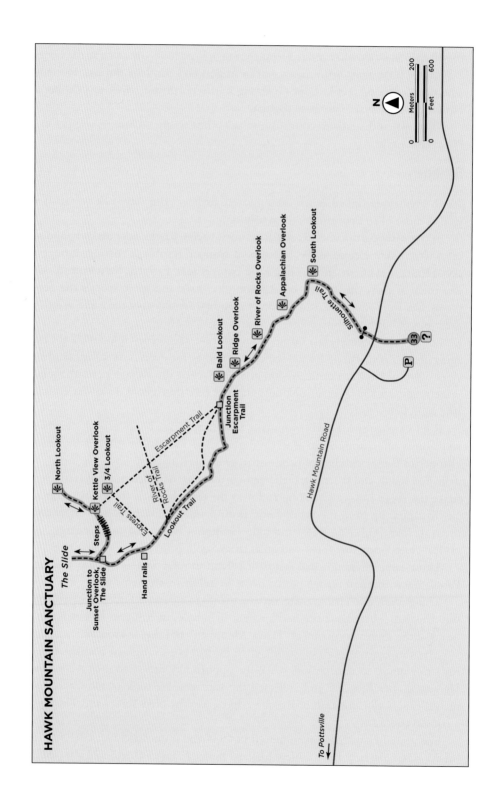

HAWK MOUNTAIN SANCTUARY

The Slide

North Lookout

Kettle View Overlook

3/4 Lookout

Steps

Junction to
Sunset Overlook,
The Slide

Hand rails

Express Trail

River of Rocks Trail

Lookout Trail

Escarpment Trail

Junction
Escarpment
Trail

Bald Lookout

Ridge Overlook

River of Rocks Overlook

Appalachian Overlook

South Lookout

Silhouette Trail

Hawk Mountain Road

To Pottsville

P

33

?

N

Meters   200

Feet   600

0

0

as warden responsible for guarding the property. Shooting of raptors stopped immediately. A year later, Edge opened the property to the public. In 1938 she bought the land outright and donated it to the Hawk Mountain Sanctuary Association, creating the world's first site for raptor conservation.

Always, the goal was to showcase the birds of prey as something worth conserving. That would take time. The Game Commission offered bounties on some raptors until as late as 1968. Such persecution became illegal in 1973 with the passage of the federal Migratory Bird Act. It, along with other legislation, makes it illegal to trap, shoot, or otherwise harm birds of prey.

All that's helped change the reputations of the birds, if not with everyone, certainly most. Indeed, now they're viewed as partners in conservation in a way. Generalists that eat a variety of prey, raptors are sometimes indicators of environmental health. When their populations decline, it's often a sign of some other problem, be it habitat loss or pollution, like that from DDT.

Hawk Mountain continues to study raptors around the world and educate people as to their value. It's an ongoing job, but one paying dividends. Visitors today travel here not to kill, but to admire.

That's just what Pough, Edge, Braun, and others would have wanted.

Miles and Directions

0.0 Start at the visitor center. Follow the sign for sanctuary trails, passing a deer exclosure and native plant garden before crossing Hawk Mountain Road.

0.1 Enter the sanctuary through a gate and past the last restrooms on the hike.

0.2 Come to the South Lookout on the right. Check it out, then go left on Lookout Trail. Soon the Appalachian Trail is on the right.

0.3 River of Rocks Overlook is on the right.

0.4 Ridge Overlook is on the right, then Bald Lookout, also on the right.

0.5 The trail Ys. Escarpment Trail goes to the right. Go left and stay on Lookout Trail. Follow the orange blazes past Express Trail on the right.

0.8 Notice the handrails as you start to climb.

0.9 The trail Ys. To the left is Sunset Overlook and The Slide. Go right toward North Lookout.

1.0 Rocky stairs mark the final ascent to North Lookout, elevation 1,521 feet. Soon Kettle View Overlook is to the right. Go left to North Lookout. After a few hundred yards the trail Ys. Skyline Trail goes right. Go left and immediately arrive at North Lookout. After checking out the birds and views, turn back and walk to The Slide.

1.4 Arrive at The Slide. Take in the view—often limited by vegetation—and the informational panels, then return back to the starting point via the route you took on the way up.

2.2 Reach the sanctuary gate to close the loop.

2.3 Arrive back at the start.

34 Daniel Boone Homestead

Start: At the visitor center
Distance: 1.1 miles
Type: Loop
Hiking time: 1 hour
Difficulty: Easy
Best season: Year-round
Traffic: Hikers and horseback riders

Fees and permits: None to enter the park; fees to enter the visitor center and historic area
Maps: Available at www.danielboone homestead.org/historic-area-map.html
Trail contact: Daniel Boone Homestead, 400 Daniel Boone Rd., Birdsboro 19508; (610) 582-4900; www.danielboonehomestead.org/index.html

Finding the trailhead: From Pottstown, take Route 422 West for 4.5 miles to a right turn onto Daniel Boone Road. Go 1.3 miles and make a left onto Old Daniel Boone Road. Follow it for 0.3 mile to the visitor center parking lot. GPS: N40 17.820' / W75 47.674'

The Hike

Daniel Boone explored a lot of country in his day, from Pennsylvania, North Carolina, and Virginia to Kentucky, Missouri, and Florida. Always, he knew where he was.

Sort of. "I have never been lost, but I will admit to being confused for several weeks," he once famously said. You don't have to worry about that on this hike.

This walking tour of the Daniel Boone Homestead is an easy one, following wide, flat gravel paths for little more than a mile. It's definitely a walk worth taking, though. It offers a glimpse of pioneer life as Boone would have lived it, with some more-modern touches added.

One piece of advice? If possible, visit here on one of the occasions when volunteer staff from the Friends of Daniel Boone Homestead are hosting an event. You won't necessarily get any access you wouldn't otherwise, but the stories and history the volunteers tell while dressed in period clothes adds so much to the experience.

Either way, start the hike at the visitor center. From there the first place you'll visit is the Boone home—or more specifically, the home built on the Boone home.

When Boone's father, Squire Boone, built here, he constructed a one-room log cabin on a stone foundation above a spring for his family of eleven to live in. It's long gone. The foundation remains, however. In fact, it's the only original piece of the home you see now. Those who came after the Boones built over it, adding to the house bit by bit over the years to produce the structure you see today.

The hike next goes past a blacksmith shop and Pennsylvania German–style barn. The barn houses an original Conestoga wagon, one that would have been driven by a "teamster." Perhaps you've heard of the International Brotherhood of Teamsters union? It's because of wagons like these that its logo features a pair of horses.

A costumed reenactor looks out from the second floor of the barn at the Daniel Boone Homestead.

The barn at the Daniel Boone Homestead dates to the late eighteenth century, and some of the structure is still original.

The hike then takes you past the Bertolet House and a bakehouse. Frontier families typically set one day aside for baking, producing breads and pies and drying herbs in an all-day marathon. This oven is a 20-some-second one. What that means is, the baker would fire it up and wait for the coals to burn. When he could stick his hand in and hold it there for 20 or more seconds without the heat forcing him to retreat, it was ready for baking. Volunteers actually bake in it on occasion today, so if you're here to see that, it's pretty cool.

The hike then takes you to a vertical, water-powered sawmill and a small pond, with a trail around it. Just be aware that, when I last visited, a bridge needed to circle the pond was out. If you want to make this trek, plan to do some bushwhacking. Otherwise, you'll head back from here to the start—all without wandering off course.

The History

Mention Daniel Boone and a lot of people immediately think of a coonskin-capped frontiersman wandering the woods of Kentucky.

Well, yes and no.

Boone certainly spent a lot of time in that state, and achieved his most lasting fame there. He twice led settlers through the Cumberland Gap at a time when that was the western edge of America's frontier.

A few young visitors to the Daniel Boone Homestead get a lesson in frontier-era firearms.

The first trip didn't go so well. Boone and his following were ultimately beaten back by Native Americans, with Boone's eldest son among those killed. Two years later he tried again, though, and succeeded in establishing Fort Boonesborough. It became a thriving settlement. Tragically, he lost his second son there, too, seven years later, in one of the final battles of the American Revolution.

But before all that, he got his start right here in Pennsylvania. Born on the grounds in 1734, he spent his youth much like any other pioneer boy, helping his family to raise crops, tend livestock, and—eventually—hunt for food. He got his first rifle at age 13 and soon proved to be an excellent marksman. By age 15, though, he was gone, his family having moved to North Carolina. He would bounce around after that, living in several different places, though he did wind up back in Pennsylvania for a while. He served as a blacksmith and wagoneer with General Braddock, George Washington, and the rest of the British near Pittsburgh during the French and Indian War.

Boone lived to age 86, passing away in 1820. Long before then, books written about him in the 1780s solidified his status as a frontier legend. Comic books, television shows, toys, and more kept him popular throughout the twentieth century.

It was that popularity that led to this site surviving. The homestead passed through at least ten owners over the years, but by 1919 was abandoned. That's when Rev. Arthur Vossler bought it with the goal of making sure it got the respect he felt it deserved. A grassroots preservation effort was begun, one that ultimately

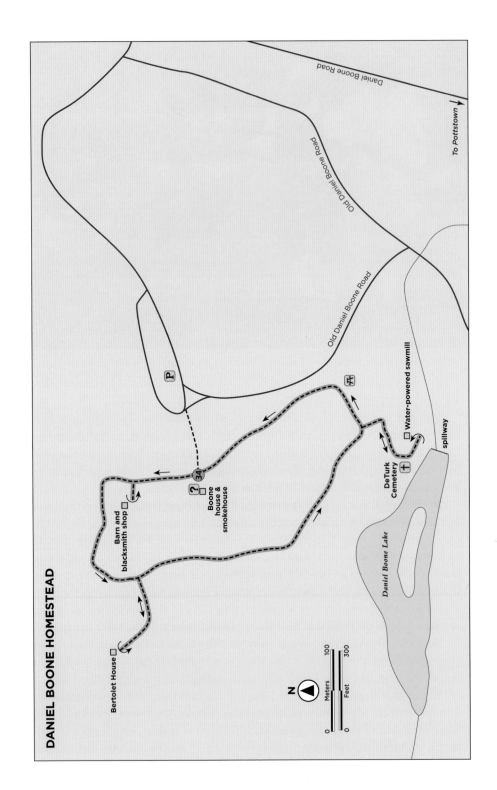

DANIEL BOONE HOMESTEAD

led to the state buying the property for $7,000 in 1937. The homestead as a historic site was born.

Interestingly, Daniel Carter Beard—founder of the Boy Scouts of America—was one of those who led the charge. A fan of Boone and his skills, he felt it important to memorialize the spot where he was born. His own son even took part in the dedication.

Since then, the site has come to house the historic buildings you'll see. The irony? Daniel Boone would likely have recognized them, architecturally speaking. But he never lived or worked in any of them.

The blacksmith shop, for example, dates to 1769, or nearly twenty years after Boone left. It is, though, similar to one Squire Boone would have had on-site. It was moved here in 1947. Likewise, the Pennsylvania German–style bank barn was also built in the late 1700s. That's also the time frame when the Bertolet smokehouse and bakehouse were likely constructed. They were moved here in 1968, along with the Bertolet House itself. A typical Pennsylvania German log cabin with two rooms and a loft, built in 1737, it's thought to be very much like the home Daniel Boone would have lived in while here. Then there's the vertical, water-powered sawmill. It's one of just three in the country like it that are still operable. It was built in the late eighteenth or early nineteenth centuries and moved to the homestead in 1972.

So there's a lot of history here, some of it tied directly to Daniel Boone, some tied to the history of the surrounding Oley Valley. It's all interesting.

Oh, and as for the coonskin cap? That's perhaps more fiction than fact. Boone preferred one made of beaver.

Miles and Directions

0.0 Start by going out the back door of the visitor center. Follow the path into the historic area. After 150 feet come to a smokehouse and, straight ahead, the Daniel Boone house. Explore those, then turn right into the path.

0.2 Arrive at the Boone barn, with Conestoga wagons and other artifacts.

0.3 The trail Ts. Go left, toward the Bertolet House.

0.4 The trail Ys. Go right to check out the Bertolet House and bakehouse. Then return to the trail, continuing in the same direction as before.

0.6 Pass a small stone building on the right.

0.7 Arrive at the old sawmill. It sits to the left; another stone building is on the right. The John and Samuel DeTurk cemetery is here, too. Check it all out, then walk to the dam.

0.8 Arrive at the dam overlook. Take a look at the lake from above, then walk down the steps to see the spillway from below. When done, return to the trail by the sawmill.

0.9 Cross over a bridge. Soon the trail meets the bus parking lot. Turn left and follow the gravel road.

1.0 See a bench on the left. Soon you're back at the Boone smokehouse. Turn right to the visitor center.

1.1 Arrive back at the start.

35 Hopewell Furnace National Historic Site and French Creek State Park

Start: At the visitor center
Distance: 3.3 miles
Type: Loop
Hiking time: 3 hours
Difficulty: Easy
Best season: April to October
Traffic: Hikers only
Fees and permits: None

Maps: Available at www.nps.gov/hofu/plan yourvisit/maps.htm
Trail contacts: Hopewell Furnace National Historic Site, 2 Mark Bird Ln., Elverson 19520; (610) 582-8773; www.nps.gov/hofu/index .htm. French Creek State Park, 843 Park Rd., Elverson 19520-9523; (610) 582-9680; www.dcnr.pa.gov/StateParks/FindAPark/ FrenchCreekStatePark/Pages/default.aspx.

Finding the trailhead: From Birdsboro, take Route 724 East for about half a mile. Turn right onto Route 345 South for 5 miles and turn right onto Mark Bird Lane. GPS: N40 12.401' / W75 46.427'

The Hike

Spend time in the main picnic area of French Creek State Park on a busy weekend and English will surely be just one of the languages you hear spoken. It draws a multicultural crowd.

This hike is equally diverse.

It follows gravel roads in places. Paved roads in others. Blacktopped sidewalks in spots. Then there are sections that run through the woods, sometimes on official trails, sometimes on homemade ones, all while alternately following stretches of hard-packed earth and swampy, muddy ground where beavers have been at work.

It's mostly a level walk, so it's pretty tame. That comes with one caveat, though. The state park was, as of this writing, redrawing its maps to better match the trails on the ground. So there are spots that are confusing. At the dam, for example, is a map that says "you are here." But it shows no trails at all. So be prepared to perhaps have to figure a few things out on your own.

Anyway, this hike starts at Hopewell Furnace National Historic Site and offers the chance to see old buildings and industrial structures. It's an interesting look at how a self-contained village would have appeared in the nineteenth century. Be sure to check out the visitor center. You'll learn a lot about what you're looking at, especially if you get the chance to take part in one of the frequent educational programs.

Next, this hike leads through adjacent French Creek State Park. Why is that noteworthy? Two reasons.

This "breast" wheel at Hopewell Furnace National Historic Site is the latest of several to have been in operation.

First, and historically speaking, French Creek—the stream, not the park that came later—is the reason Hopewell Furnace was established here. The creek was dammed to pool its water, with that in turn used to power the waterwheel at the furnace. One begat the other. The creek, of course, was later dammed again, this time to form Hopewell Lake. At 68 acres, it's the larger of two lakes in the park. It's the centerpiece of the facility now. This hike offers lots of good views of it.

Second, and in terms of recreation, French Creek is part of what's known as the "Hopewell Big Woods." That's the moniker given to this region at large because the woods here comprise the last large, unbroken woods in southeastern Pennsylvania. This hike winds through that.

From Hopewell, you'll travel to the dam, then turn to walk downstream of it. This is an attractive area. The larger spillway is a concrete affair, efficient if industrial looking. Next to it is the original smaller spillway, made of field stone. It may be antiquated, but it's very pretty, its white waterfall contrasting with green cattails.

The hike then follows the shore of the lake, on official trails for part of the way and on an unofficial one, too. The "unofficial" trail isn't blazed, but it's well worn, used by hikers and anglers alike. There's no mistaking it.

One section can be tricky, though. At around the 1.5 miles mark, the hike leads to a swampy backwater. Expect mud here. There's a wet seep—not a stream really, so much as a tiny finger-like extension of the lake—you'll need to cross on some logs. Someone's arranged them like a crude bridge, but the emphasis is on crude, so be careful where you step. Shortly thereafter, the hike leads to the boat launch.

From here you'll cross roads, zip across the corner of a parking lot or two, and follow gravel maintenance roads back to the dam. Then it's a case of retracing your steps to the starting point.

Uniquely, you can end this hike with dessert.

Hopewell is home to an apple orchard. In season, visitors can pick as many as they want—some bring long-handled pickers and baskets just for that reason—and pay by the pound at the visitor center. Picking is allowed from 9 a.m. to 4 p.m. on days the site is open.

Of course, you could pick and buy a few apples first and take them on the hike. The walk is a treat, so why not enjoy another while making it, right?

The History

It was the revolution that ultimately fed *the* revolution.

In the mid-1600s, colonists settling in American brought with them the skills and technology to build and operate blast furnaces. Such facilities made cast- and wrought-iron goods. That put Great Britain on edge.

America was vast, with seemingly unending forests, the very resource needed to make the charcoal that powered furnaces. The fear was that if the colonists started making their own products, British manufacturers and merchants would suffer. Indeed they did.

Laws limiting colonists to only making pig iron, or rough cast-iron bars, were put in place. The idea was that they would ship those to the British, who would turn them into finished goods—and sell them back to the colonists. The colonists routinely ignored all that, though, and by the start of the American Revolution were indeed making 15 percent of the world's iron goods.

That paid dividends. When the war for independence broke out, furnaces— Hopewell Furnace among them—went to work making cannon barrels, shot, and shell. Hopewell's furnace fired up for the first time in 1771. Between 1775 and 1778, under the guidance of ironmaster Mark Baird, it turned out 115 cannons for the Continental navy. It also made shot and shell, including some of the ordnance used at the final battle at Yorktown.

American victory didn't secure Hopewell's future, though. In fact, in some ways, it largely doomed it, at least for a while. A bankrupt Continental Congress never did

Visitors to the ironmaster's mansion at Hopewell Furnace can see how it would have been deco-rated during its heyday.

The village of Hopewell Furnace was home to many buildings, including cottages where workers lived.

pay Baird for supplying the militia. And when British goods flooded the new nation post-war, the furnace was sold at sheriff's sale in 1788.

The furnace continued to operate under several sets of owners in the succeeding century. That meant work for all kinds of people. It took miners to collect ore, fillers to pour charcoal into the furnace stack, founders to manage the furnace, colliers to tend the charcoal, farmers to feed everyone, teachers to educate children of workers, and others.

Hopewell Furnace operated from 1788 to 1808, went under again, then reopened—and enjoyed its greatest period of relative prosperity—from 1816 to 1831, under the direction of manager Clement Brooke. It made finished goods then, including lots of kitchen stoves. The financial "Panic of 1837" wreaked havoc with the operation, though. It enjoyed another, smaller, boom of sorts with the onset of the Civil War, but never again was as profitable.

It finally closed for good on June 15, 1883. It might have finally faded into oblivion for good were it not for the keen eye of an architect. Clement Brooke's descendants had sold the property to the federal government in 1935. The site was set to become the French Creek Recreational Demonstration Area, or basically a park for "poor urbanites." But Civilian Conservation Corps architect Gustavus Mang recognized the site for its historical value and put his crews to work stabilizing five of its original structures. Three years later, in 1938, the area became a National Historic Site.

Visitors today can see the original ironmaster's mansion—and tour a portion of it inside—as well as see homes where some of the furnace's families would have lived. There's a blacksmith shop and barn, too. The latter structure is full of period equipment, with each piece's purpose illustrated.

Of special note is the furnace's waterwheel. It provided the power to get the furnace to the needed 1,800 degrees Fahrenheit. The first waterwheel here was the "overshot" type, meaning water made the wheel turn by pouring over its top. It was eventually replaced by a "breast" wheel. Those work when water flows in halfway up the wheel and fills "buckets" on one side. That makes that side heavier than the other, and gravity causes it to turn.

A number of such wheels have turned in the cast house over time. The last original wheel went out of operation in 1883. Civilian Conservation Corps workers were restoring it in 1941 when World War II interrupted. That wheel was finally re-created in 1952. It was replaced again in 1988 and most recently in 2006. The new wheel is historically accurate, if not really old.

But you'd never know it. To stand in the lowest floor of the cast house, in cool shadow, surrounded by stone walls and mellow light filtered through a dusty haze, listening to the wheel groan gently as it rolls on and on, all in place, is to listen to history come alive, one slow turn at a time.

Miles and Directions

0.0 Start at the Hopewell Furnace visitor center. Turn left out the door and follow the sidewalk down to the historic area. Check out the charcoal area, ironmaster's mansion, and barn.

0.1 Go down the historic stone steps to the lower village area. Check out the waterwheel.

0.2 Horseshoe Trail is on the right. For now, continue straight to see the other historic buildings here, some of which you can enter. When done, return to this spot.

0.3 Turn left onto Horseshoe Trail/Big Woods Trail.

0.5 Go through a gate, leaving the historic property to go into French Creek State Park.

0.6 Arrive at the dam. Turn right to follow the blue blazes.

0.7 Cross a bridge downstream of the spillway.

0.8 The trail Ys. Go left. Soon the trail Ys again. Go left again, then left at another Y just a few feet on.

0.9 Cross a small bridge. Soon you cross a series of plank bridges over wet spots.

1.0 The trail Ys. Go left, keeping the lake on your left.

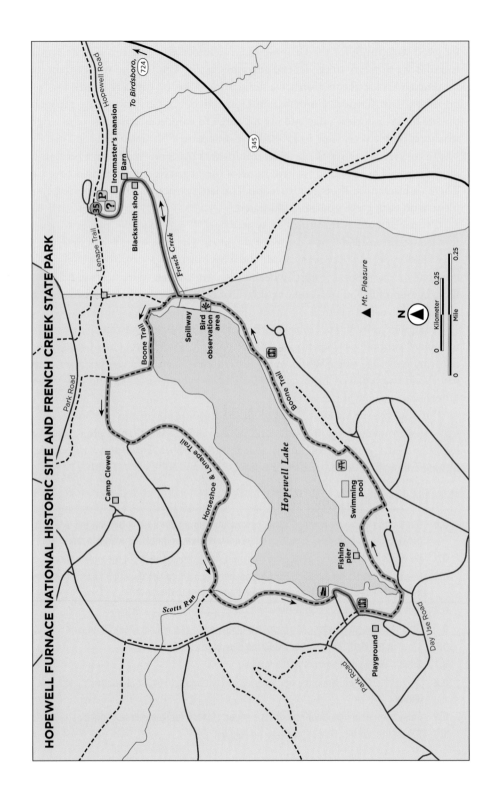

HOPEWELL FURNACE NATIONAL HISTORIC SITE AND FRENCH CREEK STATE PARK

To Birdsboro, 724

Hopewell Road

Ironmaster's mansion

Barn

Hopewell Road

345

Lenape Trail

35

P

?

Blacksmith shop

French Creek

Boone Trail

Spillway

Bird observation area

Park Road

Camp Clewell

Horseshoe & Lenape Trail

Hopewell Lake

Boone Trail

Scotts Run

Fishing pier

Swimming pool

Playground

Park Road

Day Use Road

Mt. Pleasant

N

Kilometer   0.25

0

Mile   0.25

0

1.1 Nice view of the lake on the left. Stay left when a grassy path goes off to the right.

1.2 The road leading to Camp Clewell goes to the right. Stay left.

1.3 To the right is Horseshoe Trail. Stay left on the grassy road.

1.4 Another lake view is to the left.

1.5 At this weedy end of the lake, look for evidence of beavers. Soon you cross a wet seep on logs. The trail here is grassy and indistinct, so pay attention to where you walk.

1.6 A lake view to the left offers some pretty views when the water lilies are in bloom.

1.8 Arrive at the picnic area and boat launch. Cross the parking lot and follow the sidewalk.

1.9 Cross the road again and follow the sidewalk past the restrooms. Follow the road into another parking lot, so the playground is on the right. The entrance to the outdoor classroom is on the left. Soon after, turn left into the woods to follow the blue blazes.

2.0 Cross a bridge, then hit a road. Turn left, go maybe 50 feet, then follow the trail back into the woods on the left.

2.1 Hit the path leading to the fishing pier on the left. Turn right, then make an immediate left to go up the hill toward the disc golf area.

2.2 Cross the road, with a basketball court on the left, to follow the blue blazes. Soon the road Ts. Go left. Enter French Creek's main picnic area and follow the path. The swimming pool is on the left.

2.4 Leave the picnic area behind and reenter a bit more woods.

2.5 Pass restrooms on the right.

2.7 Look on the left for some benches surrounded by informational panels identifying common birds and waterfowl.

2.8 Arrive back at the dam. Continue straight here, returning to Hopewell Furnace to close the loop, then retrace your steps back to the beginning.

3.3 Arrive back at the visitor center.

36 John James Audubon Center at Mill Grove

Start: At the John James Audubon House and Museum
Distance: 1 mile
Type: Loop
Hiking time: 1 to 1.5 hours
Difficulty: Easy to moderate
Best season: April to November
Traffic: Hikers only

Fees and permits: Museum admission is $5 adults, $4 seniors and students 6–17, free for children under 6
Maps: Available at http://johnjames.audubon.org/trails-mill-grove-0
Trail contact: John James Audubon Center at Mill Grove, 1201 Pawlings Rd., Audubon 19403; (610) 666-5593; http://johnjames.audubon.org

Finding the trailhead: From Phoenixville, follow Route 23 East. Turn left onto Pawlings Road and follow it 2.9 miles to the entrance. GPS: N40 07.382' / W75 26.646'

The Hike

There are 9 miles of trails to explore at the John James Audubon Center at Mill Grove. They're a series of interconnected loops, so you can mix and match and dodge and weave to create whatever combination you like.

This particular hike is officially 1 mile long, but expect to cover just a bit more ground. Why? It starts at the Audubon house. But because you can't drive right up to it, figure on walking a few hundred yards to get to the "start" from the parking area.

From the house this hike winds around the property and finishes at what will be, when it opens, a brand-new museum on the other end. So it begins and ends with a couple of highlights.

Pay close attention on your tour of the house. Audubon's home was built decades before he ever got there, in 1762. That makes it more than 250 years old. It's undergone changes and renovations in that time, as you'd expect. But hints of the original home remain. Can you find them? There may be two or three original yellow pine boards on the second floor. The fireplace surround, also on the second floor, is thought to be the only original woodwork. The gray-green paint in the lower two cupboards to the right of the fireplace may be original; at least it's the oldest paint in the house. And some of the window glass is old.

Once you leave the house, you'll see some birds inside an enclosure. They're some of the resident mascots, owls maintained in captivity because they're unable to be returned to the wild for various reasons.

This hike then winds past some old structures—a pump house and foundations related to its mining past—and provides views of Perkiomen Creek. It's entirely wooded along this stretch, with some short but relatively steep walking down to the creek and back up.

The John James Audubon house and museum

The hike also takes you to a bird observation blind. It's a three-sided structure with holes in the front that allows for hidden watching of birds, butterflies, and other wildlife. If you want to make the best use of it, hike early and late in the day, to be in position when wildlife gets active.

One last thing to be aware of when visiting and walking? Mill Grove is a popular site for weddings and other events. There may be times when you'll share the grounds with such gatherings.

The History

He had unusual knowledge, skill, physical prowess, talent, artistry, and woodsmanship, there's no denying any of that. But he clearly knew how to play to a crowd, too. The best salesmen always do.

John James Audubon was a master naturalist who—more than a century and a half after his death—remains as synonymous with birds as anyone who's ever walked the planet. Born in Haiti in 1785, he grew up in France. His parents worried he'd be

One of the rooms in the John James Audubon house museum contains a collection of birds' eggs that Audubon himself put together.

conscripted into Napoleon's army, so in 1803 they shipped him off to America to care for the 284-acre family property at Mill Grove.

It was his first home in America.

The idea was that he would learn to manage the estate while pursuing a career in mining. Mill Grove had substantial deposits of ore, especially lead and copper. Audubon, however, had other thoughts, or at the very least pursued other interests. "Mill Grove ever to me was a blessed spot . . ." he would write later. "Hunting, fishing, drawing and music occupied my every moment; cares I knew not, and cared naught about them. . . . I was as happy as happy could be."

His time here was not long. He lived at Mill Grove only until 1806. But those were formative years. While at Mill Grove, Audubon delved deeply into the study of birds. He spent long hours in the woods, observing their movements, coloration, and habitats. Then he used what he learned to forever set himself apart.

For starters, he launched the nation's first experiments in bird banding. Most notably, though, he developed a unique way of positioning birds on a wire armature—or skeletal framework of his own design—so that they looked lifelike. That allowed him to paint the birds, complete with background details, in a way that no one ever had before. His works are not only largely scientific in their accuracy, but fine art in their execution. They were, and remain, stunning. That's why *Birds of America*—his later book, with 453 life-size paintings—cemented his legacy.

All the while, he made quite the impression.

He met his wife, Lucy Bakewell, at Mill Grove. The daughter of an adjacent landowner, it's perhaps no wonder she fell in love. Audubon was a man's man, but a handsome one, too. "He was an admirable marksman, an expert swimmer, a clever rider, possessed of great activity (and) prodigious strength, and was notable for the elegance of his figure and the beauty of his features, and he aided nature by a careful attendance to his dress," said his brother-in-law, William Bakewell. "Besides other accomplishments he was musical, a good fencer, danced well, and has some acquaintance with legerdemain tricks, worked in hair and could plait willow baskets."

And he could sell a story.

Audubon was a man who liked to dress well. He often preferred formal French attire. But when he traveled to Europe to speak about his ornithological work, he played the part of an American frontiersman. He'd dress in rugged clothes, to better meet the expectations and stimulate the adoration of his fans.

Fortunately, one of the families who bought his home at Mill Grove recognized his importance historically. The Wetherill family purchased Mill Grove in 1813. They forever maintained its connection to Audubon, even going so far as to have the name of the surrounding community changed from Shannonville to Audubon.

Still later, in 1951, Herbert and Mary Wetherill sold the home and property to Montgomery County. It became the Audubon Shrine and Wildlife Sanctuary. The Audubon Society took over operations in 2004. Today the home is listed on the National Register of Historic Places and is a National Historic Landmark.

Visitors can see some of Audubon's works and even check out a re-creation of his room, which was regularly decorated with everything from paintings to drying bird eggs to stuffed squirrels to preserved fish. There's a room full of murals here, too. Between 1954 and 1956, artist George Harding and an apprentice, John Hanlen, painted several walls to showcase Audubon, his works, and his travels.

Still more is coming. A new museum is scheduled to open on-site in the fall of 2018. That will further help tell the tale of Audubon and his time at Mill Grove.

Miles and Directions

0.0 Start at the Audubon house. Turn left out the front door and go down the steps, past the owl enclosure, onto the green-blazed John's Trail.

0.1 The trail Ys at the base of the steps. Go left. Soon the trail Ys again by a bench. Go right and enter the woods by the ruins of an old pump house.

0.2 By a set of steps leading to Perkiomen Creek, turn right to go up the hill. A little farther the trail Ys by a sign about mallards. Go left.

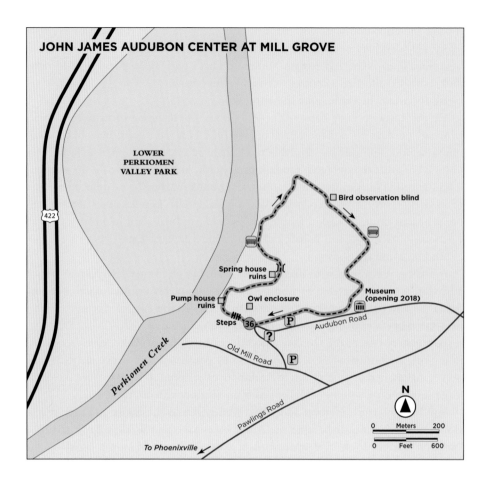

JOHN JAMES AUDUBON CENTER AT MILL GROVE

0.3 Come to a trail intersection with two right turns and one left. Go left and cross the bridge, then turn uphill. Soon the trail Ys. Go left.

0.4 Come to a bench overlooking the river. Notice an overlook on the left. Go right up the hill, where it gets steep. Then the trail Ys. Go left, around a big boulder, and cross the bridge.

0.5 The trail Ys. Go left. Then the trail Ys again. Go right this time.

0.6 The trail butts up against Audubon Loop Trail, at a bird observation blind. Check out the blind—it's a good spot to see birds and butterflies—then go left to follow the orange-blazed Bird Habitat Trail.

0.7 Notice a bench on the left. Continue straight.

0.8 The trail comes to a dilapidated bench on the edge of the field. A trail straight ahead enters the woods. Instead, turn left toward the evergreens.

0.9 Turn right on the dirt path/road toward the new museum, set to open in fall of 2018. After a hundred yards or so, arrive at the museum. Check it out, then turn right back toward the parking lot and Audubon house.

1.0 Arrive back at the Audubon house to close the loop.

37 Norristown Farm Park

Start: At the park office
Distance: 2.6 miles
Type: Loop
Hiking time: 1.5 to 2 hours
Difficulty: Easy to moderate
Best season: March to November
Traffic: Hikers, cyclists, and occasional mainte-nance and farm vehicles

Fees and permits: None
Maps: Available at www.dcnr.state.pa.us/cs/groups/public/documents/document/dcnr_003561.pdf
Trail contact: Norristown Farm Park, 2500 Upper Farm Rd., Norristown 19403; (610) 270-0215; www.dcnr.state.pa.us/stateparks/findapark/norristown

Finding the trailhead: From King of Prussia, follow Route 202 North for 3.4 miles. Take a left onto Elm Street and go 0.4 mile, then a right onto Stanbridge Street for 0.25 mile, and then another left onto Sterigere Street. Go 1 mile and turn right onto North Whitehall Road. Go 1.2 miles and turn right onto West Germantown Pike. Go less than half a mile and turn right onto Upper Farm Road. Follow that to the park office. GPS: N40 08.737' / W75 20.538'

The Hike

There was a time when to stroll around a farm in southeastern Pennsylvania, pass-ing fields of growing crops while seeing all kinds of wildlife, would have been a common thing.

No, seriously.

It's OK if that seems hard to believe. After all, that time was long, long ago. This area of the state—home to Philadelphia, the nation's fifth-largest city, and plenty of suburban sprawl—is densely populated and heavily developed. Agricultural fields have been replaced with housing plans, shopping centers, businesses, and more. That's just the reality.

Except for here. Norristown Farm Park has survived. It's an oasis of green and, most interestingly, still a working farm. That makes it unlike any other facility in the state park system.

Fittingly, the hike starts at the park office and visitor center, which was once the "milk house." There's a dairy barn here, too, along with some impressive silos. The hike follows the edges of cornfields in places.

Watch for eastern bluebirds along the way. Their brilliant plumage really stands out against the green. Keep an eye out for white-tailed deer, too. At dawn and dusk especially they're common around those same fields. In fact, be on the lookout for wildlife in general. The park is said to be home to 71 species of mammals, fish, reptiles, and amphibians. There are 173 kinds of birds, too, along with 89 tree species and 216 varieties of flowers.

Silos dominate the skyline at Norristown Farm Park.

The variety of habitats is the reason. This hike winds between fields, along wood edges, and past streams. A habitat improvement project underway in one area should only make the park more attractive to wildlife.

As for history, this walk offers the chance to see lots of that, as well. Not only is the farmland itself historic, but there are some old buildings—the remains of the Happy Hollow Cottage and a spring house, as well as the still-standing Getty Cottage and Shannon Mansion—worth checking out.

Just be sure to pack sunscreen and water. On those portions of the hike where the path runs under full sun, it can be hot. If you're not careful, you might wind up with a farmer's tan.

The History

Four hundred consecutive years. Maybe five. Maybe more. That's how long what is now Norristown Farm Park has been actively farmed. How's that for staying power?

The Lenni Lenape, a tribe of Native Americans, was here first—or, at least, was the first with a name to take up residence. The women farmed the land while the men hunted. European settlers came next—the Dutch initially, then the Swedes. Sometimes the two cultures got along. As often as not, they didn't.

Peace didn't really come until William Penn arrived with his Quaker followers in 1682. Penn—granted what is Pennsylvania, or "Penn's Sylvania," by Great Britain's King

Norristown Farm Park remains a working farm, with fields of corn a common scene.

Charles II in payment for a debt—explained his religious principles to the natives. He didn't stop there, though. Penn took the extra step of asking their permission to share the land they called home. He also educated himself about them as a people. He learned their language, participated in their festivals and games, and lived among them.

He only spent five years in the state, with that broken into two time periods. He was here from 1682 to 1684 and then again from 1699 to 1701. But his influence was large.

Sadly, it didn't last. Penn's son sold the land to Isaac Norris, for whom Norristown is named. He in turn sold it to James Shannon, who in 1764 built the Shannon Mansion that still stands here. Other buildings followed, some of which you can still see. Happy Hollow Cottage—it's just ruins now, though there are plans to restore it—followed in 1800. The Getty Cottage was built near the mansion in 1802. Erected that year, too, was the Castner House. It's in the park, but not on this hike. Be sure to drive over and check it out, however. Built by shoemaker, or "cordwainer," John Castner, it features a stone with that date engraved, surrounded by a circle of brick. Below that is a boot-shaped stone. It's very nice.

All the while, the park never went out of operation as a farm. In fact, farming was at one point valued—and specifically maintained—for its healing qualities. That's one of the most unique parts of Norristown's history.

In 1876, Pennsylvania lawmakers allocated money to buy land for construction of state hospitals. Norristown State Hospital—a "lunatic" asylum in the harsh wording

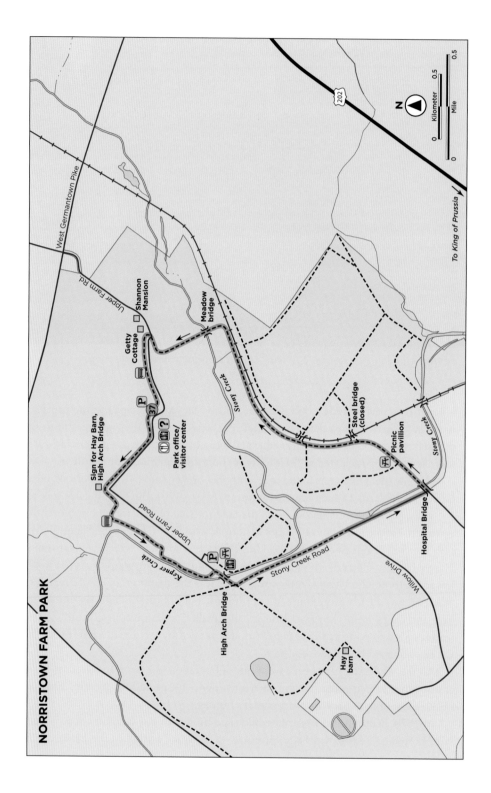

NORRISTOWN FARM PARK

of the day—was established. Male and female patients started arriving by 1880, with 4,000 of them there at one point, living in buildings connected by underground tunnels. They underwent all manner of treatments. Some seem crude today: electroshock therapy and lobotomies, for example. In time, though, the hospital was renowned as a state-of-the-art facility.

It's still in operation, though it's undergone plenty of changes over the years. One of those, interestingly enough, involves farming. For decades, all the way up to 1975, patients at the hospital worked Norristown Farm Park. They grew crops and raised livestock, sometimes working under the guidance of farm managers in training. The thinking was that the work helped patients recover more quickly, while also allowing them to produce some of the food they ate. Working alongside them sometimes were conscientious objectors. Men and women who could not take part in military service because of their religious beliefs put in time here under the guidelines of an "alternative service program."

Both of those programs have come to an end. But farming goes on. Roughly 450 of Norristown's 690 acres are still actively worked by a tenant. At this point, what else would you expect?

Miles and Directions

0.0 Start at the park office. Follow the sidewalk to the parking lot, then turn left and follow the paved trail. There are fields left and right.

0.4 The trail Ts. Go left and follow the sign for the Hay Barn and High Arch Bridge.

0.5 Look for a bench on the right, then another just a short ways ahead.

0.6 See picnic tables and parking lot #2 on the left.

0.7 Overlook of Kepner Creek on the right.

0.8 Near parking lot #3, cross over High Arch Bridge.

0.9 Come to a four-way intersection of Upper Farm Road and Stony Creek Road. Turn left onto Stony Creek.

1.1 Go straight through the gate.

1.2 Reach another gate. Willow Drive is on the right. Stay straight on Stony Creek.

1.4 The trail meets a four-way intersection near the boiler plant. Turn left and cross the bridge to follow Lower Farm Road.

1.6 Pass a picnic table and pavilion on the left.

1.7 See more cornfields on the left.

1.8 Pass a closed bridge on the right.

2.0 Notice railroad tracks on the right. Stay straight, continuing past a restroom.

2.1 Cross Meadow Bridge.

2.3 The trail meets Upper Farm Road and Ys by Getty Cottage and the Shannon Mansion. Cross the street, check out these two buildings, then turn left to follow the paved trail along the Millennium Grove.

2.5 Pass a bench on the right.

2.6 Arrive back at the park office to close the loop.

38 Washington Crossing State Park and Delaware Canal State Park

Start: At the Route 532 parking lot area, near the lagoon
Distance: 4.7 miles (one-way)
Type: Car shuttle (or out and back)
Hiking time: 3 hours
Difficulty: Easy
Best season: March to October
Traffic: Hikers and bicyclists
Fees and permits: None
Maps: Available at www.docs.dcnr.pa.gov/ cs/groups/public/documents/document/ dcnr_20031894.pdf, www.dcnr.pa.gov/ StateParks/FindAPark/DelawareCanalState Park/Pages/Maps.aspx, and www.fodc.org/ visit-the-canal/towpath-trail
Trail contacts: Washington Crossing State Park, 1112 River Rd., Washington Crossing 18977; (215) 493-4076; www.dcnr.pa.gov/State Parks/FindAPark/WashingtonCrossing HistoricPark/Pages/default.aspx. Delaware Canal State Park, 11 Lodi Hill Rd., Upper Black Eddy 18972-9540; (610) 982-5560; www.dcnr.pa.gov/StateParks/FindAPark/ DelawareCanalStatePark/Pages/default.aspx.

Finding the trailhead: From Norristown, take I-276/PA Turnpike East toward New Jersey for 17.8 miles. Take exit 351 onto Route 1 toward Philadelphia/Trenton. Merge onto Route 1 North toward Morrisville for 7.2 miles, then merge onto I-95 North toward Trenton. Go 6 miles and take exit 51 toward New Hope, then turn left onto Taylorsville Road. Go 2.9 miles and then go right on Route 532 for 0.3 mile, then enter the park by making a left at Newton Gate, on General Saint Claire Road. GPS: N40 17.455' / W74 52.582'

The Hike

The Delaware Canal Towpath stretches for 60 miles, but gains only 165 feet in elevation in all that way. So yeah, it's pretty flat. But to walk it anywhere is an out-and-back affair. There are no opportunities to do loops unless you travel some fairly busy roads.

It's worth the effort, though. There's plenty of history to see canal-wise, while the path connects the upper and lower sections of Washington Crossing State Park.

Just expect company. On nice weekends the trail is busy with hikers, nature photographers, joggers, bicyclists, and—sometimes to the side, in the canal itself— kayakers. Indeed, the sounds that often break the silence are cries of "bikes on the left" or "coming up on the left" as cyclists and runners go by. Listen for others, too, when going under the bridges that cross the towpath in many places. The sight lines are blocked just enough that a cyclist or hiker coming one way or the other without blowing a horn or twinkling a bell or calling out or at least paying attention can be a hazard.

Along the way, look for historic canal remnants. Stone markers on the right going north—they're level with the ground, so look for them in the grass—mark each

A plaque and headstones mark the spot where New York Artillery captain James Moore and many unknown soldiers of the American Revolution are buried.

mile. To the left and right, too, you'll see stone walls marking where there were once bridges or other structures.

Note the lock on the left at about mile 4.1 on this hike. Locktenders would raise and lower canal boats here by manipulating water levels to account for differences in elevation. The highest lock on this canal raised boats 17.3 feet; this one had to do just a fraction of that.

Later the trail takes you past the grave site of New York Artillery captain James Moore. He's buried alongside many unknown soldiers of the American Revolution who died here during Washington's 1776–1777 encampment.

Finally, the trail takes you to a picnic area at the lower section of Washington Crossing State Park. There are several historic buildings to see on the left. Most notable is the Thomson-Neely House. On the National Register of Historic Places, it was built in phases starting in 1740 and ending in 1788. In between, in 1776–1777, it housed wounded Continental Army soldiers.

The Delaware Canal Towpath stretches for 60 miles between Easton and Bristol and connects the two sections of Washington Crossing State Park.

Also here is the Thompson-Neely gristmill (and, if you want to drive to them later, Bowman's Hill Wildflower Preserve and Bowman's Hill Tower, a 125-foot-tall tower built in 1931 to offer views of the countryside). Check out the house and gristmill, then return to the start.

Back at the start, follow one of the roads through the park picnic area—or drive a quarter mile or so on Route 532—to the upper portion of Washington Crossing State Park. That's where you'll find the visitor center, the stone marking the approximate site of Washington's crossing of the Delaware, and several other old buildings. McConkey's Ferry Inn served as a guard post and is where Washington ate dinner prior to the Christmas Day battle in Trenton. There are 1820s- and 1830s-era homes that housed a blacksmith and other craftsmen, as well as the home of the founders of Taylorsville.

It's at this end of the park that you can see some living history on occasion, such as open hearth cooking demonstrations, among other things. Most famously, on Christmas day and usually once the week before, costumed reenactors cross the Delaware in the same kind of Durham boats Washington and his army would have used. The boats are bigger than you might think, though using them on a river cold enough to be carrying big chunks of ice downstream would have been incredibly dangerous.

There's often one on display at all times, so if you can't be here for a crossing, you can at least check it out.

The History

Never will you be able to check out two such distinct historic sites—so important for such different reasons—in one spot as you will here.

Washington Crossing State Park and Delaware Canal State Park are tied together in eastern Pennsylvania, right on the border with New Jersey. One is the base from which George Washington may have saved the nation; the other is a narrow path that helped bind the new nation together.

First, Washington Crossing. December 1776 was a dark time for the Continental Army. The mood of the country was as bleak as the weather. Just months after the Declaration of Independence was read in Philadelphia to cheers, there were fears the city would fall into the hands of the British. They'd already forced Washington out of New York. Much of New Jersey and Rhode Island then fell to the enemy, too. Washington's army was now on the banks of the Delaware River, cold, hungry, ill, and dispirited. What's more, a lot of his men were scheduled to leave, as their enlistments expired early in 1777.

Washington—whose nature was to go on the attack anyway—needed a victory to turn the tide. This is where he got it.

He was reinforced with 2,000 men on December 20. More joined him near McConkey's Ferry on Christmas Day. That was a day typically set aside by armies of the time for peace. A desperate Washington broke with tradition. Under cover of darkness, in the face of driving snow, sleet, and rain, he ferried 2,400 men, cannons, and horses across the icy Delaware. It all took much longer than expected, until 4 a.m. Some supporting troops never did get across. Everything was going wrong, and one more defeat—especially were Washington himself to be killed or captured—would likely have ended the Revolution and changed the course of history.

Still, Washington—committed to the bold and daring raid—attacked at 8 a.m. The move was a stunning success. His troops captured many Hessian soldiers and, just as importantly, their supplies. They carried all that back across the river with them. Additional attacks followed, with Washington crossing the river two more times, but the first successful attack was the game changer. It was that pivotal. It gave the army hope, convinced some soldiers to stay in the ranks and others to join, and convinced patriots across the young nation to dig in and stay the course.

Today a marker in Washington Crossing State Park marks the approximate spot from which Washington launched his offensive.

A statue of George Washington stands outside the visitor center at Washington Crossing State Park, not far from where a stone marks his approximate crossing of the Delaware on Christmas Day, 1776.

Very nearby lies Delaware Canal State Park. This is a park shaped unlike any other. It's 60 miles long, yet only a few dozen yards wide in most places. Its original purpose is the reason for the unusual layout.

In the early 1800s, America was expanding rapidly, not only geographically, but also in terms of population. With the development of railroads still years away, there was a real need for a fast, reliable way to move goods around the country. Cities, especially, needed raw materials, from food to coal to wood. The canal era was the result.

Pennsylvania had several. This particular canal was known, officially, as the Delaware Division of the Pennsylvania Canal. Its main purpose was to make possible the movement of coal from Easton to Philadelphia.

It took work and money to bring it to life. Construction—ultimately costing $1.43 million—began in 1827. It involved digging not just a trench, but building ten aqueducts, twenty-one waste gates, eight stop gates, nine dams, twenty-seven overflows, 125 bridges, two guard locks, one weigh lock, one outlet lock, and one tide lock. Construction finally wrapped up in 1832. And then . . . business started to drop off.

It took a few decades. But by the late 1860s, railroads were already starting to supplant canals as the chief way of moving goods. Each and every year thereafter, things got tougher and tougher. The Delaware Canal stayed afloat—pun intended—until 1931, but it was losing money long before then.

Fortunately, it didn't pass into history. It became a state park in 1940 and today is the only remaining, continuously intact canal of the great towpath canal building era of the early and mid–nineteenth century. It retains almost all of its features as they existed during its century of commercial operation. Visitors can see locks, aqueducts, historic towns, and more along its path.

Congress officially recognized the canal's importance to the economic development of America by establishing the Delaware & Lehigh National Heritage Corridor in 1988. What's more, the canal is a Registered National Historic Landmark, and its towpath is a National Recreation Trail.

So how's that for a combination? The launching point for a battle that saved America and a pathway that helped build it thereafter, all together.

Miles and Directions

0.0 Start at the parking off General Saint Claire Road, by the lagoon. Follow the dirt path through the grass to the Delaware Canal Towpath. After a few hundred feet you connect to the towpath. Go right.

0.6 Walk beneath the first of several bridges.

0.8 Notice homes on both side of the trail. There are sections that are surrounded by residences, sections bounded by agricultural fields, and sections with just woods.

0.9 Notice how the remnants of old canal walls have been incorporated into homes, often as patios.

1.3 Go beneath another bridge.

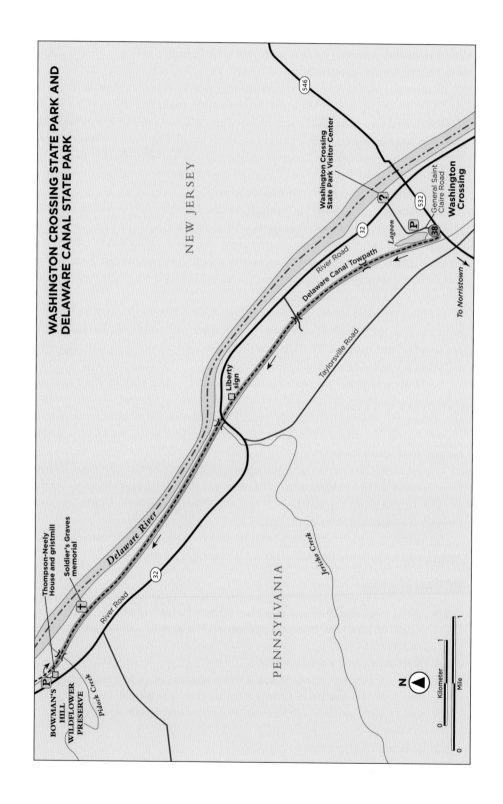

WASHINGTON CROSSING STATE PARK AND DELAWARE CANAL STATE PARK

NEW JERSEY

PENNSYLVANIA

Delaware River

Pidcock Creek

Jericho Creek

River Road

River Road

Delaware Canal Towpath

Taylorsville Road

Lagoon

Liberty sign

BOWMAN'S HILL WILDFLOWER PRESERVE

Thompson-Neely House and gristmill

Soldier's Graves memorial

Washington Crossing State Park Visitor Center

Washington Crossing

General Saint Claire Road

To Norristown

32

32

546

532

38

N

Kilometer

Mile

0   1

0   1

1.5 Impressive trees, some 4 feet in diameter, line the trail to the right.

2.0 A sign on the right honors those who fought for liberty.

2.2 The trail crosses beneath Route 32, then goes over a wooden bridge.

2.6 Starting about here, the trail drops off steeply to the Delaware River on the right in this section.

3.7 Cross another bridge.

4.1 Look on the left for remnants of an old lock. These were used to raise and lower boats to account for changes in elevation.

4.3 Come to the Soldier's Graves memorial. Turn right here to check out the memorial, then return to the trail.

4.6 Arrive at another bridge.

4.7 Hit the road. Go right to reach the parking lot, left to visit the Thompson-Neely House. Finish here if doing a shuttle; otherwise turn around and retrace your steps to the start for a 9.4-mile hike.

39 Valley Forge National Historical Park

Start: At the visitor center

Distance: 5.2 miles

Type: Loop

Hiking time: 4 hours

Difficulty: Easy

Best season: April to October

Traffic: Hikers and bicyclists, with automobiles adjacent to the trail

Fees and permits: None

Maps: Available at www.nps.gov/vafo/plan yourvisit/maps.htm

Trail contact: Valley Forge National Historical Park, 1400 North Outer Line Dr., King of Prussia 19406; (610) 783-1000; www.nps.gov/vafo/index.htm

Finding the trailhead: From Phoenixville, take Route 23 east for about 6 miles. Turn right onto North Outer Line Drive and go 0.4 mile, then left again to stay on that road. Go less than 0.1 mile and turn left to the visitor center. GPS: N40 06.071' / W75 25.361'

The Hike

Joseph Plumb Martin joined the Continental Army in 1776 as a 15-year-old boy. He served through the entire length of the war and left it in 1783 a 22-year-old man. Along the way, he was one of the few common soldiers to write about his experiences. His notes provide invaluable and colorful details about what it was like to be a Revolutionary War soldier. The hike here follows—for the most part—a trail named in his honor.

Begin at the Valley Forge Visitor Center. It's home to a tremendous amount of information, with informational panels and exhibits, not to mention a life-size George Washington mounted on a white horse. You enter the center on one floor, then exit it on one higher. Be sure to check out the theater for the movie shown there.

From there, this hike takes you past several of the more interesting points in the park. Understand that you'll be walking in direct sun almost the entire way, though. It can get hot, too. Be sure to pack sunscreen and water. There's enough to see to make the effort worthwhile, though.

For example, you'll get to explore reconstructed huts of Gen. Peter Muhlenberg's Virginia brigade. There's also an example of one of the earthen works soldiers like those under Muhlenberg's command defended.

The hike also takes you to the National Memorial Arch. Congress authorized its construction to memorialize Washington and his soldiers in 1910. It was completed in 1917. It stood as is for the next eighty years, until deteriorating conditions mandated repairs. Funded in part by the Freemasons—Washington himself was one—the work involved welding 9 tons of structural steel into the top, among other things. It's an impressive structure, one you can walk up to and around.

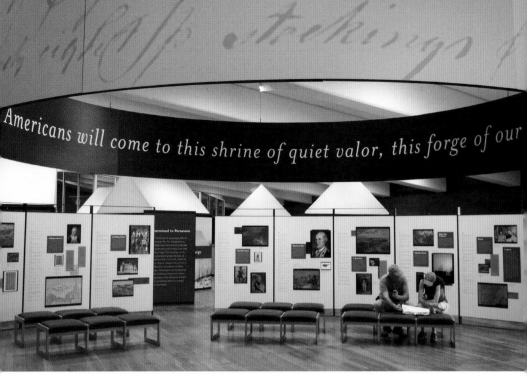

Any hike at Valley Forge National Historical Park should start at the visitor center, which offers a wealth of information about the grounds.

Other highlights are Redoubts #3 and #4, Artillery Park, the Baron von Steuben statue, Varnum's Quarters, Washington Memorial Chapel, Maurice Stephens House, and the Patriots of African Descent Monument.

This hike as described here makes a loop. To walk the entire Martin Trail would also require doing two additional out-and-back legs. We don't walk them—together, they add 2.1 miles to the trip—but at least one leads to an absolute must-see aspect of the park, so be sure to drive to it.

Located off West Inner Line Drive is the site of Washington's headquarters during the Valley Forge encampment. Ironmaster Isaac Potts, one of the owners of the actual "valley forge" iron furnace, had built a house here, sometimes between 1768 and 1770. His aunt, Deborah Hewes, was renting it at the time Washington appeared. Washington—rather than take over the house, as was British practice—paid 100 pounds in Pennsylvania currency for its use.

As one ranger pointed out while we were here, it is in some ways the most historic home in America. When you think about the precarious state of the fledgling nation that winter and spring, and the patriots who spent time here—Washington and his lieutenants—and the decisions that were made, it's truly hallowed ground.

It's possible to walk through the house and explore the rooms. It seems cozy enough for one family. When Washington was here, though, it was likely crowded, as up to twenty-five of his staff lived with him here at a time.

The National Memorial Arch is an imposing structure at Valley Forge.

There's some other history here, too. Signs note that in September 1777 the only real fighting that took place around Valley Forge occurred. The British burned the actual "valley forge" furnace and the supplies stored there, killing one Continental soldier in doing so.

To see all that's here, even if you drive, means walking about a mile or so, counting the distance from the parking lot to more soldier huts, a statue of Washington, the Potts house, and a working train station.

Just be sure to visit, however you get here.

The History

It was not the coldest encampment of the Revolutionary War, as common myth holds. But it was savagely brutal nonetheless.

In the fall of 1777 the Continental Congress was forced to flee Philadelphia just head of the British, who would go on to establish their own winter quarters in the city. Those Brits lived relatively well, too. The enlisted men had to deal with disease, but at least got to stay in warehouses or barracks. Officers billeted in commandeered private homes.

The Americans, meanwhile, had things significantly worse.

Washington took his troops to Valley Forge on December 19. He chose the site because of its strategic importance. It was on a hill, close enough to Philadelphia to keep an eye on the enemy, but far enough away to be out of reach of a surprise attack. It also allowed the Americans to protect the Congress, civilian refugees, and the limited supplies they had.

From day one, though, Washington's situation was critical. Many of his soldiers were sick; all were hungry. Supplies were few. Washington wrote a desperate letter to Congress early in winter, saying that if he wasn't resupplied soon, his army might "starve, dissolve or disperse."

Little help was forthcoming, and the army adapted as best it could. Men who lived in tents initially were soon put to work building huts—each 14 by 16 feet and sleeping twelve enlisted men—for shelter from the weather. Latrines were established, rules were put in place requiring men to wash hands and faces daily, and nurses tended to the sick and wounded. Water was treated with vinegar and whiskey to purify it.

Still, over the coming months, the Americans would suffer severely. A poorly organized supply system, inflated prices, and a devaluation of American currency all conspired to make Valley Forge a place of want and misery. Men often went days without meat or vegetables. Diseases like influenza, typhus, typhoid, and dysentery claimed many, with the worst mortality actually seen when winter abated and warmer spring temperatures settled in. At one point, more than 4,000 Americans were considered unfit for duty. By June, when the army moved on, one in ten men had perished, typically from disease.

Still, the troops were far from beaten. Hessian officer Major Baumeister reported the Americans are "bold, unyielding and fearless" and "by no means conquered."

The home of ironmaster Isaac Potts served as George Washington's headquarters at Valley Forge. It's open for tours.

Indeed, the encampment has rightly come to symbolize both the perseverance and fortitude of the Colonial Army and the nation that was to come.

Gen. Friedrich Baron von Steuben trained the formerly resistant, independent-minded colonial soldiers in drill and tactics. They learned, for example, how to execute and defend against bayonet charges. His model company in turn trained others, leaving the army more ready to go on the offensive than ever before. At the same time, Nathaniel Greene took over as quartermaster. He organized what had been a chaotic system and, in the end, outfitted 15,000 men in ways they hadn't been before.

Common men learned to live and work together here, too. Valley Forge was home to not only soldiers, but women and children, too. They came from rich and poor, representing all kinds of occupations. There were Protestants, but also Catholics and Jews. There were people of African, American Indian, French, English, Dutch, German, Irish, Italian, Polish, Portuguese, Prussian, Scottish, Spanish, and Swedish descent. They all survived together through guile and ingenuity. Faced with cruel hardship, troops figured out ways to overcome. Merit, not background, proved out. Determination was supreme.

All those developments, together with a new alliance with France—the first recognition of the United States by a foreign power—left Washington's troops organized, prepared, and ready for battle. "Naked and starving as they are, we cannot enough

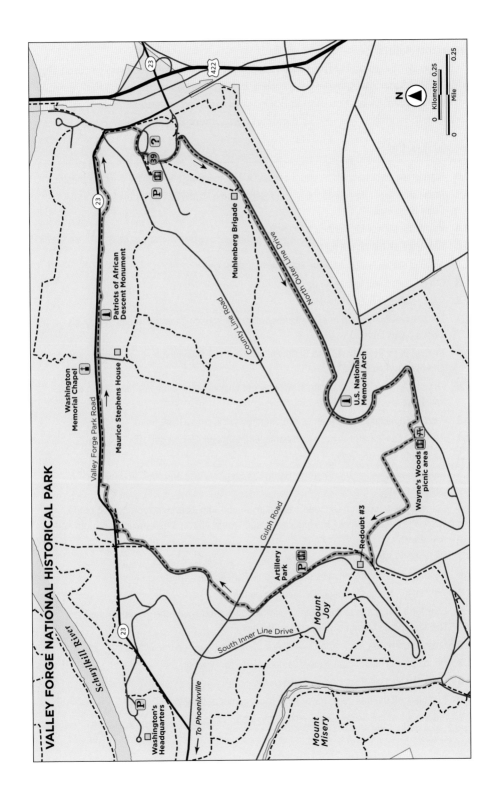

VALLEY FORGE NATIONAL HISTORICAL PARK

Schuylkill River

Washington Memorial Chapel

Patriots of African Descent Monument

Maurice Stephens House

Washington's Headquarters

Valley Forge Park Road

County Line Road

North Outer Line Drive

Muhlenberg Brigade

U.S. National Memorial Arch

Wayne's Woods picnic area

Redoubt #3

Artillery Park

Gulph Road

South Inner Line Drive

Mount Joy

Mount Misery

To Phoenixville

23

422

39

N

0   Kilometer 0.25

0   Mile   0.25

admire the incomparable patience and fidelity of the soldiery," Washington wrote of his men that winter.

The war would go on for five more years, so plenty more suffering was to come. But the legendary American spirit—born earlier, in other engagements—was here refined, hardened, and sharpened. Freedom and self-governance were national goals that would be realized, in large part because of the defining moment that was Valley Forge.

Miles and Directions

0.0 Start at the back door of the visitor center. Go left, following the walkway, past the theater.

0.1 At the stop sign turn right to follow the Joseph Plumb Martin Trail as it parallels North Outer Line Drive.

0.4 Reach the huts of Muhlenberg's Brigade.

1.0 Pass another hut on the right.

1.1 Arrive at the roundabout for the National Memorial Arch.

1.3 Cross Gulph Road to stay on the trail.

1.6 Pass additional huts on the left.

1.7 The trail leaves the road near the Pennsylvania Columns to enter the woods at Wayne's Woods picnic area.

2.4 The trail Ts by Redoubt #3 and South Outer Line Road. Going left leads to Knox's Quarters. Turn right and go up the hill.

2.6 Arrive at Artillery Park on the right. Walk over to check out the cannons, then return to the trail. There are restrooms here, too.

2.9 Pass two huts on the left. After several hundred yards cross Gulph Road.

3.1 Pass a "redan," or arrow-shaped embankment, with cannons on the left.

3.3 Three huts sit on the right.

3.5 Reach the statue for Gen. Friedrich Baron von Steuben, who organized and trained colonial troops.

3.6 Come to the house that Gen. James Varnum shared with its owners for a portion of the Valley Forge encampment. His brigade included many African American soldiers, both free and slaves.

3.7 Redoubt #1 sits on the left.

3.8 Another hut is on the left, across Valley Forge Park Road.

3.9 Washington Memorial Chapel Cemetery is on the left.

4.0 Look for a Daughters of the American Revolution monument on the ground on the right. The Washington Memorial Chapel is on the left.

4.2 Cross the driveway leading to the Maurice Stephens House on the right.

4.3 On the right is the monument for "Patriots of African Descent."

5.0 Cross County Line Road and continue uphill.

5.1 Turn right, off the trail, to go toward the visitor center parking lot.

5.2 Arrive back at the visitor center to close the loop.

40 Independence National Historical Park

Start: At the visitor center
Distance: 3.2 miles
Type: Loop
Hiking time: 4 hours
Difficulty: Easy
Best season: March to October
Traffic: Hikers, bicyclists, and automobiles
Fees and permits: Free unless you order tickets to Independence Hall ($1.50 in advance).

There are fees for parking and visiting many of the independent museums along the route.
Maps: Available at www.nps.gov/inde/plan yourvisit/maps.htm
Trail contact: Independence National Historical Park, 143 S. Third St., Philadelphia 19106; (215) 965-2305; www.nps.gov/inde/index.htm

Finding the trailhead: From the west, take I-76/PA Turnpike to I-676. Continue to the Sixth Street exit (Independence Hall exit), then turn right onto Sixth. Parking may be available at the Independence Visitor Center underground garage on Sixth Street between Arch and Market Streets. GPS: N39 56.990' / W75 09.033'

The Hike

The question is not whether there's anything historic to see in Philadelphia. It's how to see it all. This hike hits quite a few of the highlights, not least among them the "big three": where America's founding fathers talked business, spent their leisure time, and worshipped.

It starts at the park's visitor center. There are movies to see here and a few other exhibits, not to mention a gift shop and a cafe. While here—if you haven't done this in advance, by phone or online—be sure to get tickets to tour Independence Hall. Admission is on a timed basis from March through December; without a ticket, you don't get in.

Next you'll go to the President's House Site and then the Liberty Bell. There's typically a line; visitors have to go through metal detectors and that takes a bit. But there are a lot of informational panels documenting the history of the bell inside, then the bell itself. Just expect crowds. People gather around to take pictures of themselves with the bell in the background—park folks call those shots "bellfies."

From there it's on to Independence Hall, the first of the big three. It's a UNESCO, or United Nations Educational, Scientific and Cultural Organization "world heritage site" because of its importance to democracy. The Hall is where George Washington, Thomas Jefferson, Benjamin Franklin, and all the other luminaries of the American Revolution debated the fate and direction of the new country. It's surprisingly small. For its time it was likely one of the biggest and grandest buildings in the city. In comparison to modern buildings, though, and given the importance of what went on within its walls, it seems a tiny place.

Independence Hall is where the US Constitution and Declaration of Independence were created.
Tours are available, but on a timed, ticketed basis.

Visitors get to see two halves of it on the lower floor. On one side is a courtroom. The building was originally constructed in 1732 to be Pennsylvania's State House, so this is where the state supreme court met.

The other side is the more interesting. Known as Assembly Hall, it's where George Washington was appointed commander of the Continental Army and where the Declaration of Independence and US Constitution were signed. The room is set up the way it would have been when representatives of the thirteen colonies were here. Most of the furniture dates to the era, but is not original—with one exception.

The "rising sun" chair—so called because of the intricate carving of a sun atop the backrest—is the actual chair Washington sat in when attending meetings. Franklin is said to have remarked that he never knew whether it had a rising or setting sun until the Revolution succeeded and America became free.

This hike next moves on to Washington Square, one of five original squares from when the city was first laid out. A burial ground and pasture in the eighteenth century, it's today home to the Tomb of the Unknown Soldier of the American Revolution (as well as a clone of the NASA moon tree; information about that is available at https://nssdc.gsfc.nasa.gov/planetary/lunar/moon_tree.html).

From there the hike leads to the portrait gallery in the Second Bank of the United States, Franklin Court and the Market Street Houses, and then City Tavern, the second of the big three. Originally built in 1773, it served as a favorite meeting place of the founding fathers; they often took their meals here. It hosted the country's first Fourth of July celebration in 1777, too.

It didn't last forever. The building's roof caught fire in 1834, causing heavy damage. In 1854 it was finally torn down. The National Park Service built a replica in 1976, though, and today it's home to a themed restaurant where diners are served by waitstaff in period clothes. Be sure to sample the sweet potato biscuits, a favorite of Thomas Jefferson.

From here, the hike moves on to Christ Church. Third of the big three highlights and known as the birthplace of the Episcopal Church in America, it hosted many of the founding fathers who came to worship. Benjamin and Deborah Franklin, Betsy Ross, Robert Morris, and John Penn, William Penn's grandson, were all members. (Franklin and four other signers of the Declaration of Independence are buried in the church's burial grounds, at the corner of Fifth and Arch Streets, about two blocks from here, if you want to see that.) The church is also where the nation's first black priest received his ordination. It's not just a historic site, though. Services are still held on Sunday mornings.

From here, the trail winds back to the start. There are other sites to see, including many private museums in the city. It's up to you how to fit them all in.

It takes a bit of time to see the Liberty Bell—expect to stand in line—so those who do usually mark the occasion by taking photos, including "bellfies."

The History

It's easy in hindsight to just assume that the American Revolution was a sure thing, an upheaval destined to succeed on the basis of its inherent righteousness. In reality, it was a dangerous and iffy uprising.

It's one that many didn't even want to pursue initially. In 1774, Great Britain's Parliament passed the "Intolerable Acts," punishing Massachusetts for the Boston Tea Party. Boston's harbor was closed to commerce. That caused considerable economic hardship and, if anything, had the opposite effect of what the British were hoping for. America's colonists were not cowed. Rather, they rallied together in ways previously unthinkable.

In May of that same year, the Virginia Assembly called for a meeting of representatives from all the colonies to plan a response. That gathering—the first Continental Congress—was held here in Philadelphia, then America's largest and most prosperous city. The Revolution began less than a year later, in April 1775, with the firing of shots

Washington Square is home to the Tomb of the Unknown Soldier of the American Revolution.

at Lexington and Concord. A month later the second Continental Congress met and appointed George Washington commander in chief of American forces.

Still, there was debate about whether the colonies should seek outright independence or just a new kind of relationship with Great Britain. Congress sent to King George III an "Olive Branch Petition," which outlined its grievances, but also affirmed its loyalty to the crown. King George was in no mood to negotiate, however. He declared the colonies to be in a state of rebellion and set out to quash it.

The course of history was then set, the war for independence on. At the urging of Virginian Richard Henry Lee, Congress severed ties to Great Britain and signed the Declaration of Independence. Now officially outlaws, ones who could be punished by hanging, the members of Congress set about directing the war.

It would prove to be a long one. The Revolution lasted seven years and, at several points, came perilously close to failing.

A Philadelphian is partly to credit for keeping it going. Robert Morris, a merchant and banker in the city, was appointed by Congress to solve the young would-be nation's financial woes. The young government's debt was rising rapidly, while inflation was driving the power of American currency down. Morris became the driving force behind the Bank of North America and, in effect, helped successfully finance the war effort.

In the meantime, though, Philadelphia itself would suffer during the war. The city had earlier been occupied by the British, who were none too squeamish about taking food from private citizens and furnishings from public and private buildings to make their stay more to their liking.

In the end the colonists gained independence, of course, with the war culminating in the Battle of Yorktown. The Treaty of Paris ending the war officially came later, in 1783. Britain's army and navy were recalled, leaving the Americans at peace for the first time in nearly a decade.

That's not where the story of independence and Philadelphia's role in it end, though. The Articles of Confederation that had governed the colonies during the war would prove totally inadequate as a form of government soon thereafter. By 1787 five delegates would again convene in Philadelphia to revise the Articles "for the preservation of the union."

Instead, they ditched the Articles altogether and came up with the Constitution as we know it. A result of what was called the "Great Compromise," it established a two-chamber system of government, with a Senate and House of Representatives, so that small states as well as large ones would have a voice. Most importantly, the central government—with executive and judicial branches—was given more power, enough to build a nation around.

The US Constitution was ratified in 1788; the Bill of Rights would follow a year later. And a year after that, in 1790, Philadelphia became the nation's temporary capital. It wouldn't hold that title long. The government moved to Washington, DC, a decade later, in 1800.

But there's no doubt, Philadelphia's place in American history is secure.

Miles and Directions

0.0 Start at the Independence Visitor Center. Cross Market Street at the light where it intersects Sixth Street. After 400 feet arrive at the President's House, where you can see remnants of the home George Washington called "the best single house in the city" and the Liberty Bell. When through the line, exit the Liberty Bell Center and continue down Sixth Street.

0.9 Opposite Sansom Street, turn left and go up a few steps to the back of Independence Hall. You'll probably have some time until your tour of the Hall, so check out the courtyard here. Then cross through to Fifth Street.

1.1 At Fifth Street, turn left. Pass the Library of the American Philosophical Society on the right and the American Philosophical Society Museum on the left. Turn left onto Chestnut Street.

1.5 Arrive at the East Wing entrance to Independence Hall, where tours start. The brick and stone of the Hall are close to 100 percent original; the woodwork is about 70 percent. Inside you'll see some interesting artifacts, including the silver inkstand believed to be the

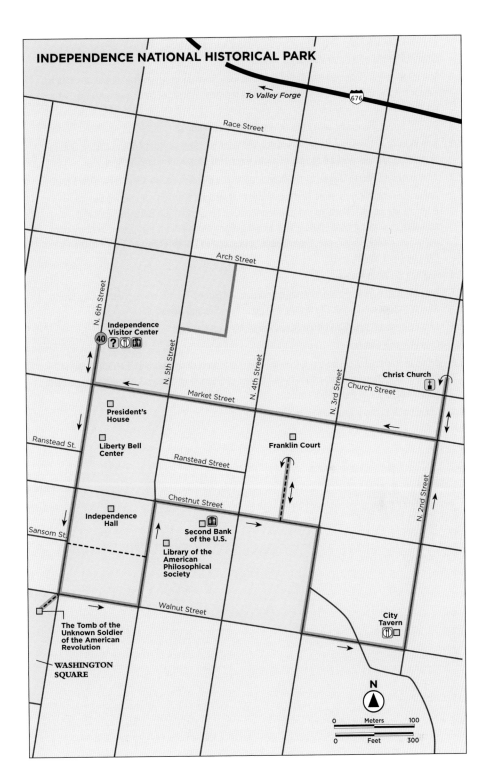

INDEPENDENCE NATIONAL HISTORICAL PARK

To Valley Forge 676

Race Street

Arch Street

N. 6th Street

Independence Visitor Center
40 ? 🍴 🏛

N. 5th Street

N. 4th Street

N. 3rd Street

Church Street

Christ Church 🏛

Market Street

☐ **President's House**

Ranstead St.

☐ **Liberty Bell Center**

Ranstead Street

☐ **Franklin Court**

N. 2nd Street

Chestnut Street

Sansom St.

☐ **Independence Hall**

☐ 🏛 **Second Bank of the U.S.**

☐ **Library of the American Philosophical Society**

Walnut Street

☐ **The Tomb of the Unknown Soldier of the American Revolution**

WASHINGTON SQUARE

🏛 ☐ **City Tavern**

N

0 — Meters — 100
0 — Feet — 300

one used to sign the US Constitution and Declaration of Independence. Do the tour, then exit and turn left onto Sixth Street again. Follow it to the intersection with Walnut Street. Soon turn right and enter Washington Square.

1.6 The Tomb of the Unknown Soldier of the American Revolution. An eternal flame burns here. Check out the exhibits—and enjoy a peaceful moment—then exit the Square and go right on Walnut.

1.8 Walnut Street intersects with Fifth Street. Turn left on Fifth.

1.9 Turn right onto Chestnut Street. Soon you will pass the Second Bank of the United States, home to a famous portrait gallery of more than 150 of the Founding Fathers.

2.1 After crossing Fourth Street, turn left and follow the signs down an alley to Franklin Court.

2.2 Arrive at Franklin Court. Here find remnants of Benjamin Franklin's home, visible via a "ghost structure" aboveground and foundations below, and the Benjamin Franklin Museum, a working post office and a working reproduction of an eighteenth-century printing office. Check all this out, then retrace your steps to Chestnut Street. Turn left, then go right on Third Street.

2.4 Turn left on Walnut again.

2.5 Turn left at the intersection of Walnut and Second Street. On the corner here is City Tavern. After a tour or lunch, exit the tavern and go left on Second Street.

2.6 Cross Chestnut Street and then Black Horse Alley on the right.

2.7 Cross Market Street.

2.8 Arrive at Christ Church, on the left, which can be toured during normal operating hours. Check it out, then go right, return to the corner of Second and Market Streets, and go right on Market, back to the visitor center.

3.2 Arrive back at the visitor center to close the loop.

Hike Index

About the Author

Bob Frye is outdoors editor and manager of eveybodyadventures.com, a website focused on outdoor adventure, from hiking and paddling to hunting and fishing and everything in between. He's also the longtime outdoors editor of the *Tribune-Review* newspaper. Both are based in southwestern Pennsylvania.

Frye—writing for newspapers, magazines, and books—has won nearly fifty national and state awards for his work. He's been recognized by the Outdoor Writers Association of America, Professional Outdoor Media Association, Pennsylvania Outdoor Writers Association, Pennsylvania Newspaper Association, Society of Professional Journalists, Associated Press Managing Editors, and the Press Club of Western Pennsylvania, among others.

Frye lives east of Pittsburgh, in Westmoreland County. From there he explores the state with his wife, Mandy, always looking for new adventures.